The Jumbo Book of
200 Indoor & Outdoor Things for Kids to Do

The Jumbo Book of
200 Indoor & Outdoor Things for Kids to Do

Petra Boase   Clare Bradley   Marion Elliot

Cecilia Fitzsimons   Judy Williams

LORENZ BOOKS

First published in 1998 by Lorenz Books

© Anness Publishing Limited 1998

Lorenz Books is an imprint of
Anness Publishing Limited
Hermes House
88–89 Blackfriars Road
London SE1 8HA

ISBN 1 85967 822 X

A CIP catalogue record for this book is available from the British Library

Publisher: Joanna Lorenz
Project Editor: Zoe Antoniou
Designers: Peter Laws, Lilian Lindblom, Alan Marshall and Adrian Morris
Jacket designer: Ian Sandom
Photographers: James Duncan, John Freeman and Anthony Pickhaver
Stylists: Petra Boase, Madeleine Brehaut, Susan Bull and Judy Williams
Extra recipes: Sam Dobson
Illustrations: Lucinda Ganderton and Andrew Tewson

Previously published in two separate volumes, *100 Things for Kids to Make and Do* and *The
Best-ever Book of 100 Things for Kids to Make, Do and Play*

Printed and bound in Italy

1 3 5 7 9 10 8 6 4 2

CONTENTS

INTRODUCTION

It's always great fun to make something, and this book is full of all kinds of brilliant ideas. Whatever you like to do, there is something special here for everyone.

There are lots of toys to make and play with, from rag dolls to robots. Or, if you like to play outside, this book can show you how to explore your garden. It is really interesting planting seeds and watching them grow into plants. If you want to impress your friends, cook them a fantastic meal or throw a wild fancy dress party! Show everyone how to make up their faces so they look like spooky monsters or wild animals.

Next time it's a friend's birthday, make a special badge or bracelet using a jamjar lid or plastic bottle. Recycling things that you find around the house is very cheap and fun to do. It's amazing what you can do with a few plastic straws or coloured paper clips!

Some of the projects you can make yourself, following the step-by-step pictures and the simple instructions. You may need to ask an adult to help you to make some of the toys, or when you are in the kitchen. Always be very careful if you are using sharp tools or are cooking on a hot stove.

Indoors and outdoors, summer and winter – there's always something incredible to make, do or play!

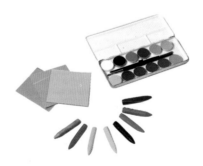

Getting Started

All the projects for indoors can be made easily at home, although some may need adult help. Before you start, read the instructions below to make sure you don't make too much of a mess, and don't have an accident. Remember to ask permission before starting a project and collecting all your materials – you don't want to 'recycle' items which are new!

Right: *To prevent your clothes from getting covered in paint and glue, wear a smock or apron, or ask an adult for an old shirt. That way, you can make as much mess as you like!*

Left: *When you have decided which projects you are going to make, lay out all the materials you will need on your work surface. You will then find it much easier to get to work.*

Below: *Before you start work on any project, cover the surface you will be working on with newspaper or an old piece of material.*

Above: *If you can find a clear surface to work on, you'll find it much easier to make your projects. If you are using a desk or kitchen table, clear everything away before you begin so you have plenty of room.*

Left: *It is very important to keep all art materials away from your mouth. Not only will they taste very unpleasant, but they could also be dangerous.*

BASIC TECHNIQUES

Papier-mâché

Papier-mâché is made by shredding paper, usually old newspapers, and combining it with glue. The paper can be used in a number of ways to make a huge variety of objects which are either useful or just for decoration.

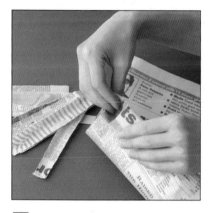

1 For most projects, paper should be torn into fairly short strips approximately 2 cm (¾ in) wide.

2 Mix some non-toxic PVA (white) glue with water to the consistency of single (light) cream.

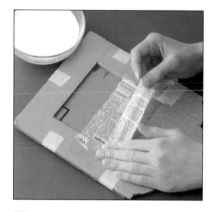

3 Papier-mâché can be pressed into lightly greased moulds or wrapped around cardboard shapes like this.

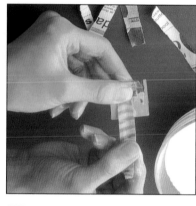

4 To cover smaller shapes, use small, thin pieces of newspaper.

5 Your papier-mâché object may have a slightly rough surface when it has dried out. To make it uniformly smooth, lightly rub the paper with fine sandpaper.

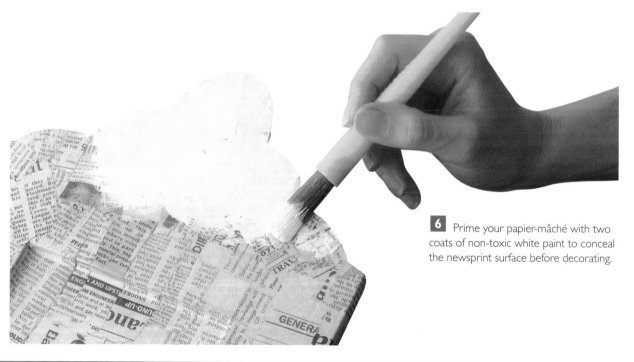

6 Prime your papier-mâché with two coats of non-toxic white paint to conceal the newsprint surface before decorating.

Salt dough

Salt dough can be used like clay and baked in the oven until hard. Use this recipe for the salt dough projects in the book.

YOU WILL NEED
300 g/11 oz/3 cups plain flour
300 g/11 oz/2 cups, plus 30 ml/2 tbsp salt
wooden spoon
large bowl
30 ml/2 tbsp vegetable oil
200 ml/8 fl oz/1 cup water

1 Put the flour and 300 g/11 oz/2 cups salt into a large bowl.

2 Add the oil to the flour and salt mixture and add the remaining salt. Mix all the ingredients together with a large wooden spoon.

3 Pour in the water and mix thoroughly, making sure there are no lumps.

4 Knead the dough until it is firm.

5 When it is ready you can use it straight away or store it in an airtight container in the refrigerator.

Tracing

Some of the projects in this book have patterns that you can transfer directly to paper or use to make templates. Tracing is the quickest way to make copies of a pattern so that you can easily transfer it to another piece of paper or cardboard.

 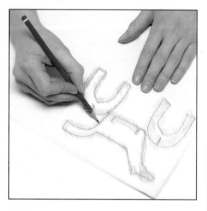

1 Lay your piece of tracing paper on the pattern and use a soft pencil to draw over the image, making a dark line. Turn the sheet of tracing paper over and place it on a scrap of paper. Scribble over the lines with your pencil.

2 Turn the tracing right-side up again and place it on an appropriate piece of paper or cardboard. Carefully draw over the lines to transfer the tracing to the paper or cardboard.

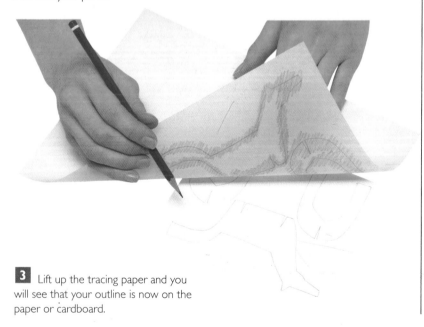

3 Lift up the tracing paper and you will see that your outline is now on the paper or cardboard.

Scaling-up

Sometimes you will want to make a project bigger than the template given. It's easy to make it larger. This is known as scaling-up. Use a scale of, say, one square on the template to two squares on the graph paper. You can use a different scale depending on the size you want.

1 If you wish to copy a template that is not printed on a grid, trace it and transfer it to graph paper. If the template you have chosen does appear on a grid, proceed directly to step 2.

2 Using an appropriate scale, enlarge the template onto a second piece of paper, copying the shape from each smaller square to a larger square.

3 Cut out the template and transfer it to card (posterboard) or paper.

Stencilling

Stencilling is a way of applying decoration to a surface using special card (cardboard), clear film or metal stencils. A shape is drawn onto the card, cut out, and then paint is applied over the cut-out portion of the stencil with a sponge or brush. It is possible to buy ready-cut stencils or you can make your own. Ask an adult to cut out your stencil motif for you – craft knives are *very* sharp, and are difficult to control.

1 Cut a piece of stencil card (cardboard) and draw your design.

2 Ask an adult to cut out the image from the stencil card.

3 Mix paint in a palette or on an old saucer. Add a little water to make a slightly sticky consistency.

4 Cut a piece of household sponge into small squares.

5 Place the stencil card on a piece of heavy paper or thin card (posterboard). Dip the sponge in paint and gently dab it over the cut-out motif.

6 Remove the stencil card carefully, one corner at a time, to avoid smudging the paint.

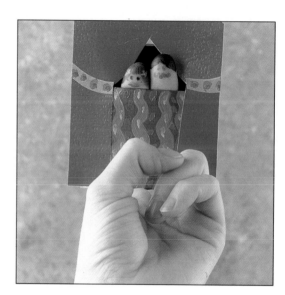

Paper Fun

Make your own personal gift wrap, stationery,
games and stand-up toys out of paper and card
(posterboard). There are many different kinds of
paper to choose from, and you can also paint
or stamp your own designs.

Materials

Coloured pencils and crayons
These must be non-toxic. They come in a huge variety of colours and are useful for decorating projects.

Cotton string
Cotton string comes in a variety of colours and is useful for binding pages together, stringing beads and making picture hangers.

Eye pins
These are small metal pins with a loop at one end. They are used mostly in jewellery to join items such as earrings together. They can be bought from specialist craft and hobby shops.

Hole punch
Use with adult supervision to make holes in paper for decoration or practical purposes.

Household sponge
This can be cut into small squares and used to apply paint with or without stencils.

Ink pad
Use an ink pad with non-toxic ink to stamp stationery and other projects.

Masking tape
Masking tape is cream-coloured paper tape that can be removed once it has been stuck down. It is particularly useful for keeping joints in position whilst glue dries.

Paintbrushes
Paintbrushes in a variety of thicknesses are used for applying glue and paint.

Paints
These must be non-toxic. Paints are used in several projects, especially for decorating papier-mâché.

Paper clips
Paper clips are very useful for holding small pieces of paper together while you are working on a project.

Paper fasteners
These are split metal pins that open out to hold pieces of paper together. They should only be used under adult supervision.

Paper glue
This must be non-toxic. Paper glue comes in a variety of formats. Perhaps the easiest to use is the solid stick of glue.

PVA (white) glue
This must be non-toxic.

Undiluted PVA glue is very useful for sticking heavy cardboard. Diluted, it can be used for papier-mâché.

Rubber cutting mat
These mats are non-slip and protect work surfaces when cutting paper and card.

Ruler
Use for measuring and drawing straight lines.

Scissors
These should be of the type made specially for children with rounded blades.

Sequins
Sequins in various shapes and sizes make very good decorations.

Stapler and staples
These should be used under adult supervision. Staples are very useful for holding paper together, especially joints in fairly thick papers and cards.

Sticky tape
Clear sticky tape is good for sticking paper, cord and card.

Strong glue
This must be non-toxic and solvent-free. Strong glue is sometimes used to fix heavyweight papers.

household sponge

masking tape

sticky tape

ink pad

coloured
pencils

rubber
cutting
mat

cotton string

crayons

paper clips

strong glue

eye pins

eraser

ruler

darning elastic

sequins

stapler

scissors

pencil sharpener

sequins

staples

paper glue

paintbrushes

paper fasteners

hole punch

paints

PVA (white) glue

Bird Mosaic Tray

This tray will make the simplest meal look exciting! Mosaic has been used as a decorative device for centuries, and especially fine examples were made by the Romans to decorate the floors of their villas. The look of mosaic has been imitated here by the use of irregular squares cut from scraps of coloured paper. The tray is sealed with several coats of varnish so it can be wiped clean with a damp cloth after use.

YOU WILL NEED
wooden tray
fine sandpaper
diluted non-toxic PVA (white) glue
paintbrushes
non-toxic white paint
non-toxic bright paint
scissors
thin paper in a variety of colours
pencil
non-toxic clear gloss varnish
    (optional)

paint

sandpaper

scissors

paintbrushes

paper glue

pencil

paper

1 Rub down the surface of the wooden tray with fine sandpaper. Seal the tray with a coat of diluted PVA (white) glue.

2 Prime the tray with a coat of white paint and allow to dry.

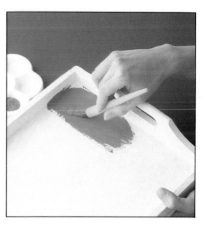

3 Paint the tray with two coats of bright paint and allow to dry thoroughly.

4 Cut mosaic squares from sheets of brightly coloured thin paper. Dip each in diluted PVA glue and use a paintbrush to stick in place around the tray.

5 Draw and cut a bird shape from paper and stick it in place in the centre of the tray. Add details cut from contrasting papers and allow the tray to dry overnight.

6 Seal the tray with several coats of diluted PVA glue or clear gloss varnish.

Rubber-stamped Stationery

If you're looking for unusual stationery, why not cut stamps from small erasers to decorate writing paper and envelopes? You could press them onto different-coloured ink pads or into bright paint to make your own personal stationery. You must ask an adult to cut the eraser for you – craft knives are *very* sharp.

YOU WILL NEED
pencil
rubber erasers
craft knife
non-toxic ink pad
writing paper

ink pad

pencil

erasers

writing paper

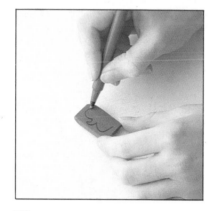

1 Draw your design onto the face of the eraser.

2 Ask an adult to trim carefully around the design with a craft knife to leave a raised image.

3 Gently press the eraser onto the ink pad. Test it first on a scrap of paper to make sure that enough ink has been absorbed to make a dark image.

4 Press the eraser firmly onto the writing paper. Remove it carefully to avoid smudging the ink.

Paper Doll

You can make all kinds of outfits for this little doll.
Make some friends and family for her to play with,
or even some pets.

YOU WILL NEED
tracing and plain paper for template
pencil
card (cardboard)
scissors
white paper
coloured paints
paintbrush
shoe box

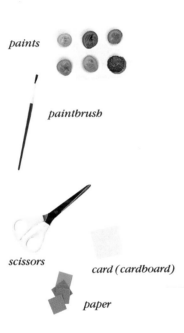

paints

paintbrush

scissors   *card (cardboard)*

paper

1 For the doll, scale-up the template from the back of the book following the instructions on page 12. Trace her onto a piece of card (cardboard). Cut out the doll carefully with a pair of scissors.

2 Paint the doll's face, hair, and underwear. Leave to dry.

3 Trace around the doll to make the clothes and paint them in bright colours. When you cut out the clothes make sure you leave small tags on them. These will bend behind the doll to stop them from falling off.

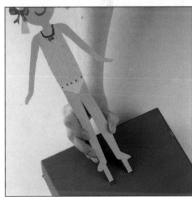

4 Paint the lid of a shoe box and make two holes with a pair of scissors to support the doll. Dress up the doll in her various outfits, remembering to bend the tags behind her.

Woven Paper Cards

Paper weaving is a fun way to achieve exciting effects from a very simple process. Pick your papers with care so that the colours complement each other, or contrast in interesting ways. You can use the weaving as a design on its own, or mount it behind shaped frames to make unusual greetings cards.

YOU WILL NEED
medium-weight card (posterboard) in
  a variety of colours
ruler
pencil
scissors
heavy paper in a variety of colours
non-toxic paper glue

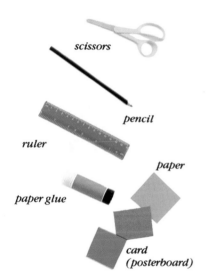

scissors

pencil

ruler

paper

paper glue

card
(posterboard)

1 Draw a rectangle measuring 16 × 24 cm (6¼ × 9½ in) on medium-weight green card (posterboard) and cut it out. Draw a line down the centre of the rectangle and, with adult help, gently score along it with scissors to form a fold.

2 Mark a 9 cm (3½ in) square on the front of the card and cut it out to form a window.

3 Cut a piece of red card measuring 10 × 10 cm (4 × 4 in). Make vertical cuts every 1 cm (⅜ in) down the card, from just below the top edge almost to the bottom, but do not cut all the way through.

4 Cut several strips of orange paper approximately 1 cm (⅜ in) wide.

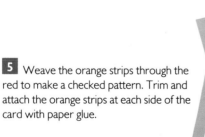

5 Weave the orange strips through the red to make a checked pattern. Trim and attach the orange strips at each side of the card with paper glue.

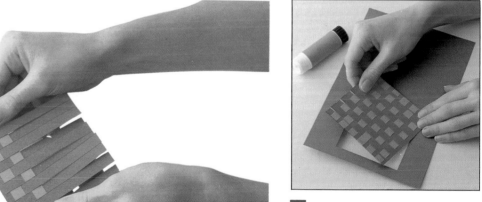

6 Stick the woven square to the inside front of the card so that it shows through the window.

Little Town

Make your own dream town out of small boxes and card (cardboard). Include all your favourite shops, your school and your friends' houses.

YOU WILL NEED

different-sized boxes (matchboxes are ideal)
card (cardboard)
scissors
PVA (white) glue
coloured paper
coloured paints
paintbrush
toothpicks
green pom-poms
green glitter
plasticine
green sticky-backed (adhesive) felt

glitter
paper
plasticine
pom-pom
paintbrush
matchbox
scissors
masking tape
toothpicks
PVA (white) glue
paints

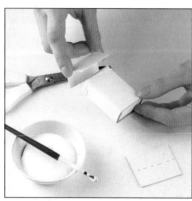

1 Remove the matches from the matchboxes and give them to an adult. For the roof tops of the houses, cut out square pieces of card (cardboard) with a pair of scissors, fold them in half and stick them onto the matchboxes with PVA (white) glue.

2 Cover the houses in different-coloured sheets of paper and paint on doors and windows.

3 For the trees, paint the toothpicks brown. Glue a green pom-pom onto a toothpick and cover it in glue. Dab the pom-pom into a ball of green glitter and paint on some red spots. To make the tree stand up, stick it into a piece of plasticine.

4 For the roads, cut out strips of card and paint them.

5 Cover a large piece of card with green sticky-backed (adhesive) felt.

6 Arrange the houses, trees and roads around the green felt to create the town. If you don't glue the pieces down, you can change the position of the buildings as many times as you like and store the town away easily.

Dressing-up Doll

Shiver me timbers! Here's a brawny brigand for you to
dress! Why not make a parrot to sit on his shoulder
and keep him company on the high seas?

YOU WILL NEED
tracing paper or graph paper
pencil
thin white card (posterboard)
cartridge (construction) paper
scissors
paintbrushes
non-toxic paint in a variety of colours

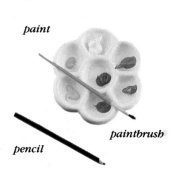

paint

paintbrush

pencil

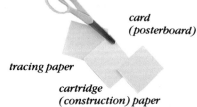

scissors

*card
(posterboard)*

tracing paper

*cartridge
(construction) paper*

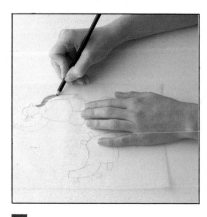

1 Trace or scale up the pirate and his
clothes from the template at the back
of the book.

2 Transfer the pirate to thin card
(posterboard), and the clothes to
cartridge (construction) paper. Carefully
cut them out.

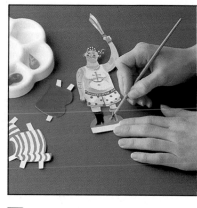

3 Fill in the pirate's features with paint.
Paint his underclothes in bright colours
and decorate the pirate's clothes.

4 With adult help, lightly score and fold
the base of the pirate so that he stands up.

5 Bend the tabs of the clothes over.
Place them on the pirate and squeeze the
tabs closed so that they fit snugly over the
paper figure.

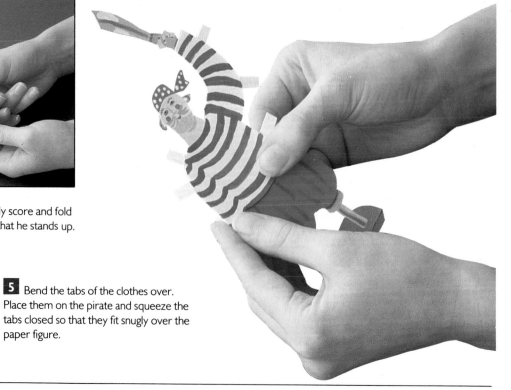

Matchbox Theatre

This must be the smallest theatre in the world – you can almost carry it in your pocket.

YOU WILL NEED
kitchen matchbox
scissors
coloured paints
paintbrush
coloured paper
felt-tip pen
coloured sticky tape

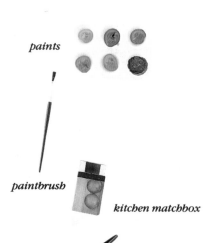

paints

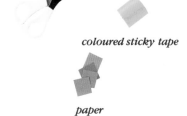

paintbrush

kitchen matchbox

scissors

coloured sticky tape

paper

1 Remove the matches from the box and give them to an adult. Take the matchbox apart and cut one-third off the sleeve with a pair of scissors. Paint both the sleeve and tray and leave them to dry before putting them back together.

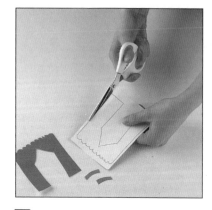

2 Draw the curtains on a piece of coloured paper with a felt-tip pen and cut them out.

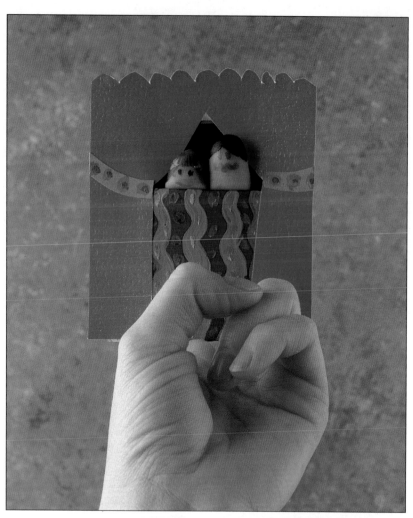

3 Attach the curtains to the matchbox using coloured sticky tape.

4 Paint a face onto the palm side of your middle and index fingers and put them inside the theatre to start acting.

Jigsaw Puzzle

Challenge your family and friends with this home-made jigsaw puzzle.

YOU WILL NEED
colourful picture or large photograph
  of your choice
card (cardboard)
PVA (white) glue
scissors
pencil
paintbrush

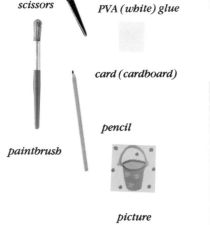

scissors

PVA (white) glue

paintbrush

card (cardboard)

pencil

picture

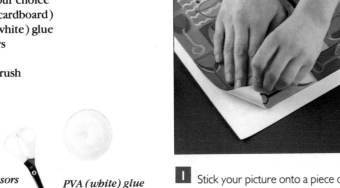

1 Stick your picture onto a piece of card (cardboard) with PVA (white) glue. Rub the palm of your hand over the picture to make sure it is completely smooth. Allow it to dry.

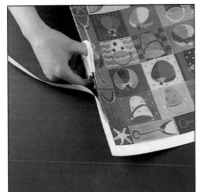

2 Cut around the picture with a pair of scissors to remove the excess card.

CRAFT HINT
You could cut out a picture from a magazine rather than using a photograph.

3 Draw the jigsaw pieces onto the reverse of the picture with a pencil.

4 Carefully cut out the jigsaw shapes and keep them in a safe place.

Eye Masks

Even if you're not going to a masked ball, you'll have fun making and wearing these disguises! They're especially good if you're in a play or pantomime – you'll be surprised how difficult your friends find it to recognize you!

YOU WILL NEED
tracing paper or graph paper
pencil
thin card (posterboard) in a variety of colours
scissors
paper in a variety of colours
non-toxic paper glue
thin wooden sticks
paintbrush
non-toxic paint
non-toxic strong glue
wax crayons
gold paper

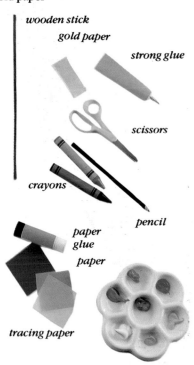

wooden stick
gold paper
strong glue
scissors
crayons
pencil
paper glue
paper
tracing paper
paint

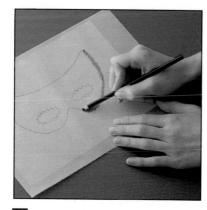

1 Trace or scale up the fiery mask shape from the template at the back of the book and transfer to orange card (posterboard). Cut it out.

2 Place the card on purple paper. Extend the sides and top of the eye mask with small spikes. Cut out this shape.

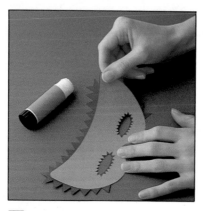

3 Using paper glue stick the orange shape in place on top of the purple one. Carefully trim the lower edge of the mask if necessary.

4 Paint the wooden stick a bright colour. You may have to use two coats of paint.

5 Attach the wooden stick to the side of the mask with strong glue. Stick it the right of the mask if you are right-handed and vice-versa if you are left-handed.

6 To make the leopard mask, use yellow card and apply the spots with wax crayon. The king has a crown made of gold paper, and his eyebrows are applied with wax crayon.

Paper Plate Tennis

A fun game for two or more players to play around the house or outdoors.

YOU WILL NEED
4 paper plates
coloured paints
paintbrush
scissors
coloured sticky tape
ping-pong ball

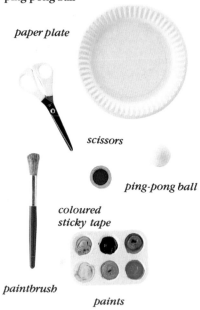

paper plate

scissors

ping-pong ball

coloured sticky tape

paintbrush

paints

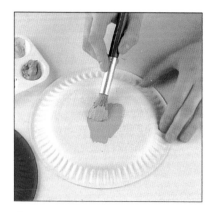

1 For each 'racquet' you will need two paper plates. Paint each plate a plain colour. Allow to dry.

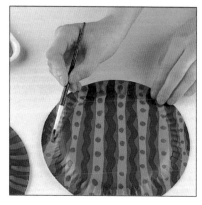

2 Paint patterns onto the plates and leave to dry.

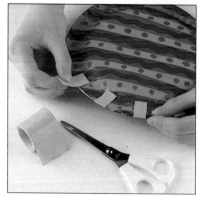

3 Attach the plates with pieces of coloured sticky tape, leaving a gap big enough for your hand to slide in.

4 Paint the ping-pong ball. Now you are ready to start playing.

Origami Water Bomb

Seek revenge outdoors with this crafty piece of paper work, but be sure to clear up afterwards!

YOU WILL NEED
pencil
ruler
coloured paper
scissors
water

scissors

paper

1 Measure a piece of paper 20 cm × 20 cm (8 in × 8 in). Cut it out with a pair of scissors. Draw lines across the square following the template at the back of the book and fold along them to make creases. Take the two creases either side of the square and pinch them into the centre. Press flat to form a triangle.

2 Fold back the corners of the triangle on both sides to form a square shape.

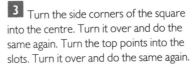

3 Turn the side corners of the square into the centre. Turn it over and do the same again. Turn the top points into the slots. Turn it over and do the same again.

4 At one end of the bomb there is a small hole. Blow into it hard to make a cube. Through the hole, fill the bomb with water and you are ready to have some outdoor fun!

Paper Beads

These fun and colourful beads are made from the pages of a magazine, but no one will guess when you wear them.

YOU WILL NEED
tracing and plain paper for templates
felt-tip pen
scissors
colourful pictures from magazines
PVA (white) glue
wooden stick or knitting needle
embroidery thread

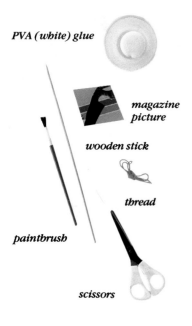

PVA (white) glue

magazine picture

wooden stick

thread

paintbrush

scissors

1 Trace the templates from the back of the book following the instructions on page 12. Place the templates onto the colourful magazine pictures and draw around them.

2 Cut out the shapes with scissors.

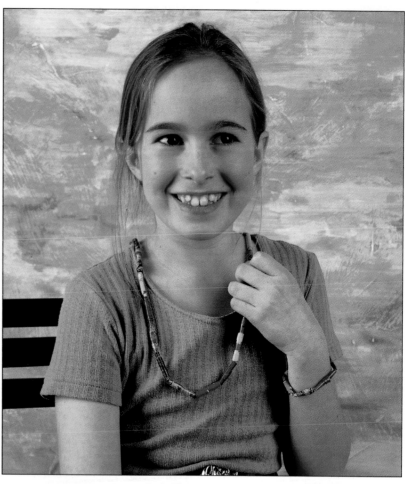

3 Paint a line of PVA (white) glue in the middle of the shapes and wrap them tightly around a wooden stick or a knitting needle. Carefully remove the stick or knitting needle.

4 When the glue has dried, thread the beads onto a piece of embroidery thread to make either a necklace or a bracelet and tie a knot.

Cowboy Face Mask

Ride the range in this cowboy mask! Wear a bright scarf around your neck for added authenticity and you'll be the envy of every cowpoke in town!

YOU WILL NEED
heavy light blue, dark blue and orange paper
pencil
scissors ruler
non-toxic paper glue
sticky tape
stapler

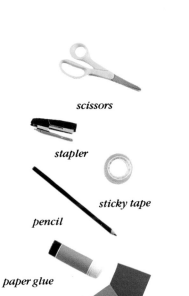

scissors

stapler

sticky tape

pencil

paper glue

paper

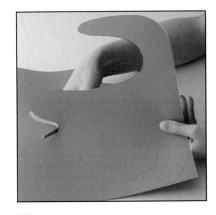

1 Draw a hat on the light blue paper. Draw a thin band approximately 5 × 60 cm (2 × 24 in) on the same paper. Cut them out.

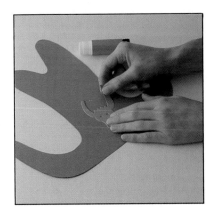

2 Draw a steer's head on the orange paper and cut it out. Stick it to the front of the hat with paper glue.

3 Draw and cut out the eye mask from the dark blue paper. Stick it to the back of the hat with sticky tape.

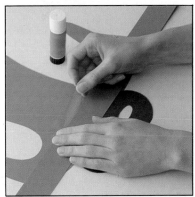

4 Stick the hat band to the back of the hat with paper glue. Make sure that it is not visible from the front. To give additional strength, hold the band in place with a strip of sticky tape. Hold the hat band around the head and ask a friend to mark where the two ends overlap. Remove the hat and with adult help, staple or glue the ends neatly together.

Papier-mâché Necklace

Papier-mâché is made by recycling old paper and cardboard; why not carry on this ecological theme by decorating a papier-mâché necklace with daisies and insects – you'll blend in well at any garden party!

YOU WILL NEED
large coin, for tracing circles
corrugated cardboard
pencil
scissors
newspaper
diluted non-toxic PVA (white) glue
non-toxic white paint
paintbrush
non-toxic paint in a variety of colours
non-toxic clear gloss varnish
darning needle
non-toxic strong glue
eye pins
coloured cord

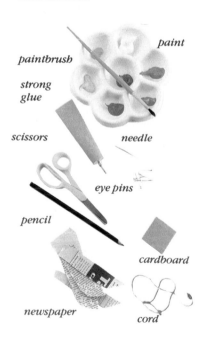

paint

paintbrush

strong glue

scissors

needle

eye pins

pencil

cardboard

newspaper

cord

1 Place a round object such as a coin on the cardboard. Draw around it to make 12 discs and cut them out.

2 Cover each disc with three layers of thin papier-mâché strips. Leave them to dry overnight.

3 Prime each disc with two coats of white paint and leave to dry.

4 Draw a daisy or ladybird (ladybug) on each disc. Fill in the design with paints.

5 Seal each disc with two coats of gloss varnish. When they are dry, with adult help, make a hole in the top of each with a darning needle. Dab a little strong glue over each hole and push in an eye pin.

6 Cut a length of cord. Pass the cord through the eye pin of each disc and tie it before adding the next.

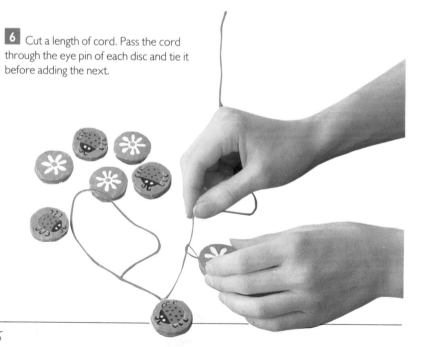

Painted Postcards

Be original and make your own cards. This ingenious method of applying and scratching off paint gives very professional looking results, and the cards could be used for place names and invitations to special events as well as birthdays and Christmas.

YOU WILL NEED
heavy coloured paper
ruler
pencil
scissors
gold paper
paintbrush
non-toxic paint in a variety of colours
non-toxic paper glue

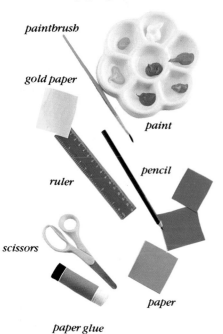

paintbrush

gold paper

paint

ruler

pencil

scissors

paper

paper glue

1 Measure and cut out rectangles of coloured paper measuring 10 × 12 cm (4 × 4¾ in).

2 Cut smaller rectangles of gold paper.

3 Apply a coat of paint to the gold paper, and while it is still wet draw a simple design in the paint with a soft pencil. Allow the paint to dry thoroughly.

4 Cut around the scratched images leaving a small border. Stick each one to a rectangle of coloured paper with paper glue and allow to dry.

Printed Wrapping Paper

If you don't like the gift wrap you see in stationery shops, print your own using stamps cut from foam rubber. It is very satisfying to be congratulated on wrapping paper *and* gift!

YOU WILL NEED
heavy corrugated cardboard
pencil
ruler
scissors
non-toxic strong glue
foam rubber approximately 6 mm
    (¼ in) thick
non-toxic paint in a variety of colours
thin coloured paper

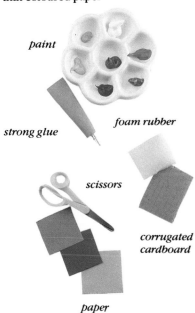

paint

strong glue

foam rubber

scissors

corrugated cardboard

paper

1 To make the stamps, cut several rectangles of heavy cardboard measuring 5 × 6 cm (2 × 2¼ in). Cut an equal number of smaller rectangles measuring 6 × 1.5 cm (2¼ × ⅝ in) to form the handles. Stick the handles to the top of the bases and leave to dry.

2 Draw the image for each stamp onto the piece of foam rubber. Carefully cut around each shape with scissors ensuring that the edges are smooth.

3 Stick the shapes to the base of each stamp and allow to dry thoroughly.

4 Spread a thin layer of paint onto a saucer to act as an ink pad. Press each stamp into the paint, varying the colours as desired, and print the wrapping paper.

Fancy Wrapped Parcels

Turn the humblest present into an exciting parcel by
making the wrappings interesting and fun. All sorts of
characters are appropriate for decorating parcels.
Think of the person who will receive the parcel, and of
their favourite characters when choosing a design.

YOU WILL NEED
items to wrap
crêpe paper
sticky tape
paper ribbon
pencil
thin paper in a variety of colours
scissors
non-toxic paper glue
non-toxic strong glue

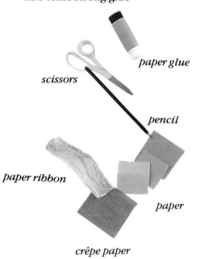

paper glue

scissors

pencil

paper ribbon

paper

crêpe paper

1 Wrap the parcels in crêpe paper.

2 Open out lengths of paper ribbon
and secure each parcel.

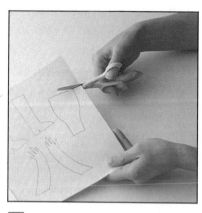

3 Draw designs onto pieces of thin
coloured paper to make the head, arms
and legs for each parcel (or head, legs and
tail if an animal). Cut out the shapes.

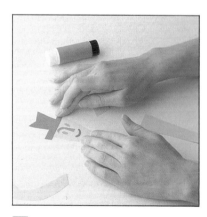

4 Stick the decorative details onto each
main body piece with paper glue.

5 Stick the decorations around the
corners of each parcel with strong glue.

Christmas Wreath

Celebrate the festive season with this Christmas wreath. The leaves are lightly scored so that they have a three-dimensional effect. Use gold paper to impart an extra sparkle to the musical angel.

YOU WILL NEED
heavy red paper
ruler
pencil
scissors
tracing paper
green, white, gold and pink paper
small stapler
non-toxic paper glue
paper ribbon
thin cord

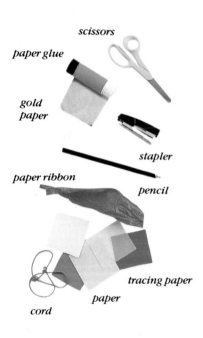

paper glue

scissors

gold paper

stapler

pencil

paper ribbon

tracing paper

paper

cord

1 Draw a circle measuring 24 cm (9½ in) in diameter on a square of heavy red paper. Cut it out.

2 Trace the leaf shape from the template and transfer it to the green paper. Cut out approximately 30 leaves.

3 To make the leaves appear three-dimensional, ask an adult to help you score the centre of each one with a pair of scissors and curve the paper. Score half the leaves on the front and half on the back, so that they curve around the right- and left-hand sides of the wreath.

4 With adult help, staple the leaves around both sides of the wreath, overlapping them slightly.

5 Trace the angel pieces from the template and transfer them to white, gold and pink paper. Cut out each of the pieces, and stick them in place on the front of the wreath.

6 Open out a length of paper ribbon and tie it to form a bow. Stick it in position at the bottom of the wreath. Stick a loop of cord to the back to form a hanger.

Craft Fun

Try your hand at sewing, papier-mâché, decoupage and salt dough, and make your own Christmas decorations. Get out your paints or experiment with string or potato prints. There are so many exciting crafts to choose from.

Materials

You will need some materials for this chapter.

Badge pins
These are glued onto the backs of badges. They can be bought from specialist shops.

Coloured pencils and crayons
These come in a huge range of colours and should be non-toxic.

Coloured sticky tape
This is a strong tape which can be used for fastening heavy materials.

Crêpe and tissue paper
These come in lots of colours and can be used for making and decorating projects.

Cress seeds
These are scattered on moist cotton wool (balls) and left to grow into cress.

Face paints
These are used for decorating the face and body and can be removed easily with soap or cleansing cream.

Felt
This can be used in sewing projects. It is easy to cut and won't go ragged at the edges.

Felt-tip pens
These are always good to use on paper. The colours can't be mixed like paint, so it's best to use them separately.

Flour
This is one of the ingredients used for making salt dough.

Glitter
This can be glued onto projects as decoration. If there is any left over it can be poured back in the tube.

Needle and thread
These are used to sew with. Needles are very sharp so you must be careful not to hurt yourself. Threads come in a large range of colours.

Paintbrushes
These are used for applying paint and glue. They should be washed after use.

Paints
These must be non-toxic. Different colours can be mixed together to form new ones.

Paper glue
This comes in various formats but is easiest to use when in a tube.

Pencil sharpener
Use this to keep your pencils nice and sharp.

Pins
These are used to hold fabric together when sewing. They are very sharp.

Pom-poms
These can be bought from specialist shops or you can make your own. They can be glued or sewn onto projects.

PVA (white) glue
This must be non-toxic. When undiluted it is very useful for sticking heavy materials together. It can be diluted with water and used for papier-mâché.

Rolling pin
This is used for rolling out salt dough or cookie dough.

Ruler
This is used for measuring and drawing straight lines.

Safety pin
This can be used instead of a badge pin.

Salt
Use large amounts for the basic salt dough mixture.

Scissors
These should not be too sharp and must be handled safely at all times.

flour

salt

felt

crêpe and tissue paper

PVA (white) glue

paints

cress seeds

paintbrushes

rolling pin

scissors

needle and thread

face paints

safety pin

wax crayons

badge pins

glitter

pencil sharpener

coloured
sticky tape

paper glue

pins

felt-tip pens

ruler

pom-poms

coloured pencils

Potato Printing

Create your own wrapping paper with this simple and fun technique.

YOU WILL NEED
potato
knife
felt-tip pen
coloured ink
paper towel
paper plate or saucer for the ink
white or coloured paper

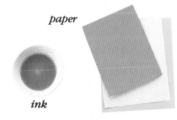

paper

ink

knife

paper towel

potato

paper plate

felt-tip pen

1 Cut a potato in half with a sharp knife and draw out a shape with a felt-tip pen.

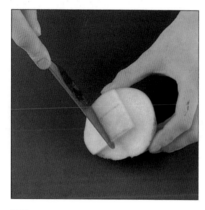

2 With the help of an adult, cut out the area around the shape.

3 Pour a few drops of ink onto a piece of paper towel placed on a paper plate or saucer and dab the potato into it.

4 Place the potato onto some white or coloured paper and press down hard. Repeat this process until the paper is covered with the design.

String Printing

Print this string design on coloured paper and cover your school textbooks.

YOU WILL NEED
cardboard
scissors
PVA (white) glue
felt-tip pen
string
saucer or paper plate
coloured paints
paintbrush
coloured paper

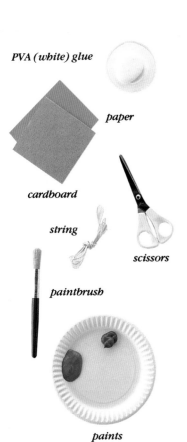

PVA (white) glue

paper

cardboard

string

scissors

paintbrush

paints

1 Cut out a few pieces of cardboard with a pair of scissors and stick the pieces together with PVA (white) glue to make a thick block.

2 Draw a design onto the cardboard with the felt-tip pen.

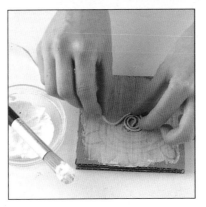

3 Cover the cardboard with glue and stick the string around the outline of the design. Allow to dry.

4 Dab paint onto the block with a paintbrush. Press down onto the paper. Repeat this process until the paper is covered with the design.

Teasel Mice

In days gone by, teasels were used to comb or 'tease' tangled wool before it could be spun. You can use them to make a family of animals.

YOU WILL NEED
teasels
scissors
circle of material 23 cm (9 in) in
    diameter for the body
needle, thread and pins
soft toy stuffing
rectangle of material 23 cm × 10 cm
    (9 in × 4 in) for the arms
rectangle of material 40 cm × 10 cm
    (15 in × 4 in) for the skirt
PVA (white) glue
beads for nose and eyes
fishing line or thread for whiskers
bits and pieces of felt, string, lace
    and ribbon

teasel

soft toy stuffing

PVA (white) glue

material

lace

scissors

! 1 Collect teasels from hedges and roadsides. Cut the heads from the stalks. Be careful, they are extremely prickly. If you have trouble finding any, teasels are often sold in florists' shops for dried flower arrangements. Alternatively, you can make these mice with pine cones instead.

! 2 Sew a running stitch around the edge of the circle of cloth for the body. Pull the threads to gather.

3 Put some of the toy stuffing in the middle.

4 Put a teasel on top of the stuffing. Draw the gathering thread in tightly around the base of the teasel. Knot to secure.

5 To make the arms, fold the small rectangle of material in half. Fold in half again. Pin and stitch along its length.

6 Sew a running stitch along one long side of the large rectangle of material for the skirt. Gather. Place around the neck of the teasel and stitch so that the skirt hangs over the body. Put the arms around the neck and stitch them in place above the skirt. Finish by gluing on beads for the eyes and nose, whiskers of fishing line or thread, felt ears and string for the tail. Decorate with ribbon, lace, hats, aprons, cloaks and other clothes. Make a whole family of mice!

Papier-mâché Piggy Bank

You won't find a friendlier pig to look after your pocket money!

YOU WILL NEED
PVA (white) glue
water
vaseline (optional)
large bowl
newspaper
wooden stick
balloon
pin
egg carton
scissors
masking tape
coloured paints
paintbrush

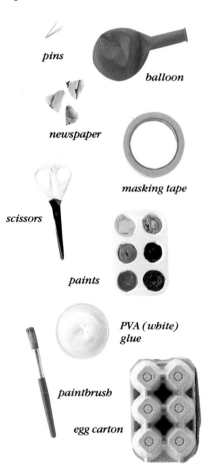

pins

balloon

newspaper

masking tape

scissors

paints

PVA (white) glue

paintbrush

egg carton

1 For the papier-mâché, mix some PVA (white) glue with water in a large bowl and stir in several layers of torn-up newspaper with a wooden stick. Blow up the balloon and tie a knot in it. Cover the balloon with water or vaseline and apply a layer of newspaper, then apply five layers of papier-mâché. Leave the balloon to dry overnight in a warm place. (This may take a little longer depending on the time of year.)

2 Once the papier-mâché is completely dry, burst the balloon with a pin and remove it. You may need to make a small hole to take out the balloon. For the feet and snout, cut up an egg carton with a pair of scissors, dividing up the egg tray and attaching the parts onto the balloon with masking tape.

3 Cut out triangles from the egg carton for the ears and attach them to the balloon with masking tape. Use papier-mâché to cover over the feet, snout and ears.

4 For the tail, roll up a piece of newspaper tightly and apply glue to secure it. Wrap the strip around your finger and let go. It should now have a coil shape. Attach it to the balloon with strips of papier-mâché.

5 When all the papier-mâché is completely dry, apply two coats of paint to the pig.

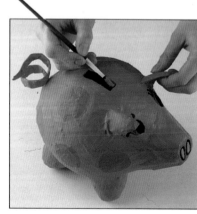

6 Cut out the money slot and finish painting the details onto the pig.

Decoupage Frame

Decoupage is a form of decoration using pictures cut from magazines, newspapers, even wallpaper. The pictures are then stuck onto mirror frames, screens and all sorts of objects to make a new and interesting design. Black and white pictures can be hand-tinted with paint that matches or contrasts with the object you are decorating. You can dip the pictures in cold tea to give the paper a pleasing 'aged' effect similar to old photos, or you can colour them with paints.

YOU WILL NEED
painted picture frame
sandpaper
assorted black and white pictures
scissors
non-toxic paint that matches the
    colour of the frame
undiluted non-toxic PVA (white) glue
paintbrush
non-toxic clear gloss varnish

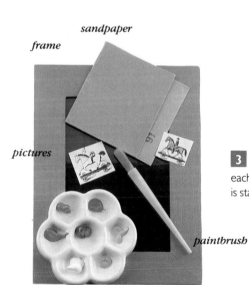

sandpaper
frame
pictures
paintbrush
paint

1 Remove the glass and backing from the picture frame. Lightly rub down the paint with sandpaper to give a patchy, antiqued effect.

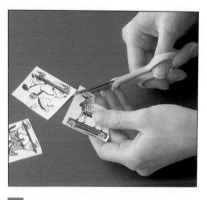

2 Carefully trim the pictures, leaving a slight border around the edges.

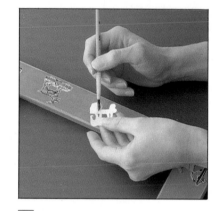

4 Arrange the dried cut-outs around the frame. When you are pleased with the composition, stick them in place with PVA (white) glue.

3 Make a thin solution of paint and dip each cut-out briefly into it until the paper is stained. Leave the cuttings flat to dry.

5 Seal the frame with three or four coats of gloss varnish. Leave to dry.

6 Fit your picture inside and replace the glass and backing.

Juggling Squares

Keep practising your juggling skills and impress everyone around you.

YOU WILL NEED
squares of colourful fabric
pencil
ruler
scissors
pins
needle
thread
crumpled paper or newspaper

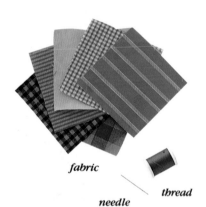

fabric

needle

thread

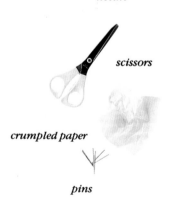

scissors

crumpled paper

pins

IMPORTANT SAFETY NOTE

You may need an adult's help for the sewing.

1 For each juggling square you will need six squares of fabric, 12 cm × 12 cm (4¾ in × 4¾ in). Cut these out with a pair of scissors. With the right sides facing each other sew the first two squares together with a needle and thread, allowing a 1 cm (½ in) seam allowance.

2 Sew all the squares together to form a letter 'T' shape.

3 Join the sides together to form a cube, leaving one side open for the stuffing. Turn the cube right side out.

4 Fill the cube with the crumpled paper or newspaper, and, when it is full, sew up the last side.

Teddy Bear's Outfit

Spoil your teddy with a new set of clothes.

YOU WILL NEED
scissors
colourful felt
needle
cotton thread
ribbon
PVA (white) glue
paintbrush
tracing and plain paper for templates
pencil
buttons
ruler
cotton fringing

thread

needle

PVA (white) glue

buttons

felt

fringing

ribbon

paintbrush

scissors

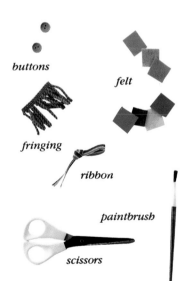

1 With a pair of scissors, cut out two semi-circular pieces of colourful felt to fit the width of your teddy's head. Sew the two pieces together with a needle and thread. To decorate the hat, stick on some felt shapes and ribbon with PVA (white) glue.

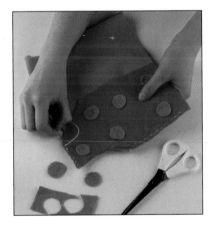

2 For the waistcoat, scale-up and trace the templates from the back of the book following the instructions on page 12. Place the templates onto pieces of felt and cut out. Glue on some felt spots and sew the three pieces together.

3 Sew three buttons onto one side of the waistcoat.

4 For the scarf, cut out a 30 cm × 6 cm (12 in × 2½ in) strip of felt. Glue on strips of coloured felt for the stripes and pieces of cotton fringing for the ends.

Painted Terracotta Flowerpots

Store your bits and pieces in these colourful pots, or use them to plant bulbs.

YOU WILL NEED
terracotta flowerpot
coloured paints (acrylic or emulsion)
paintbrushes
varnish (optional)
PVA (white) glue (optional)

paints

flowerpot

varnish

paintbrushes

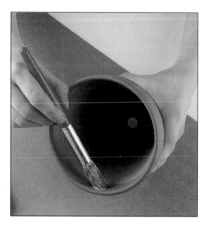

1 Paint the inside of the flowerpot in a single colour. Allow to dry.

2 Paint the outside rim of the pot in another colour. Allow to dry.

3 Paint the rest of the outside in a third colour.

4 Paint spots on the inside of the pot.

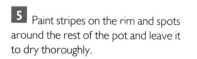

5 Paint stripes on the rim and spots around the rest of the pot and leave it to dry thoroughly.

6 Complete the design with more spots. Varnish the pot completely and leave it to dry before using. If you don't want to use varnish, you can use PVA (white) glue thinned with water. Use a paintbrush to cover the pot. It will dry clear, like varnish.

IMPORTANT SAFETY NOTE

Always use varnish in an area where there is plenty of air. Do not breathe in the varnish fumes, and clean your brushes thoroughly afterwards.

Salt Dough Buttons and Beads

Make your own personalized fashion accessories.

YOU WILL NEED
salt dough
toothpick
baking tray (sheet)
oven gloves
fish slice (spatula)
cooling rack
coloured paints
paintbrush
embroidery thread
rolling pin
tracing paper and card (cardboard)
   for templates
pencil
scissors
knife

1 Make the salt dough following the instructions on page 11. For the beads, mould a small piece of salt dough on the palm of your hand to form either a round, oblong or flat shape.

2 Pierce a hole through the beads with a toothpick. Lay the beads out on a greased baking tray (sheet). With the help of an adult, heat the oven to 100°C/ 225°F/Gas 2 and put in the baking tray. Cook for approximately 6 hours or until the beads are hard. Wearing oven gloves, remove the baking tray from the oven. With a fish slice (spatula) slide the beads onto a cooling rack. The beads will be very hot. Allow to cool before painting.

3 Paint the beads in lots of different colours and patterns. Allow each coat of paint to dry before adding the next so the colours don't smudge.

knife   *paintbrush*

wooden spoon

rolling pin

thread

paints

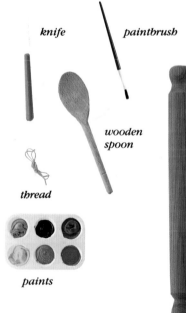

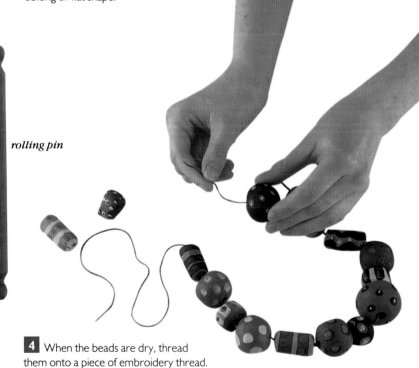

4 When the beads are dry, thread them onto a piece of embroidery thread.

5 For the buttons, sprinkle some flour onto a flat surface and roll out a piece of salt dough until it is 5 mm (¼ in) thick. Trace the templates from the back of the book following the instructions on page 12. Place the templates onto the dough and cut around them with a knife. Pierce 4 holes on each button. Bake them in the oven in the same way as the beads in step 2.

IMPORTANT SAFETY NOTE

You will need an adult to help you to heat the oven and remove the salt dough once it has been baked. Use oven gloves, and do not touch the baking tray (sheet) until it has cooled completely.

6 Paint the buttons when cool and allow to dry. Sew them onto a shirt, cardigan or even a hat. You will have to remove them before washing the clothes. Salt dough should not be washed with water or in a washing machine.

Cress Eggs

These funny eggs have hair that grows. You can give them a haircut and use the 'hair' as a tasty sandwich filling!

YOU WILL NEED
2 eggs
small bowl
cotton wool (ball)
water
cress seeds
coloured paints
paintbrush

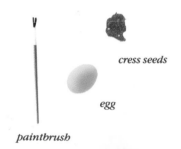

cress seeds

egg

paintbrush

cotton wool (ball)

paints

1 Carefully crack the eggs in half and empty the contents into a small bowl.

2 Moisten a piece of cotton wool (ball) in cold water and place it inside each egg shell half.

3 Sprinkle the cress seeds sparingly onto the cotton wool. Store the egg shells in a dark place for two days or until the seeds have sprouted, then transfer to a light area such as a windowsill.

4 Paint a jolly face onto each egg shell.

Papier-mâché Napkin Ring

Add some colour to the dinner table with fun napkin rings. You can make your own designs for different occasions.

YOU WILL NEED
tracing and plain paper for template
pencil
scissors
card (cardboard)
PVA (white) glue
cardboard toilet roll
masking tape
water
large bowl
newspaper
wooden stick
coloured paints
paintbrush

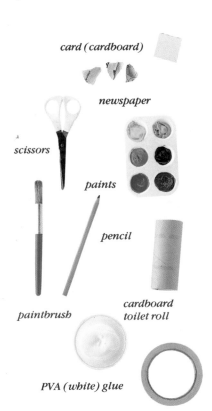

card (cardboard)

newspaper

scissors

paints

pencil

paintbrush

cardboard toilet roll

PVA (white) glue

masking tape

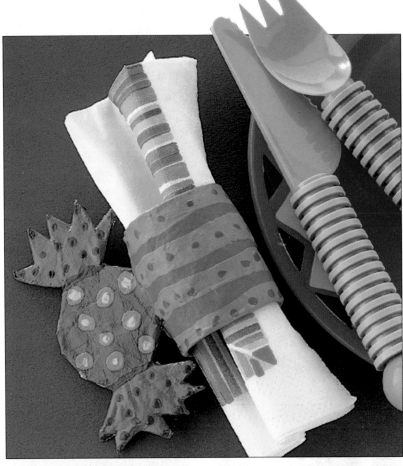

1 Trace the sweet (candy) template from the back of the book following the instructions on page 12. Place the template onto the card (cardboard) and cut it out. Stick the sweets together with PVA (white) glue. Do not stick the tags because they have to be bent outwards.

2 Cut a toilet roll in half and attach the sweet to it with masking tape.

3 For the papier-mâché, mix some glue with water in a large bowl and stir in several layers of torn-up newspaper with a wooden stick. Cover the napkin ring with three layers of papier-mâché and leave to dry overnight in a warm place.

4 When completely dry, paint the napkin ring in an assortment of colours and patterns.

Magic Box

Build your own fantasy world within a box. You could choose any theme you like – a jungle, a circus, or the bottom of the sea, as here.

YOU WILL NEED
coloured paints
paintbrush
cardboard box
scissors
pictures of shells and fish (cut from wrapping paper)
PVA (white) glue
netting
blue cellophane
card (cardboard)
pencil
glitter
tracing and plain paper for templates
cotton thread
wooden sticks

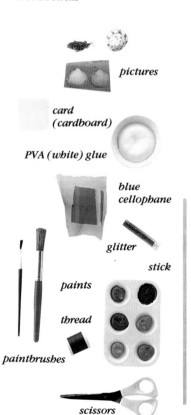

pictures

card (cardboard)

PVA (white) glue

blue cellophane

glitter

stick

paints

thread

paintbrushes

scissors

1 Paint the cardboard box both inside and out. Allow to dry. With a pair of scissors, cut out a rectangle from the top of the box and a circle from the front.

2 Decorate the opening with pictures of fish. Decorate the inside of the box with netting and cut-outs of shells stuck down with PVA (white) glue. Glue a piece of blue cellophane to the back wall.

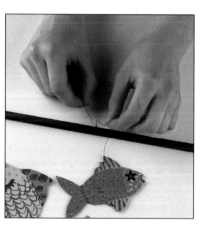

3 Draw a wave onto a piece of card (cardboard) with a pencil. Cut it out and dab on some spots of glue. Sprinkle glitter over the glue and allow to dry. Cover the wave in blue cellophane.

4 Trace the fish and seaweed templates from the back of the book following the instructions on page 12. Place the templates onto a piece of card and cut them out. Paint the shapes in an assortment of colours and leave to dry.

5 Tie a piece of cotton thread to each fish and seaweed shape and tie them to wooden sticks.

CRAFT HINT

If you can't find pictures of shells on wrapping paper look in magazines for pictures. You could also draw your own if you don't find any you like.

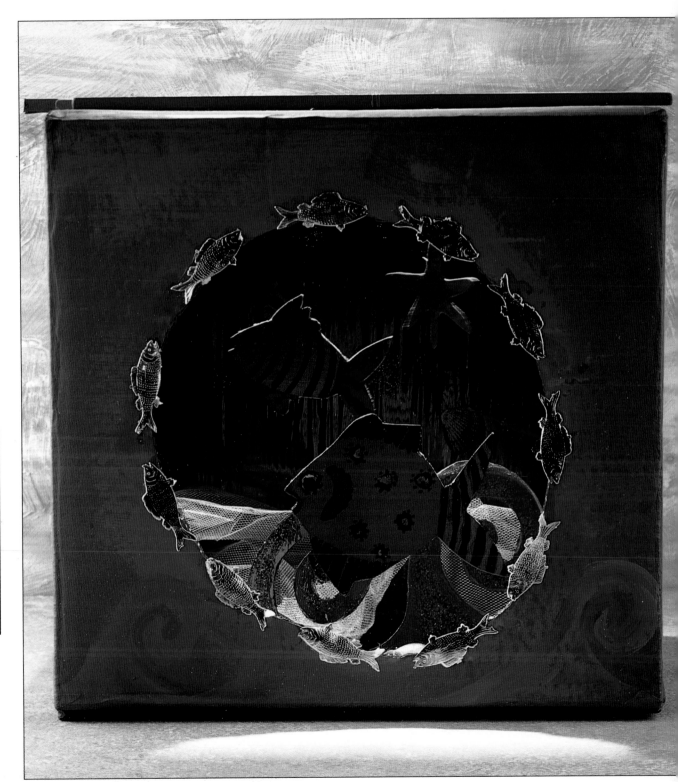

6 Place the sticks across the rectangle and dangle the sea-shapes inside the box.

Space Rocket

Travel in time with your very own rocket, made from objects around the house.

YOU WILL NEED
clear plastic bottle
tin foil
scouring pad
scissors
double-sided sticky tape
shiny paper
PVA (white) glue
paintbrush
tinsel
foil pie dishes (pans)

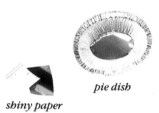

pie dish

shiny paper

1 Fill the bottle with scrunched-up pieces of tin foil.

2 Cut the scouring pad in half with a pair of scissors and attach it to the top of the bottle with double-sided sticky tape. Cut out two spots from the shiny paper and stick onto each side of the pad with PVA (white) glue.

3 Attach a piece of double-sided sticky tape onto the lid end of the bottle and wrap the tinsel around it.

sticky tape

scouring pad

PVA (white) glue

tinsel

scissors

plastic bottle

4 Cut the pie dishes (pans) in half and fold them in half again. Stick to the bottom of the bottle with sticky tape.

5 Cut out some stars from a piece of shiny paper and stick them onto the bottle with glue or sticky tape.

6 Cut out two pieces of shiny paper for the wings and glue them onto either side of the bottle.

Painting Eggs

The perfect Easter gift for your friends and family.
Put them in baskets or hide them for an egg hunt.

YOU WILL NEED
eggs
pin
small bowl
coloured paints
paintbrush

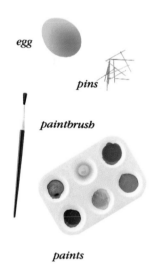

egg

pins

paintbrush

paints

CRAFT HINT

Make a whole batch of eggs in different colours. You could paint on names or paint faces to look like your friends and family.

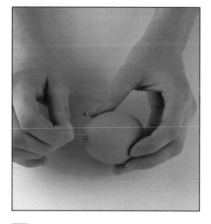

1 Pierce a hole in both ends of each egg with a pin.

2 Carefully blow the contents of the egg into a small bowl.

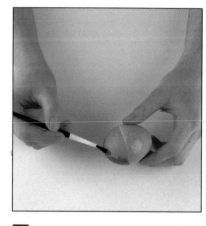

3 Paint one half of the egg and leave it to dry. Paint the other half in a different colour if you wish.

4 When the paint is dry, add a spotty bow.

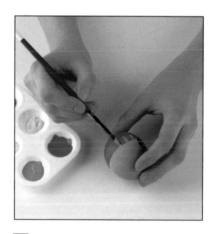

5 When the bow is dry, paint a band of different colours around the egg.

6 Finish decorating the egg with coloured spots.

Papier-mâché Treasure Box

Keep your favourite treasures hidden away in this box.

YOU WILL NEED
small cardboard box
pencil
scissors
cardboard
PVA (white) glue
paintbrush
tracing and plain paper for template
card (cardboard)
masking tape
water
large bowl
newspaper
wooden stick
coloured paints
foil sweet (candy) wrappers

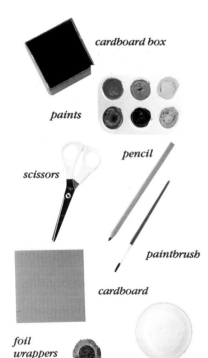

cardboard box

paints

pencil

scissors

paintbrush

cardboard

foil wrappers

PVA (white) glue

newspaper

masking tape

1 For the lid, draw round the box with a pencil on a piece of cardboard and cut it out with a pair of scissors. Cut out a slightly smaller piece and stick this onto the slightly larger piece with PVA (white) glue. Leave to dry.

2 Trace the jewel template from the back of the book following the instructions on page 12. Place the template onto the card (cardboard) and

cut it out. Bend along the marked lines to join the jewel together and fasten with masking tape.

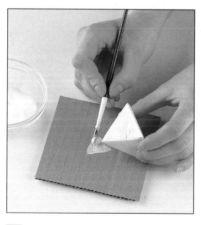

3 Glue one of the jewel's triangular sides onto the lid.

4 For the papier-mâché, mix some glue with water in a large bowl and stir in several layers of torn-up newspaper with a wooden stick. Apply three layers of papier-mâché to the box and the lid and allow them to dry overnight in a warm place. (This may take a little longer depending on the time of year.)

5 When the box is completely dry, paint the inside and the outside of both the box and the lid. Allow to dry.

6 Flatten the sweet (candy) wrappers and cut out circles from them. Glue the circles onto the box as decoration.

Musical Instrument

Discover your musical talents with this fun, colourful instrument. You can pluck the string and run the stick over the corrugated paper. You can even hit the top or sides like a drum.

YOU WILL NEED
plain and shiny corrugated paper
cardboard box
PVA (white) glue
felt-tip pen
scissors
coloured paints
paintbrush
tinsel
double-sided sticky tape
wooden broom pole
coloured sticky tape
string

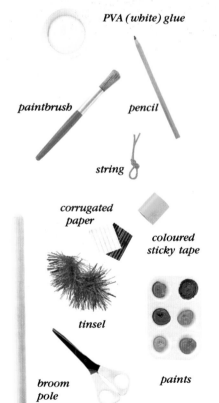

PVA (white) glue

paintbrush   *pencil*

string

corrugated paper

coloured sticky tape

tinsel

broom pole

scissors   *paints*

1 Stick a piece of corrugated paper around the upright sides of the cardboard box with PVA (white) glue.

2 With a felt-tip pen, draw a circle on one side of the box and carefully cut it out with scissors to make a hole.

3 Glue a piece of shiny corrugated paper on the top of the box. Paint the rest of the box a bright colour.

4 Stick the tinsel around the hole using either glue or double-sided sticky tape.

5 Paint the wooden broom pole and attach it to the side of the box using coloured sticky tape.

6 Thread the string through the hole at the top of the pole and tie a knot. Make a hole at the top and bottom of the box and thread the string through. Tie a knot to secure. It will need to be very tight to make a noise.

Natural Christmas Decorations

In ancient times people in Europe worshipped many different gods of nature. Holly, ivy, mistletoe, yew and other plants held religious meaning for these people. Memories have been passed down with our folklore. Today, these plants are still used to decorate homes at Christmas.

YOU WILL NEED
Christmas greenery
newspaper
dried seed heads
pine cones
gold and silver spray paint
florist's foam for flower arranging
candles
red berries
Christmas tree decorations
ribbon
sticky tape
string
wire
tinsel

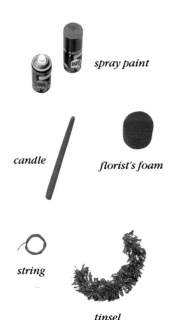

spray paint

candle　*florist's foam*

string

tinsel

1 Gather together some greenery such as holly, ivy, mistletoe, conifer sprigs and other evergreen leaves

2 Spread out the newspaper in a well ventilated area. Spray dried seed heads and pine cones with gold or silver paint. Allow to dry before using as decorations.

3 To make a table decoration, stick greenery into florists' foam.

4 Push a candle into the middle of the foam. Decorate with sprayed seed heads, cones, berries, Christmas tree decorations and tinsel.

5 To make a Christmas wreath, tape or tie greenery around a circle of wire, cane or twigs.

6 Decorate with pine cones and ribbons and other pretty objects. Look at the picture opposite. Can you see some other ideas for natural Christmas decorations?

Christmas Stocking

Hang this stocking at the end of your bed for Santa to fill with plenty of Christmas presents.

YOU WILL NEED
paper
pencil
scissors
colourful or patterned fabric
red felt
needle
thread
pins
velvet ribbon
rik-rak braid
PVA (white) glue
paintbrush
buttons

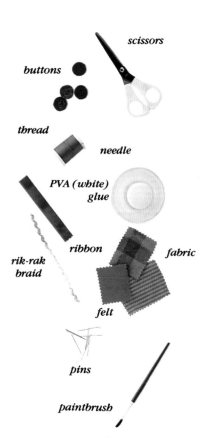

scissors

buttons

thread

needle

PVA (white) glue

rik-rak braid

ribbon

fabric

felt

pins

paintbrush

1 Draw a stocking shape on a piece of paper, and use it as a pattern. You will need to make the pattern 1 cm (½ in) bigger all around to allow for the seam. Cut out 2 pieces of fabric for the main part of the stocking. Cut out a spiky border from red felt for the top.

2 Fold over the top edge of each stocking piece and sew with a needle and thread.

3 Pin the two stocking pieces together making sure the right sides are facing each other. Sew around the bottom and sides leaving a 1 cm (½ in) seam allowance. Turn the stocking right-side out.

4 Pin the red spiky felt around the top edge of the stocking together with a piece of velvet ribbon for the loop, and sew.

5 Stick some more velvet ribbon and some rik-rak braid onto the red felt with PVA (white) glue.

6 Sew some buttons onto the red felt.

IMPORTANT SAFETY NOTE

You may need an adult's help for the sewing. If you don't want to sew, you could make the entire stocking from felt, and glue the sides together with a thin layer of PVA (white) glue.

Recycling Fun

It is amazing what you can do with a plastic bottle,
an empty washing-powder box and a few bottle tops.
Even an old pair of socks or a collection of empty
matchboxes can be turned into something to
play with or wear.

Materials

These are just some of the materials you will need.
Some you will already have, others you can buy.

Cardboard tubes
These come in a variety of sizes in the centres of toilet rolls, kitchen-paper rolls and rolls of silver foil.

Coloured cord, thin
This is very strong and is good for necklaces and mobiles.

Coloured sticky-paper dots
These come in a variety of colours and sizes and are available from most stationers.

Corks
Corks are good for making small dolls, animals and other toys.

Cotton thread
This comes in lots of bright colours and thicknesses and is used for patchwork and sewing.

Darning needles
These are wide needles with large eyes and rounded ends that are not very sharp. Use them for sewing, for stringing beads and for threading elastic.

Elastic
It is possible to buy thin elastic in different colours, such as silver, gold and glitter-effect.

Fabric and felt scraps
Scraps of fabric and felt are useful for making fabric pictures, toys' clothes and patchwork. Felt comes in lots of lovely colours and doesn't fray.

Felt-tipped pens
These must be non-toxic. They are good for adding decoration to paper and card (posterboard).

Masking tape
Masking tape is made from paper and is easy to remove after it has been stuck down.

Measuring tape
You sometimes need this for measuring fabric.

Natural objects
These include twigs, acorns and fir cones, which can be picked up in parks and during country walks. Always show an adult what you have found before you use it, to make sure that it is safe.

Paintbrushes
Paintbrushes come in a variety of sizes. Use a medium-thick brush for general painting and for applying glue. Use fine brushes to paint more detailed designs.

Paints
These must be non-toxic. Poster paints are good because they come in lots of lovely colours.

Palette
A palette is a useful container for paint. If you don't have one, use an old saucer or carton.

Paper clips
Paper clips may be plain or patterned and come in lots of sizes. They are meant for holding pieces of paper together, but some are very colourful and attractive and can be used as decoration as well.

Paper glue
This must be non-toxic and comes in liquid or a solid stick.

Pencils
A soft pencil is useful for making tracings and transferring them to card (posterboard) and paper.

PVA (white) glue
This must be non-toxic. PVA (white) glue is very sticky and is good for gluing cardboard and fabric. It can also be mixed with poster paints to make them stick to plastic surfaces. It is useful as a varnish and, if you dilute it, you can use it to make papier-mâché.

Rubber bands
These come in lots of colours and different lengths.

Ruler
A ruler is useful for measuring and drawing straight lines.

Scissors
These should be specially for children with rounded blades.

Silver and coloured foil
Silver foil comes on long rolls and is good for making jewellery. Coloured foil covers sweets (candy) and biscuits (cookies).

Sticky tape
This can be used for sticking paper, card (posterboard) and foil.

Strong glue
This must be non-toxic and solvent-free. Strong glue is useful for sticking heavy cardboard and holding awkward joints together.

coloured sticky-paper dots

coloured foil

sweet (candy) wrappers

corks

silver foil

PVA (white) glue

paper glue

palette

paintbrushes

fabric scraps

paints

strong glue

felt-tipped pens

pencils

wooden spoons

scissors

ruler

natural objects

cardboard tubes

sticky tape

coloured cord and threads

rubber bands

darning needles

pins

paper clips

masking tape

Printing with Foam Rubber Stamps

Simple stamps can be cut from sheets of thin foam rubber and stuck onto cardboard bases. Use these recycled stamps to make your own special greetings cards, or even to decorate your walls.

Painting on Plastic

Sometimes you may want to paint plastic bottles and yogurt cartons but ordinary poster paint will not stick to plastic. However, if you add glue to the paint it will become sticky and will cover the plastic well.

1 To make the stamps, cut several rectangles of heavy cardboard measuring 5 x 6 cm (2 x 2¼ in). Cut an equal number of smaller rectangles measuring 1.5 x 6 cm (⅝ x 2¼ in) to form the handles. Stick the handles to the tops of the bases with strong glue.

1 Put some ordinary poster paint into a palette or small dish.

2 Pour in a little PVA (white) glue. Carefully mix the paint and the glue, until they are thoroughly mixed together.

2 Draw the stamp motif onto foam rubber. Cut it out with scissors and glue it to the cardboard base. Leave aside to dry thoroughly.

3 Mix paint with water to a stiff consistency. Gently dip the stamp in the paint and then press it onto medium-weight paper or thin card (posterboard).

3 Wash your plastic bottle in warm soapy water and dry thoroughly. Apply the paint mixture over the surface of the bottle, taking care to spread the paint smoothly. Wash your brush thoroughly, as soon as you have finished.

Flattening and Cutting Up a Box

Cardboard can be used for papier-mâché frames among other things. Old boxes are the best source, and you can flatten them out easily.

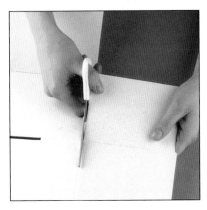

1 Remove any tape that is holding the box together and press it flat.

2 Cut the box into pieces, ready for use in your various projects.

Removing a Label From a Bottle

Plastic bottles can be used for all kinds of projects. You will need to wash them thoroughly.

1 Fill a washing-up bowl with warm soapy water.

2 Soak the bottle in the water for approximately 10 minutes.

Re-using Foil Wrappers

Coloured foil is great for decorations, and you don't have to buy it specially. Save old sweet (candy) wrappers and cases made of pretty colours, and cut them into different shapes.

1 Flatten the wrappers and cases and smooth them out. Cut them up for use in your projects.

3 Peel the label off the bottle. If the label is still sticking to the bottle, soak it in the water for a little longer.

Junk Robot

All you need to make this fabulous robot is a washing-powder box, a plastic cup, some washing line, washing-up sponges and toilet-roll tubes. Its features and control panel are added with various bits and pieces, such as bottle tops, yogurt pots and a safety pin, so keep an eye on the kitchen bin for useful robot parts!

RECYCLING TIP
Silver foil can be used more than once. If it has been used for food wash it carefully with soapy water and a sponge and leave it to dry.

YOU WILL NEED
PVA (white) glue
4 toilet-roll tubes
washing line
rubber bands
plastic cup
silver foil
scissors
sticky tape
washing-powder box
washing-up sponges
2 small yogurt pots
2 thick sponge scourers
3 round plastic scourers
bottle caps and other
  plastic bits and pieces
foil pie dishes (pans)
2 metal washers
safety pin

toilet-roll tubes

washing-up sponge

foil dishes (pans)

plastic scourer

sticky tape

1 Put a little glue on the tops and bottoms of the toilet-roll tubes. Wrap washing line around the tubes. Hold it in place with rubber bands while the glue dries. Do the same to the plastic cup.

2 Cut a piece of silver foil that is large enough to cover the washing-powder box. Loosely crumple the foil, to give it a crinkly surface, and tape it around the box.

3 Cut two circles from washing-up sponge and glue them to one end of two of the toilet-roll tubes. Glue a small yogurt pot to the other end of both tubes to make the robot's arms.

4 To make the robot's legs, glue a thick scourer to one end of the two remaining toilet-roll tubes. Stretch a round plastic scourer over each end of the tubes.

5 Glue bottle caps, foil dishes and other bits and pieces to the front of the box to make the controls. Glue two metal washers and a safety pin to the front of the plastic cup to make the face.

6 Glue the cup to the top of the box and put a plastic scourer over it to make the neck. Glue the legs to the bottom and one arm to each side; hold in place with rubber bands until the glue dries.

Peg Cowboys

These cowboys are ready to ride the range on their dappled horses. They are made from old-fashioned wooden pegs (clothespins) and look very smart in their gingham shirts and spotted neckerchiefs. The horses are made from thin card (posterboard) and they can stand upright.

YOU WILL NEED
white, dark blue and red
    poster paints
paintbrushes
paint-mixing container
wooden clothes pegs (clothespins)
scissors
yellow, red and white
    paper scraps
non-toxic strong glue
tracing paper
pencil
thin white card (posterboard)
felt-tipped pens

wooden clothes pegs (clothespins)

scissors

poster paints

pencil

felt-tipped pen

paintbrushes

paper scraps

strong glue

1 Paint the top of a peg (clothespin) white. Paint the bottom half dark blue to make the cowboy's jeans.

2 When the first coat of paint has dried, add details, such as the cowboy's face and the checks on his shirt, using poster paints.

3 Cut a hat from yellow paper. Fold up the edges and then glue the hat to the front of the cowboy's head. Cut a neckerchief from red paper and add spots with white paint. Glue the neckerchief around the cowboy's neck.

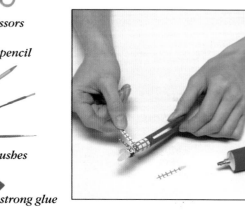

4 Cut two strips of white paper to make the cowboy's arms. Paint a hand at the end of each strip and add checks. Glue the arms to the cowboy's sides.

5 Trace the horse templates from the back of the book. Lay the tracings face-down on thin white card (posterboard) and draw over the lines to transfer them. Cut out all the pieces.

6 Using felt-tipped pens, draw in the horse's face and its markings. Push the body into the slots in its legs. Sit the cowboy on his horse.

Snake Sock Puppets

One good way to give your old socks a new lease of life is to make them into puppets. These snakes are decorated with brightly coloured felt. Once you've made a snake, why not make some other characters to keep it company?

YOU WILL NEED
scraps of coloured felt
scissors
non-toxic strong glue
1 sock

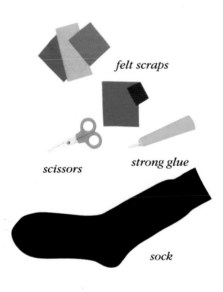

felt scraps

scissors

strong glue

sock

1 To make the snake's eyes, cut two circles of felt. Cut two smaller circles of a different colour and glue them to the middle of the larger circles.

2 Glue the snake's eyes in position at the top of the sock.

3 Cut diamonds and strips of felt in various colours. Glue the strips at equal distances along the length of the sock. Glue the diamonds between the strips.

4 Cut a forked tongue from red felt. Glue the tongue to the top of the toe of the sock, in the centre. Allow the glue to dry thoroughly before you play with your sock puppet.

Wooden Spoon Puppets

You can make puppets from all sorts of things, but wooden spoons are especially good because they are just the right shape to make a head and a body. Gather a piece of fabric to hide the spoon handle, paint a face at the top and away you go!

YOU WILL NEED
wooden spoon
pink, blue, brown and yellow poster
   paints
paintbrush
paint-mixing container
pencil
ruler
fabric
scissors
darning needle
matching thread
non-toxic strong glue
satin ribbon scrap
gold and coloured foil

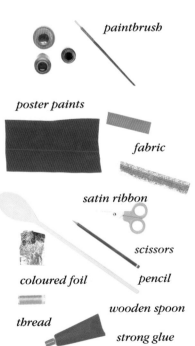

paintbrush
poster paints
fabric
satin ribbon
scissors
coloured foil   *pencil*
thread   *wooden spoon*
strong glue

1 Paint the top half of the wooden spoon pink and leave it to dry. Draw the puppet's eyes, nose, mouth and hair in pencil on the spoon and then fill in its features using poster paints.

2 Cut a piece of fabric as long as the spoon handle and 30 cm (12 in) wide. Sew two lines of running stitches along the top edge of the fabric and pull the threads tight to gather the material. Knot the ends of the threads together.

3 Glue the gathered edge of the fabric around the spoon handle, below the puppet's face. Glue a short scrap of satin ribbon around the puppet's neck, to cover the top of the gathered fabric.

4 Cut a crown from gold foil and glue it to the top of the head. Cut two circles of coloured foil and glue one to the middle of the crown and one at the centre of the satin ribbon, as 'jewels'.

Catch-the-ball Game

Test your skill with this bat-and-ball game. It takes quite a lot of practice to catch the ball in the cup but it's good fun while you are learning! Use a plastic bottle with a long neck, because this makes a better handle to hold on to.

YOU WILL NEED
coloured tissue paper
PVA (white) glue
mixing bowl
clear plastic bottle
scissors
yogurt pot
non-toxic strong glue
thin coloured cord

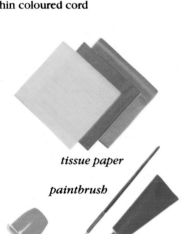

tissue paper

paintbrush

yogurt pot   *strong glue*

cord

plastic bottle

1 Take two sheets of different coloured tissue paper and tear them into strips and circles.

2 Mix some PVA (white) glue with a little water. Coat each strip of tissue paper with glue. Cover the bottle with the paper. Add some circles of paper on top of the strips. Leave to dry thoroughly.

3 Carefully cut the corners from the top of the yogurt pot. Glue the pot to the centre of the bottle.

4 Roll a sheet of tissue paper tightly into a small ball. It should be small enough to fit inside the yogurt pot.

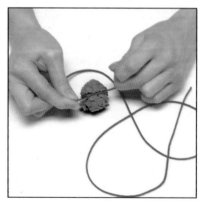

5 Cut a long piece of coloured cord. Tie one end of the cord tightly around the ball of tissue paper.

6 Tie the other end of the thin coloured cord around the end of the neck of the bottle.

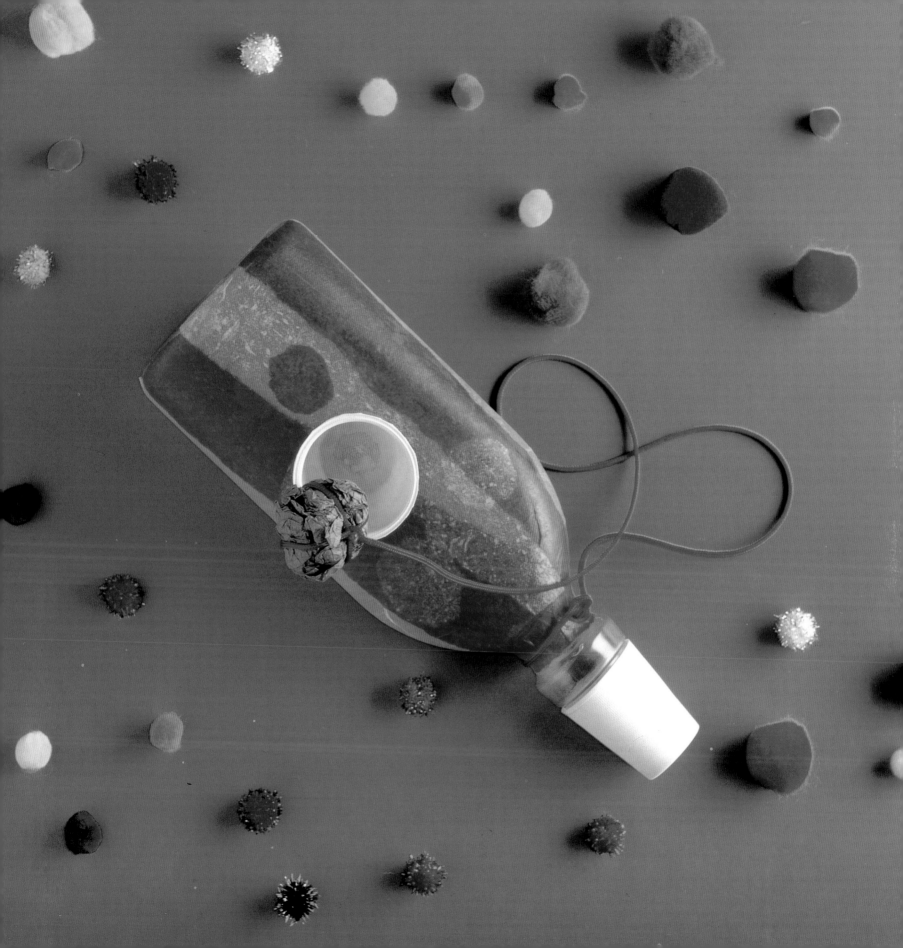

Shaker

This shaker is filled with beads and buttons, but you can use rice or dried beans.

YOU WILL NEED
clear plastic bottle, with cap
small beads and buttons
large and small coloured
   sticky-paper dots
non-toxic strong glue

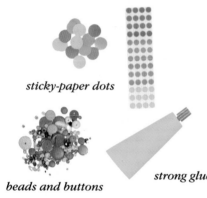

sticky-paper dots

beads and buttons

strong glue

1 Wash and carefully dry the bottle. It should be dry inside as well. Pour a mixture of small beads and buttons into the bottle. A couple of handfuls will make a good noise.

2 Spread a line of glue around the inside of the bottle top. Screw the top back onto the bottle. Stick large coloured sticky-paper dots to the outside to make a bright and decorative pattern.

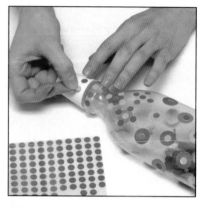

3 Stick a row of small coloured sticky-paper dots around the lower edge of the bottle top to make a pattern.

Tambourine

Two foil pie dishes (pans) can quickly and easily become a shiny tambourine.

YOU WILL NEED
ruler
thin satin ribbon
scissors
small bells
sticky tape
2 foil pie dishes (pans)
non-toxic strong glue

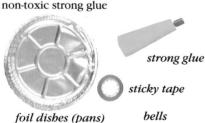

strong glue

sticky tape

foil dishes (pans)

bells

1 Cut 10 cm (4 in) lengths of ribbon, and tie a bell to each piece.

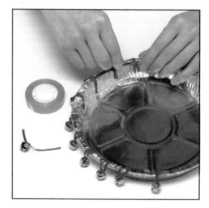

2 Tape the bells around the inside edge of one of the foil dishes (pans), making sure to space them evenly.

3 Spread glue around the rim of the second foil dish. Glue the two dishes together, rim to rim, covering the ends of the ribbons. Leave the glue to dry.

Drum

Drums are good fun to play and this one is portable, so you can play it wherever you are. The drum is made from an old plastic ice-cream tub and the drumsticks are knitting needles, with wooden beads on the ends.

YOU WILL NEED
ice-cream tub, with lid
yellow poster paint
paintbrush
paint-mixing container
PVA (white) glue
paper glue
scissors
coloured paper
thick coloured cord
dried rice
non-toxic strong glue
2 large wooden beads
2 knitting needles

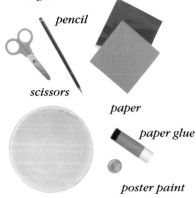

pencil

scissors

paper

paper glue

poster paint

ice-cream tub

wooden beads

rice

cord

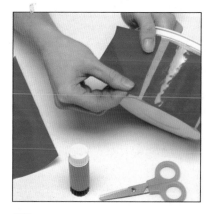

1 Paint the outside of the ice-cream tub with bright poster paint mixed with a little PVA (white) glue. When the paint is dry, cut out squares of red paper and glue them around the tub.

2 Ask an adult to punch a hole in both sides of the tub. Cut a length of thick coloured cord and poke the ends through the holes. Tie a double knot in each end of the cord.

3 Put a handful of dried rice inside the tub and replace the lid. The rice will make a swishing sound when you beat the drum.

4 Cut a circle of red paper and glue it to the top of the lid of the drum.

5 Cut diamonds of coloured paper. Glue one on top of each coloured square of paper around the sides of the drum and one to the top of the lid.

6 To make the drumsticks, use the strong glue to attach a large wooden bead to the end of each knitting needle. Let the glue dry thoroughly before you play your drum.

Pom-pom Hat

Beat the cold with this fun pom-pom hat. It's made by cutting down an old pair of wool tights. Leftover balls of wool are used to make two pompoms to decorate the top of the hat. It looks so stylish that no one will be able to guess what it is made from.

YOU WILL NEED
tape measure
pair of wool tights
scissors
darning needle
thin knitting wool (yarn)
pencil
pair of compasses
thin cardboard
knitting-wool oddments

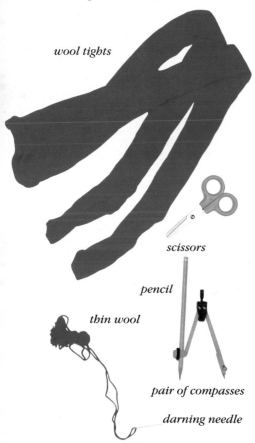

wool tights

scissors

pencil

thin wool

pair of compasses

darning needle

1   Measure 15 cm (6 in) down from the top of each leg of the tights. Cut off the legs at this point and discard them.

2   Thread the needle with the wool. Sew across the top of the cut ends, using small running stitches. Pull the stitching tight. Sew two more stitches to keep the ends gathered. Cut the thread.

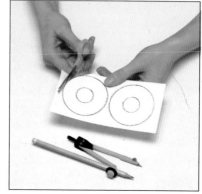

3   Draw two identical circles with the pencil and pair of compasses on the cardboard. Draw smaller circles inside. Cut out the larger circles. Ask an adult to help you to cut out the smaller ones.

4   Place the circles together. Tie the end of a length of wool around the circles. Wrap the wool around and around the circles, passing it through the central hole, until the hole is filled in.

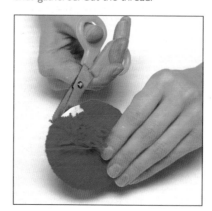

5   Snip through the wool at the edge of the circles. Pull the circles slightly apart and tie a short piece of wool around the centre of the wool between the circles, to keep it all together. Pull the circles off and trim any uneven wool.

6   Make a second pom-pom, then sew one to the end of each gathered leg. To wear the hat, roll up the waistband a couple of times to make a brim, and tie the legs loosely together.

Squeezy Bottle Dog Book-ends

These book-ends are made by covering two squeezy bottles with small pieces of papier-mâché and then painting them. The legs are made from corks, and the ears and tails are cut from scraps of thin card (posterboard).

YOU WILL NEED
2 squeezy bottles
funnel
dried rice
masking tape
newspaper
diluted PVA (white) glue
8 corks
white, red, yellow, brown and black
   poster paints
paintbrushes
paint-mixing container
pencil
thin white card (posterboard)
scissors
strong non-toxic glue

squeezy bottle

masking tape

rice   *corks*   *scissors*

PVA (white) glue

funnel

poster paints

paintbrushes

1 Wash and dry the squeezy bottles. Put a funnel in the top of each bottle and half-fill it with rice. Seal the top of each bottle with a strip of masking tape.

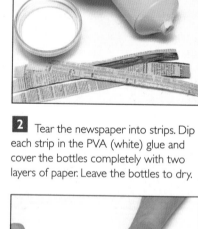

2 Tear the newspaper into strips. Dip each strip in the PVA (white) glue and cover the bottles completely with two layers of paper. Leave the bottles to dry.

3 With PVA (white) glue, stick four corks to one side of each squeezy bottle to make the legs. Leave the book-ends to dry thoroughly.

4 Paint the book-ends white. You may have to use two coats of paint to cover up the newsprint completely.

5 Draw in the dogs' faces, collars and markings with the pencil. Decorate the dogs using poster paints.

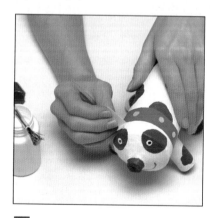

6 Draw four ears and two tails on the card (posterboard) and cut out. Bend back the edges of each shape and glue ears and a tail onto each dog, using the strong glue.

Nail Chimes

Make beautiful music with these nifty nail chimes. They are suspended from a cardboard tube and they make a lovely, clear, ringing sound when you strike them. You will need to find bolts in various sizes, so that your chimes make different notes.

YOU WILL NEED
scissors
coloured paper
cardboard tube
paper glue
coloured sticky-paper dots
strong coloured cord
bolts of various sizes
1 long bolt

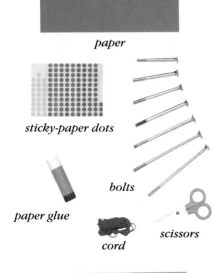

paper

sticky-paper dots

paper glue

bolts

scissors

cord

cardboard tube

1 Cut a rectangle of coloured paper as long as the cardboard tube and wide enough to fit around it. Stick the paper to the tube.

2 Stick a row of sticky-paper dots around each end of the cardboard tube, as decoration.

3 Cut a long length of coloured cord. It must be strong enough to bear the weight of all the bolts.

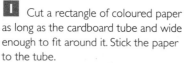

4 Tie the length of cord around the head of each bolt. Make sure that the bolts are evenly spaced along the cord.

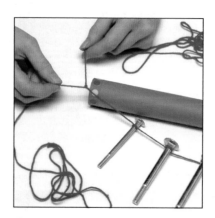

5 Thread the free ends of the coloured cord through the cardboard tube. Tie them together at one end.

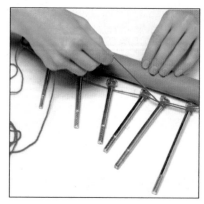

6 Loop one of the cords two or three times around the head of each bolt again, then pass it back through the tube. Tie the ends tightly together. Play the chimes using the long bolt.

Groovy Guitar

Make yourself a groovy, twanging guitar from a cardboard tube and a washing-powder box. The strings are made from elastic bands and they rest on half a toilet-roll tube, which gives them quite loud different sounds.

RECYCLING TIP
You could cover the guitar with silver foil if you have some spare.

YOU WILL NEED
washing-powder box
felt-tipped pen
scissors
long cardboard tube
brown-paper tape
toilet-roll tube
non-toxic strong glue
yellow and orange poster paints
paintbrush
paint-mixing container
6 rubber bands
5 small cotton reels (spools)
silver foil
thick cord

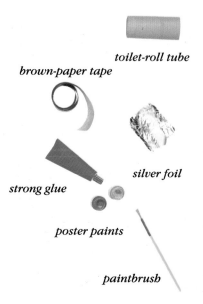

toilet-roll tube
brown-paper tape
silver foil
strong glue
poster paints
paintbrush

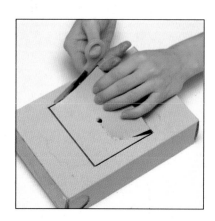

1 Draw a square on the front of the washing-powder box. Ask an adult to help you to cut the square out of the box.

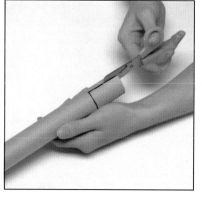

2 Draw a rectangle on one end of the cardboard tube. Ask an adult to help you cut the shape out of the tube, so that it will fit on the end of the box.

3 Put the tube on the end of the box and tape it in place with brown-paper tape to make the neck of the guitar.

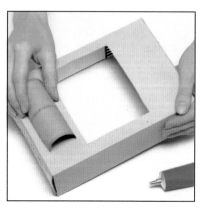

4 Cut a toilet-roll tube in half. Glue the half-tube below the hole in the front of the guitar.

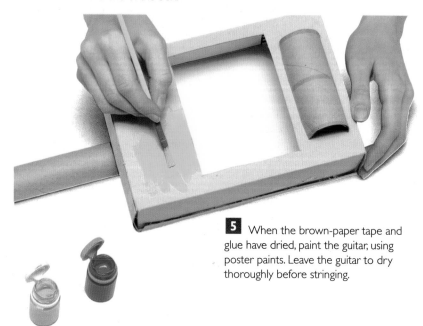

5 When the brown-paper tape and glue have dried, paint the guitar, using poster paints. Leave the guitar to dry thoroughly before stringing.

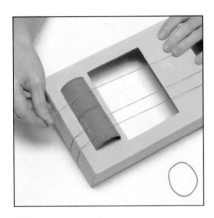

6 Stretch six rubber bands around the body of the guitar. Rest the rubber bands on the half toilet-rolls as this will make them louder.

7 Cover five small cotton reels (spools) with silver foil, then glue four reels to the neck of the guitar to make pegs. Glue the other reel to the end of the guitar. Tie a length of cord from the neck of the guitar to the reel at the base of the guitar to make a strap.

Storage Chest

This small storage chest is great for keeping little treasures safe. It is made from large, empty matchboxes and is covered with scraps of sticky-backed plastic. You can make the chest as large as you want – just keep adding more matchboxes. You can also use large and small matchboxes, so you have different-size compartments.

RECYCLING TIP
This is an ideal storage place for those buttons, beads, pins and paper clips that all good recyclers collect and keep.

YOU WILL NEED
green and red sticky-backed plastic
scissors
6 large matchboxes
non-toxic strong glue
tracing paper
pencil
thin card (posterboard)
6 coloured plastic beads

matchboxes

scissors

sticky-backed plastic

strong glue

pencil

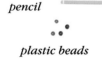

plastic beads

1 Cut three green and three red pieces of sticky-backed plastic the same width and long enough to fit around a matchbox. Glue them on.

2 Cut six thin strips of red and six of green sticky-backed plastic. Glue them to the front and back of the box trays: red in green boxes and green in red boxes.

3 Spread glue along the long side of one green box and glue it to a red box. Repeat so that you have three rows of two boxes.

4 When the glue has dried, glue the three rows of boxes on top of each other to make the storage chest. Make sure that the edges of the boxes line up.

5 Trace the template at the back of the book. Lay it face-down on a piece of card (posterboard), draw over the lines to transfer it and cut out. Cover with sticky-backed plastic and trim.

6 Cut out a small red heart and stick it to the front of the card (posterboard). Bend back the base and glue it to the top of the chest. Glue a bead to the front of each tray for handles.

Nature Box

If you go for an autumn walk in the countryside or a park you will probably find some twigs, seed pods, fir cones and so on, which make lovely decorations. This plain cardboard box is decorated with rows of acorns, seed pods and small and large fir cones have been added to make it really attractive. Always ask an adult to look at what you have found to see that it is safe. Carefully wash everything before you use it.

YOU WILL NEED
green poster paint
paintbrush
paint-mixing container
small, round cardboard box, with lid
acorns, fir cones and seed pods
non-toxic strong glue

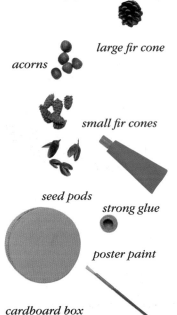

large fir cone

acorns

small fir cones

seed pods

strong glue

poster paint

cardboard box

paintbrush

1 Paint the lid and base of the cardboard box with poster paint and leave it to dry thoroughly.

2 Arrange a row of acorns around the edge of the lid of the box and glue them in position.

3 Glue a large fir cone to the middle of the lid. Glue small fir cones to the top of the lid, between the acorns and the large fir cone.

4 Glue a row of seed pods at equal distances around the sides of the box. Let the glue dry thoroughly before you use your box.

Sponge-flower Hairband

Washing-up sponges come in such pretty colours that it seems a pity not to use them in new ways. Here, pink, yellow and green sponges have been used to make a flower to decorate and brighten up a plain hairband.

YOU WILL NEED
tracing paper
pencil
thin card (posterboard)
scissors
yellow, pink and green
   washing-up sponges
thin black felt-tipped pen
darning needle
pink, yellow and green or
   blue threads
hairband

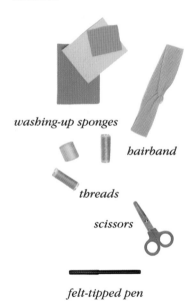

washing-up sponges

hairband

threads

scissors

felt-tipped pen

1 Trace the flower patterns from the back of the book. Lay the tracings face-down on the card (posterboard) and draw over the lines again. Cut out the shapes to make templates.

2 Place the flower template on the yellow sponge, the flower centre on the pink sponge and the leaves on the green sponge. Draw around the templates with the felt-tipped pen. Cut out the shapes.

3 Place the pink flower centre in the middle of the flower. Sew the centre to the flower with three or four small stitches, using pink thread.

4 Place the leaves, pointing outwards, on the front of the hairband. Sew the leaves to the hairband with small stitches in blue or green thread. Lay the flower on top of the leaves, and sew its centre and edges to the band with yellow thread.

Straw Mobile

Drinking straws come in wonderful bright colours and you can use them to make lots of different projects. This mobile is made from pieces of straw threaded together.

YOU WILL NEED
scissors
coloured drinking straws
ruler
coloured cotton cord
non-toxic strong glue
large buttons
wooden beads

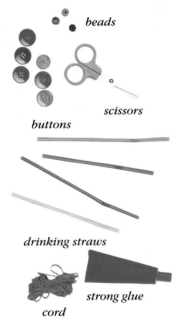

beads

scissors

buttons

drinking straws

cord

strong glue

1 Cut four different-coloured straws into 10 cm (4 in) pieces. Cut a long piece of coloured cord and thread the straw pieces onto it. Tie the ends of the cord, so that the straws make a square.

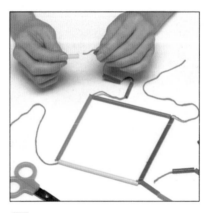

2 Cut more straws into 2.5 cm (1 in) lengths. Tie a length of coloured cord at each corner of the straw square. Thread the pieces of straw onto the cotton.

3 Tie the pieces of cotton together at the top. Tie another length of cord to the top of the mobile and thread some more short lengths of straw onto it.

4 Cut four 2.5 cm (1 in) pieces and one 5 cm (2 in) piece of the same coloured straw. Glue the longer piece of straw to the back of a large button. Glue two short pieces of straw on each side of the long piece. Glue another button on top to make a star. Make four more stars in different colours.

5 Cut four different lengths of coloured cord and tie one to each corner of the square, so that they hang down. Cut 2.5 cm (1 in) lengths of straw and thread them onto the cotton. Thread a star onto the end of each cord and one on the top of the mobile.

6 Thread a wooden bead on the end of each piece of cord, to keep the stars in place. Knot the ends of the four cords that hang down and trim the ends. Leave a long cord at the top of the mobile to hang it up.

Paper Clip Christmas Decorations

These shiny Christmas decorations will add a sparkle to your Christmas tree. Decorate them with scraps of bright foil from sweet (candy) wrappers, and sandwich paper clips between them to make the decorations look like icicles.

YOU WILL NEED
pencil
pair of compasses
thin card (posterboard)
scissors
silver and coloured foil
non-toxic strong glue
silver paper clips
thin silver elastic

coloured foil　　*strong glue*

silver foil　　*paper clips*

silver elastic

scissors

1 Using a pencil and a pair of compasses, draw two circles exactly the same size on the card (posterboard). Cut them out.

2 Cut two squares of silver foil about 4 cm (1½ in) bigger all the way around than the circles of card (posterboard). Place a circle in the middle of each piece of foil. Wrap the edges of the silver foil over the card (posterboard).

3 Cut a circle of coloured foil and snip small triangles from its edges to make a 'star' shape. Glue the star to the front of one of the card (posterboard) circles. Cut two circles from coloured foil and glue them to the middle of the star.

4 Glue a row of paper clips to the back of the other circle. Glue the two circles together. Tie a length of thin silver elastic to the top of the decoration to hang it from the tree.

Pasta-shape Christmas Tree Decorations

These Christmas tree decorations are made from plastic pudding cartons. They are painted in bright colours and then decorated with pieces of dried pasta, which comes in lots of lovely shapes and sizes. Mix the paint with PVA (white) glue first, so that it sticks to the plastic.

YOU WILL NEED
2 plastic pudding cartons
PVA (white) glue
green, pink and gold
  poster paints
paintbrush
dried pasta shapes
2 gold pipe-cleaners
non-toxic strong glue

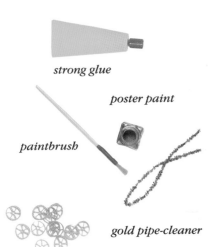

strong glue

poster paint

paintbrush

gold pipe-cleaner

dried pasta shapes

1 Wash and dry the cartons. Mix a little glue with green poster paint and paint one carton. Repeat with pink paint and the second carton. When dry, paint the top and bottom edges gold.

2 Paint the pasta shapes you have chosen with gold poster paint. Leave them to dry thoroughly.

3 Ask an adult to help you to make a hole in the top of the cartons. Push both ends of the pipe-cleaners through the holes. On the inside of the cartons, bend the ends of the pipe-cleaners outwards to keep them in place.

4 Spread a little glue around the edge of each pasta shape. Glue the shapes around the sides of the cartons. Thread a pasta shape over the top of each pipe-cleaner and glue it to the top of the decoration.

Jamjar Lid Badges

Next time you finish a jar of jam, keep the lid to make a fun badge. Cover the lids in silver foil and then cut shapes from scraps of bright foil, saved from sweet (candy) wrappers. You can buy special badge pins but a safety pin is fine.

YOU WILL NEED
scissors
silver foil
non-toxic strong glue
jamjar lid
scraps of gold and coloured foil
safety pin
sticky tape

safety pin

sticky tape

foil scraps

jamjar lid   *silver foil*

strong glue

scissors

1 Cut a square of silver foil that is about 4 cm (1½ in) larger all the way round than the jamjar lid. Spread glue on the back of the lid and then wrap it in the foil. Squash the foil down on the inside of the lid.

2 Cut a circle of gold foil and glue it to the inside of the lid. Cut shapes from scraps of coloured foil and glue them on top of the gold circle.

3 As a change, snip the edges of the gold foil circle to make a 'star'.

4 Turn the badge over and put a safety pin in the centre. Tape the pin in place to make a fastener.

Squeezy Bottle Bracelets

Sections of a squeezy bottle are perfect for making bracelets and bangles, and you can decorate them in lots of different ways. Scraps of coloured foil saved from sweet (candy) wrappers make really bright, cheerful stripes and you can also roll the foil to make glittery fake jewels.

YOU WILL NEED
squeezy bottle
scissors
sticky tape
silver foil
coloured foil scraps
non-toxic strong glue

silver foil

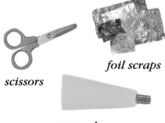
foil scraps

scissors

strong glue

squeezy bottle

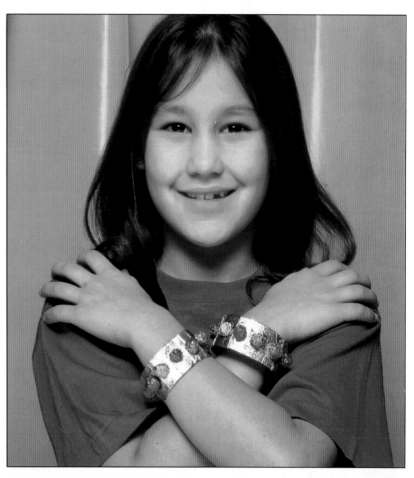

1 Wash and dry an empty squeezy bottle. Ask an adult to help you to cut a 2.5 cm (1 in) wide section from the bottle that is long enough to go round your wrist comfortably. Join the ends of the section together, using sticky tape, to make a bracelet.

2 Cut a piece of silver foil about twice the width of the bracelet. Place the bracelet on the foil and press the foil around the bracelet to cover it.

3 Smooth the scraps of coloured foil with your fingers. Cut several strips of foil long enough to fit around the bracelet. Glue the strips around the bracelet at equal distances.

4 Roll more scraps of different-coloured foil into small beads and glue them around the outside of the bracelet to make 'jewels'.

Paper Bag Animal Masks

Plain paper bags are great for making masks quickly and easily. You can cut them into all sorts of different shapes and use felt-tipped pens to add exciting decoration. Collect brown-paper carrier bags to make masks too – they're stronger than paper bags and will last longer.

YOU WILL NEED
pencil
2 large paper bags
scissors
paper glue
orange, red and black
  felt-tipped pens

felt-tipped pens

paper bag

pencil

scissors

paper glue

1 Draw three holes on the front of one paper bag, for your eyes and mouth. Cut out the holes.

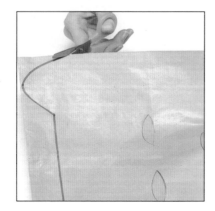

2 Draw two ears along the top edge of the bag and cut them out. Glue the top edges of the bag together again.

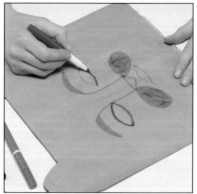

3 Draw the animal's face on the front of the bag, using felt-tipped pens. Draw red lines around the eyes so that they stand out strongly.

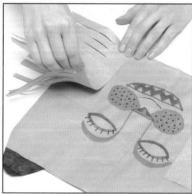

4 Cut three wide strips from another paper bag. Make long cuts along one long edge of each strip. Glue the uncut edges of the strips to the sides and top of the animal's head to make a mane.

Foil Robot

This robot is made from cotton reels (spools) and foil pie dishes (pans). Cotton reels (spools) are great because the holes in the middle mean they can easily be threaded together.

YOU WILL NEED
scissors
silver foil
17 small cotton reels (spools)
1 large cotton reel (spool)
sticky tape
darning needle
thin elastic
4 small foil pie dishes (pans)
paper clips
press studs
non-toxic strong glue

strong glue

paper clips

press studs

silver foil

scissors

foil dishes (pans)

cotton reels (spools)

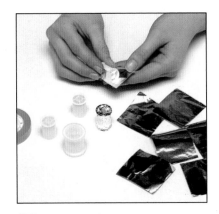

1 Cut strips of silver foil about 1.5 cm (⅝ in) wider than the reels (spools) and long enough to fit around them. Cover the reels (spools) with foil.

2 Thread a darning needle with elastic and tie a big knot in the end. Ask an adult to make a hole in the centre of two dishes (pans) and two holes in a third. Thread a dish (pan) onto the elastic; then three small reels (spools); then the dish (pan) with two holes; then three reels (spools); then a dish (pan). Tie a knot in the end and cut the elastic.

3 Ask an adult to make a hole in the centre of the last dish (pan). To make the upper body, tie a knot in the end of a piece of elastic. Thread on three small reels (spools) and a large reel (spool) for the head. Secure with a paper clip.

4 To make an arm, tie a paper clip to elastic, thread on four small reels (spools) and tie a knot in the end. Glue the dishes (pans) together. Attach the arms below the head. Use paper clips and press studs for the face and controls.

Wild West Ranch

Every cowboy needs a ranch and here's one to be proud of. The ranch house is a cardboard box covered with pieces of corrugated cardboard, which go well with the lolly-stick roof and make the house look as if it's made from wood. The floor is made from coarse sandpaper.

RECYCLING TIP
It might take you a long time to eat enough lollies for all these sticks so ask your friends to save theirs too.

YOU WILL NEED
ruler
scissors
corrugated cardboard
non-toxic strong glue
cardboard box
brown and green poster paints
paintbrush
paint-mixing container
thin card (posterboard)
sticky tape
lolly sticks
yellow paper
coarse sandpaper sheet

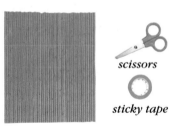

corrugated cardboard

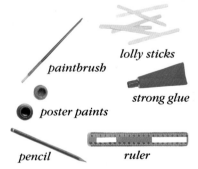

scissors

sticky tape

lolly sticks

paintbrush

strong glue

poster paints

pencil   *ruler*

1 Cut four pieces of corrugated cardboard and glue them around the box. Paint the cardboard brown.

2 To make the roof, cut two pieces of thin card (posterboard) just longer than the box. Tape them together on the back, so they fold in a roof shape. Glue lolly sticks to both sides of the roof.

3 Cut a rectangle of thin card (posterboard) as long as the top of the box and 5 cm (2 in) wider. Fold over 2.5 cm (1 in) on either side to make flaps. Glue the card inside the roof to make a base. Glue the roof to the house.

4 For windows, cut two squares of yellow paper; fold in four and cut a square out of the corner. Open it out and glue to the house. Cut a rectangle of corrugated cardboard for a door.

5 Cut a rectangle of corrugated cardboard the same size as the sheet of sandpaper. Glue the sandpaper to the cardboard.

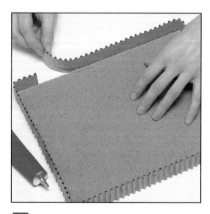

6 To make the fence, cut a strip of corrugated cardboard 2.5 cm (1 in) high and long enough to glue around the base, and paint green.

Space Station

If you like the idea of space travel, why not make yourself a floating space station like this one? It has a radar dish and a landing stage for you to park rockets and other spacecraft on. Look around for any interestingly-shaped odds and ends that would look good on your space station. Paint them silver, and start building!

RECYCLING TIP

You can use all sorts of different sized boxes but make sure the cardboard isn't too thick. If the boxes are too heavy the glue might not hold them together.

YOU WILL NEED
small and large cardboard boxes
paintbrush
paint-mixing container
silver poster paint
PVA (white) glue
4 paper bowls
cardboard tubes
2 round foil pie dishes (pans)
non-toxic strong glue
2 yogurt pots
drinking straw
round cardboard carton
rectangular foil dish

PVA (white) glue

paper bowl

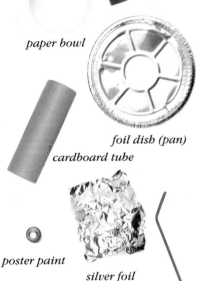

foil dish (pan)

cardboard tube

poster paint

silver foil

drinking straw

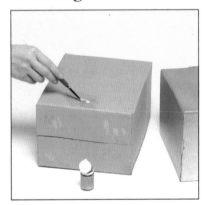

1 Paint the large cardboard box and the smaller one silver. You may have to paint the boxes twice to cover the cardboard properly.

2 Glue the rims of two paper bowls together with PVA glue. Glue two more in the same way. Stick all four together. Paint them silver and glue them between the two boxes to make an airlock.

3 Paint one of the tubes silver. Glue the rims of the foil pie dishes (pans) together with strong glue. Glue them to the top of the tube. Glue the tube to the larger box to make a landing stage.

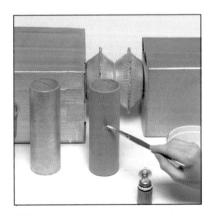

4 Add a little PVA glue to the silver paint and paint the yogurt pots, one small and two large cardboard tubes silver. Glue one pot to the small tube. Stick this next to the landing pad.

5 Stick the tubes one each side of the larger box and the yogurt pot to the end. Cover the straw with silver foil and paint the round carton silver. Join them together and stick to the smaller box.

6 Stick the rectangular foil dish upside-down next to the straw aerial.

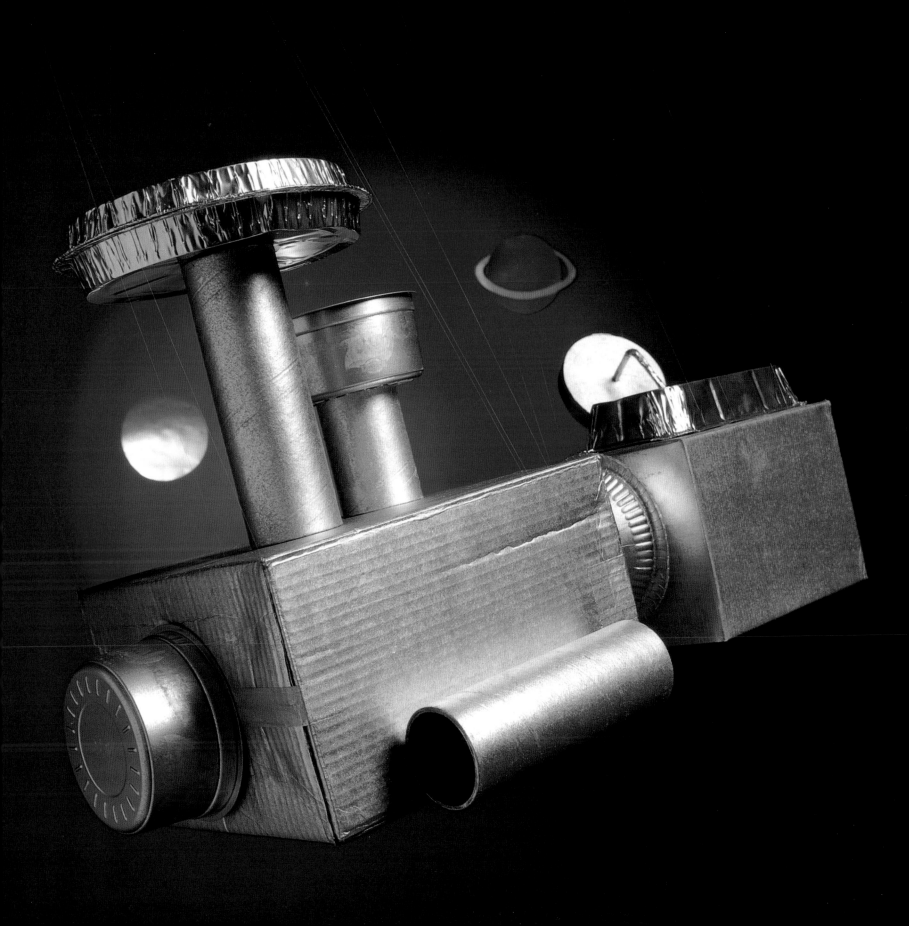

Air Soccer

A fun game for two or more players. Use the blowers
to move the ball into the opposite goal.

YOU WILL NEED
pencil
scissors
card (cardboard) or 2 shoe boxes
masking tape
coloured paints
paintbrush
coloured sticky-back (adhesive)
   plastic
2 cardboard tubes
ping-pong ball
green sticky-back (adhesive) felt

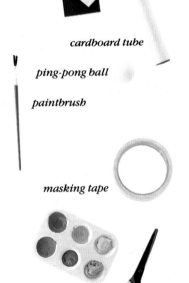

plastic covering

card (cardboard)

cardboard tube

ping-pong ball

paintbrush

masking tape

paints

scissors

1 Draw the goals onto card (cardboard) and cut out with a pair of scissors, or cut one long side off of each shoe box.

2 Bend back the two short sides about 2.5 cm (1 in) so the goal will stand up. Stick the card together with masking tape if necessary.

3 Paint the goals inside and out. Cut out some spots from the coloured sticky-back (adhesive) plastic and stick them onto the goals.

4 For the blowers, cover two cardboard tubes with coloured sticky-back plastic.

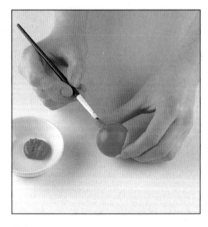

5 Paint the ping-pong ball with bright colours.

6 For the pitch (field), cover a piece of card as big as you like with green sticky-back felt. Mark out the pitch with masking tape and position the goals.

Periscope

The easy way to spy and become a secret agent. Hide behind furniture and walls and look over the top without anyone seeing you.

YOU WILL NEED
tall fruit juice or milk carton
coloured paper
PVA (white) glue
scissors
ruler
pen
2 mirrors
coloured paints
paintbrush

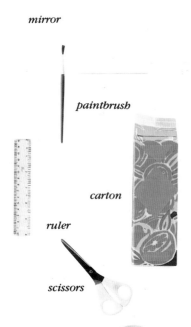

mirror

paintbrush

carton

ruler

scissors

PVA (white) glue

paints

1 Cover the fruit juice or milk carton in brightly-coloured paper.

2 Cut out two holes of the same size at the top of the front of the carton and the bottom of the back with a pair of scissors.

3 With a ruler, measure and draw two squares on both sides of the carton, level with the holes on the front and back. Divide the squares with a diagonal line. This is to ensure that the mirrors are at the same angle of 45 degrees.

4 Cut a slit along each diagonal line big enough to slide the mirrors through.

5 Slip the mirrors in place with the reflecting sides facing each other.

6 Decorate your finished periscope with painted spots. To use, look through the bottom hole at the back.

Papier-mâché Bowl

Papier-mâché is like magic because you can make all sorts of things from it, using only old newspapers and glue. This bowl is decorated by gluing bright strips of gift wrap and paper shapes to its surface. It is good for holding fruit or odds and ends.

YOU WILL NEED
petroleum jelly
plastic bowl
newspaper
PVA (white) glue
scissors
gift wrap
thin coloured paper

PVA (white) glue

newspaper

plastic bowl

coloured paper

scissors

1 Grease your chosen bowl with a thin coating of petroleum jelly, so that the papier-mâché bowl will come out. Tear newspaper into 2.5 cm (1 in) wide strips. Dip the strips in diluted PVA (white) glue and press into the mould, overlapping the edges slightly. Press in six layers and leave to dry overnight.

2 Gently pull the paper shape out of the mould. Leave the bowl upside-down to dry. When it has dried, cut away the rough edges from the rim of the bowl.

3 Tear the gift wrap into strips and glue them to the outside and inside of the bowl to decorate it.

4 Cut circles from the coloured paper. Snip segments out of the paper to make 'stars'.

5 Glue the stars to the centre and sides of the bowl, using PVA glue.

6 Cut lots of small squares from two colours of thin paper. Glue the squares around the outside edge of the bowl.

Rhythm Sticks

Thin pieces of branch make great percussion sticks. Look out for two sticks that are about the same length and thickness next time you are in a park or wood. Make sure the branches are really dry, so that they make a loud noise when you knock them together. If you wish, seal the surface of the sticks with non-toxic craft varnish after they have been painted.

YOU WILL NEED
2 sticks
white, red, green and yellow poster
  paints
paintbrush
paint-mixing container
scissors
coloured string

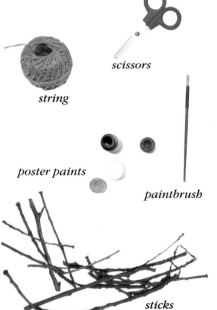
string

scissors

poster paints

paintbrush

sticks

1 Remove any leaves and loose bark from the sticks and paint them white. Leave the sticks to dry.

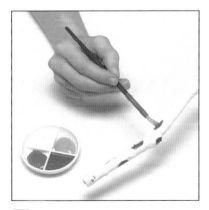

2 Paint decorative red and green spots on top of the white paint. Make the spots different sizes.

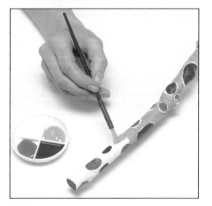

3 When the spots have dried, fill in the white space between them with yellow paint. Leave a small white space around each spot.

4 Cut two long pieces of coloured string. Tie one to the end of each stick. Wrap the string round and round the ends of the sticks to make handles. Tie the ends of the string very tightly so that they don't unravel.

Printed Stationery

Personal stationery is often very expensive, but you can make your own by printing it with these simple printing blocks. The pad of each block is made from shapes cut from washing-up sponges. Once you are used to the technique, make some blocks with your initials on.

YOU WILL NEED
pencil
ruler
thick corrugated cardboard
scissors
non-toxic strong glue
felt-tipped pen
washing-up sponge
poster paints
paintbrush
saucer
coloured writing paper

washing-up sponge

writing paper

corrugated cardboard

pencil

strong glue

ruler

poster paints

scissors

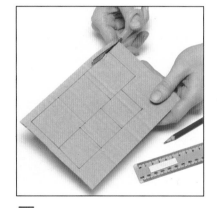

1 Draw three 5 x 5 cm (2 x 2in) squares and three 4 x 4 cm (1½ x 1½ in) squares on the corrugated cardboard. Cut out all the squares.

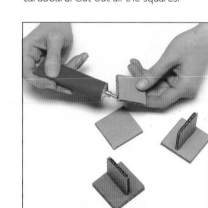

2 Glue the small squares upright on top of the larger squares to make printing blocks. (The small squares are the handles for holding the blocks.)

3 With a felt-tipped pen, draw simple shapes onto the washing-up sponge. Cut out the shapes and glue one to each printing block.

4 When the glue has dried, spread a little thick paint on a saucer. Dip a block into the paint or use the brush to coat it, so that the sponge is coated, and then press the block firmly onto a piece of writing paper to print the shape.

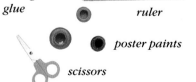

Fun with Toys

It is as much fun to make your own toys and
games as it is to play with them. You can sew a doll
or a cushion, or even make a skipping rope to take
outdoors. There are lots of other ideas here to
choose from.

Materials

These are some of the materials you will need. Many of these projects will require an adult's help, particularly when you see the sign !

Bottles
Only use plastic bottles for the projects. Save bottle tops for decoration. However, they are not suitable for decorating babies' toys.

Card (posterboard) and paper
Card (posterboard) comes in a range of thicknesses. It sometimes needs to be cut with a craft knife rather than scissors, and you must ask for help with this. Newspaper is the core material used for papier-mâché.

Decorations
These are incredibly wide-ranging and the only curb on your imagination is making absolutely sure that the decoration you have chosen for a toy is suitable for your age. All decorations should be very firmly attached. Choose from buttons (look in charity shops for unusual examples), furnishing fringing, coloured pipe-cleaners and pretty ribbons, including ribbon roses, sticky shapes or even shoelaces.

Fabrics
The choice of colours, patterns and textures is as wide as you could wish for. You may prefer to choose natural materials, such as cotton and linen. Felt is beautifully soft and has the added advantage of being easy to cut without fraying. It is also available with an adhesive backing for covering objects.

Fasteners
Paper fasteners can be used to join two pieces of card (posterboard) or paper together, while still allowing them to move. Poppers (snap fasteners) or press studs are used for fastening fabric. Velcro is also a quick and easy fastener for fabric.

Glues and tapes
Double-sided tape can be used instead of glue to stick paper or card (cardboard). Electrical tape is very strong and can be used to fasten heavy materials. It can also be used for decoration and it comes in a wide range of bright colours. Masking tape is very useful for reinforcing card (posterboard) shapes and for marking out areas before painting. PVA (white) glue is a water-based, non-toxic glue ideal for sticking wood or paper. It can also be diluted with water and used in papier-mâché or as a quick and easy varnish.

Paints
Water-based paints are non-toxic and ideal for babies' and children's toys. Choose from either poster, acrylic or emulsion (latex) paints. Enamel paints are oil-based paints that will adhere to metal, wood or plastic. Spray paints are mostly toxic when wet, so use them outdoors or in a well-ventilated room and always wear a mask.

Polymer clay
This is a modelling medium that is available in a range of colours. Always follow the manufacturer's instructions, as products do vary.

Safety pin
Use this to help thread ribbon or cord through a fabric tube.

Screw eyes
These are screwed into the back of a piece of wood (for example, a picture frame) and cord can be attached to them for hanging.

Stuffing (batting)
This is used to fill toys and shapes made from fabric.

Ties
Cord is stronger than either string or ribbon and can be threaded through a drawstring bag to pull it shut. Rope is stronger still, although nylon rope does tend to unravel at the ends unless you seal them by burning (with an adult's help).

Threads
Embroidery threads are used in hand sewing to make colourful, detailed stitches. For ordinary hand or machine sewing choose either cotton or rayon thread.

Wood
Balsa wood is a very soft wood that can be bought from model shops. Medium-density fiberboard, or MDF, is a manmade wood. Wear a mask when sawing as it produces a fine dust.

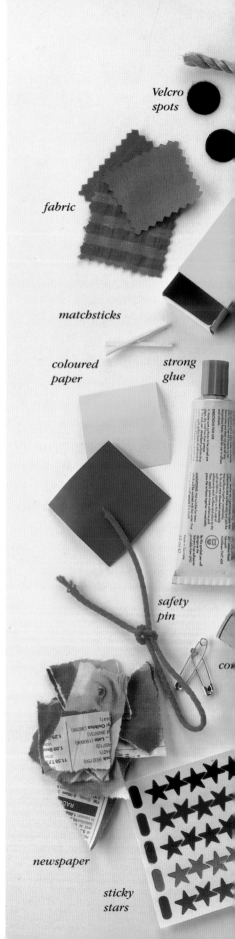

Velcro spots

fabric

matchsticks

coloured paper

strong glue

safety pin

newspaper

sticky stars

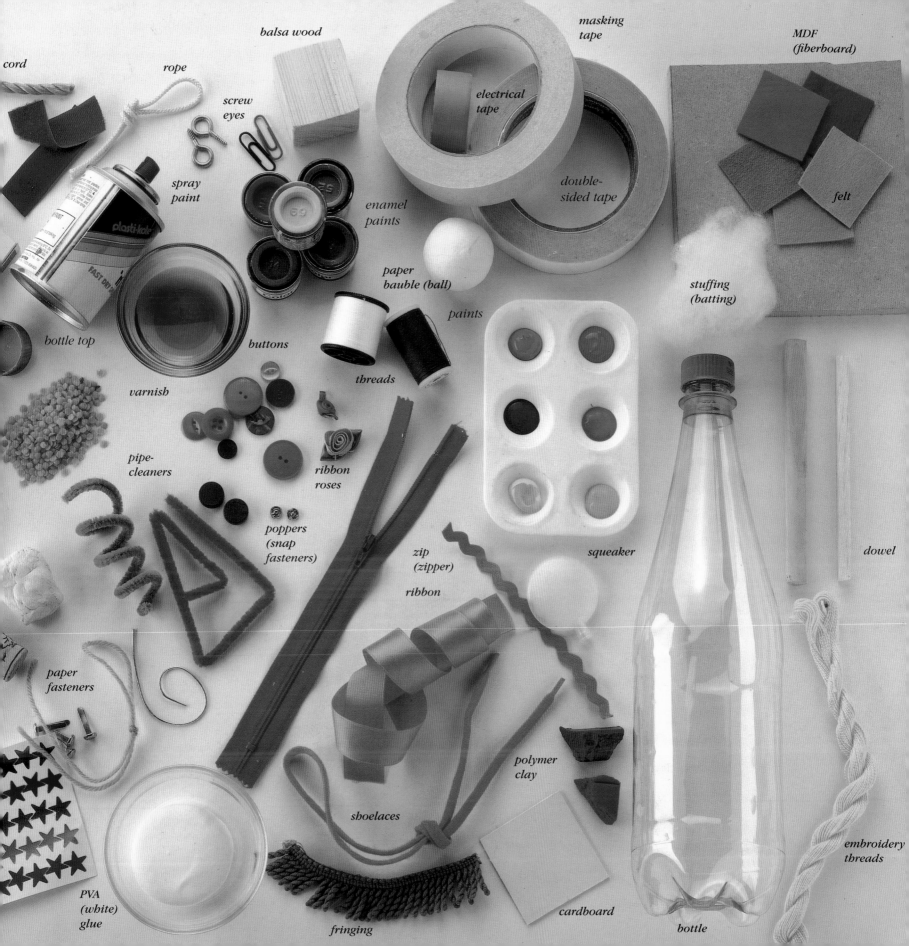

cord

rope

balsa wood

masking tape

MDF (fiberboard)

screw eyes

electrical tape

spray paint

enamel paints

double-sided tape

felt

paper bauble (ball)

stuffing (batting)

bottle top

paints

varnish

buttons

threads

squeaker

dowel

pipe-cleaners

ribbon roses

poppers (snap fasteners)

zip (zipper)

ribbon

paper fasteners

polymer clay

shoelaces

embroidery threads

PVA (white) glue

fringing

cardboard

bottle

Sanding Wood

It is very important to smooth the surface and corners of wood before painting as this will avoid splintering.

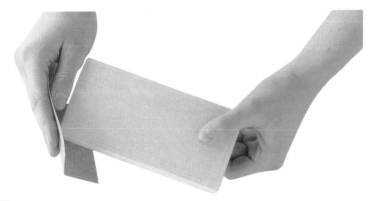

1 Use sandpaper to smooth any rough edges on sawn wood.

! Drilling Wood

Make sure that you ask an adult to drill or saw any wood that you work with.

1 Place an old piece of wood under the piece you want to drill.

! Sealing Rope Ends

Some of the projects use plastic rope and the ends can be burnt to prevent them unravelling.

1 Ask an adult to carefully burn the rope ends for you, and then put them outside on a stone or concrete surface to cool.

Stuffing Soft Toys

1 Push stuffing (batting) to the ends of toy pieces, using a knitting needle or the end of a wooden spoon to reach small or awkward shapes.

Stitches

Several of the needlework projects use decorative stitches. Some of them you may be familiar with.

French knots

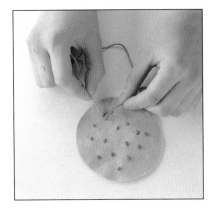 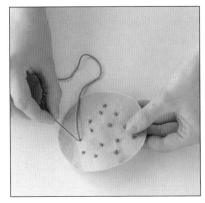

1 Tie a knot at the end of the sewing thread then stitch through to the right side of the fabric. Using the needle, make a knot close to the fabric.

2 Pass the needle back through the fabric again close to the knot.

Blanket stitch

1 Use this stitch for edging fabric to prevent it from fraying. Tie a knot at the end of the sewing thread or wool (yarn), and pass it through the fabric from the wrong side. Push the needle through the right side of the fabric 1 cm (½ in) farther on and place the needle over the loop to form a stitch. Repeat.

! Bending Wire

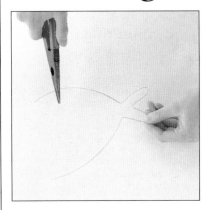 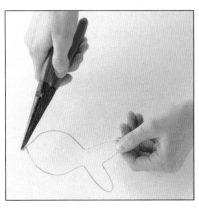

1 Ask an adult to help you use a pair of pliers to bend a piece of wire into shape.

2 To secure the two ends of the wire together, twist them and press hard with the tips of the pliers.

! Making a Hole in a Can

1 An adult must help you with this technique. Place a ball of softened modelling clay on the can where you want to make a hole then pierce it with a bradawl. The modelling clay will prevent the bradawl from slipping.

Rag Doll

Every little girl needs a calico doll like this as a best friend. First make the doll, then make her a special outfit to wear, such as a dress and matching pantaloons.

YOU WILL NEED
tracing paper
pencil
paper
scissors
50 cm x 1 m (20 in x 39 in) calico
matching sewing thread
needle
stuffing (batting)
knitting needle, optional
blue and pink scraps of felt
blue, pink, brown and red embroidery
 threads
tapestry needle
yellow knitting wool (yarn)
ribbon

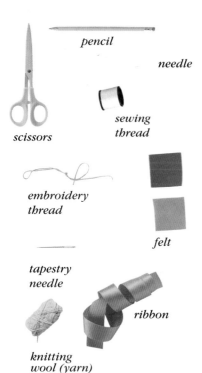

pencil

needle

scissors

sewing thread

embroidery thread

felt

tapestry needle

ribbon

knitting wool (yarn)

1 Trace the doll templates from the back of the book and cut out. Fold the calico in half and draw round the shapes. Cut the body shape out once and the arm and leg shapes twice. Stitch the shapes together in pairs, leaving an opening in each.

2 Turn all the pieces right side out and fill with stuffing (batting) until firm. Use a knitting needle if necessary to push the stuffing (batting) into the furthest corners. Slip stitch the openings to close them.

3 Pinch the tops of the arms and legs, then stitch.

4 Stitch the arms and legs securely to the body.

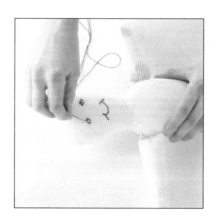

5 Cut two small circles out of blue felt for the doll's eyes, and two slightly larger circles out of pink felt for her cheeks. Stitch on to her face, using matching embroidery threads. Embroider her eyebrows in brown and her mouth in red in running stitch.

6 Stitch short lengths of yellow wool (yarn) through the top of the doll's head, using a tapestry needle. Tie each length of wool in a knot close to her head. Give her hair a neat trim. Tie the ribbon in a bow and stitch in place.

Rag Doll's Dress

The dress is decorated with a double felt collar and ribbon roses, which you can buy in craft and needlework shops. It fastens at the back with a row of poppers (snap fasteners), so is ideal for dressing and undressing the doll.

YOU WILL NEED
tracing paper
pencil
paper
scissors
50 cm x 1 m (20 in x 39 in)
  dress fabric
matching sewing thread
needle
felt
ribbon roses
poppers (snap fasteners)

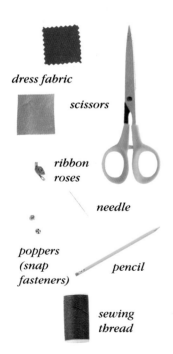

dress fabric

scissors

ribbon roses

needle

poppers (snap fasteners)

pencil

sewing thread

1 Trace the dress templates from the back of the book onto paper. Fold the fabric in half, place the pattern piece for the front on the fold and cut out. Cut two sleeves and two back pieces. Stitch the sleeve seams and hem the cuffs. Leave 6 mm (¼ in) seam allowance.

2 Stitch the two back pieces to the front piece, right sides together. Turn under 6 mm (¼ in) and hem.

3 Right sides together, stitch the shoulder seams. Turn the dress right side out. Place the sleeves through the armholes as shown and tack (baste) in position, then stitch.

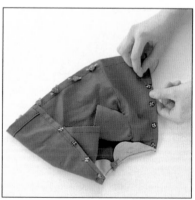

4 Turn over 6 mm (¼ in) round the neck edge to the right side and stitch. Trace the collar template on to paper and cut out twice from felt. Stitch both collars round the neck edge. Decorate the dress with ribbon roses as shown. Turn the raw edges of the back opening under 2 cm (¾ in) to the wrong side and stitch. Stitch poppers (snap fasteners) to either side of the opening at the back.

Rag Doll's Pantaloons and Boots

Make the pantaloons in plain or patterned fabric to contrast with the rag doll's dress. Her boots are easily made out of scraps of fabric.

YOU WILL NEED
tracing paper
pencil
paper
scissors
matching sewing threads
needle
FOR THE BOOTS
scrap of fabric
FOR THE PANTALOONS
70 cm x 1 m (27½ in x 39 in) dress fabric
60 cm (24 in) narrow elastic
safety pin

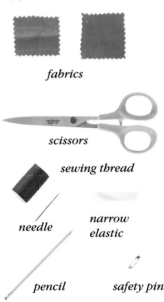

fabrics

scissors

sewing thread

needle　*narrow elastic*

pencil　*safety pin*

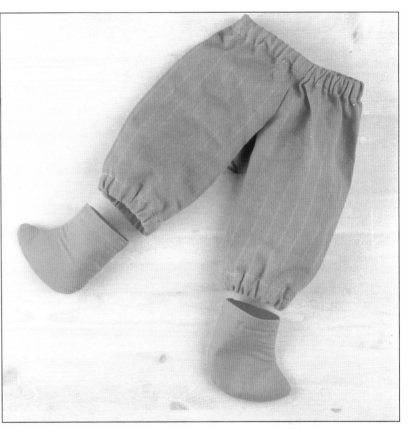

1 Trace the boot template from the back of the book onto paper. Fold a small piece of fabric in half, draw round the shape twice and cut out. Stitch two boot shapes together, right sides facing, leaving the top open. Hem the top and turn right side out. Make the other boot.

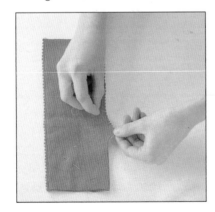

2 Trace the pantaloons template. Fold the fabric in half, right sides facing, then place the pattern piece on the fold as marked. Cut out twice. Keeping the fabric folded in half, stitch along the inside leg.

3 Turn one pantaloon leg right side out and place inside the other leg, with raw edges matching along the crotch seam. Stitch the crotch seam and turn right side out. Fold the waist edge over 3 cm (1¼ in) to the wrong side then stitch round the waist 1 cm (½ in) from the top, leaving a small opening. Repeat at the bottom of each leg.

4 Cut the elastic into one piece of 30 cm (12 in) and two pieces of 15 cm (6 in). Pin a safety pin to one end of the long piece and thread it through the waistband. Pull both ends to gather the waist and stitch firmly together. Repeat for the pantaloon legs.

Activity Blanket

Tiny fingers will love playing with this blanket, and at the same time they will learn how to use zips (zippers), buttons and shoelaces. Make sure all the pieces are securely attached, especially the buttons.

YOU WILL NEED
coloured blanket
tapestry wool (yarn), in bright
  colours
tapestry needle
scissors
coloured zips (zippers)
dressmaker's pins
scraps of contrast-coloured
  blanket or felt
buttons
pom-poms
shoelaces

felt

tapestry needle

zip (zipper)

button

pom-poms

scissors

shoelaces

tapestry wool (yarn)

1 Cut the blanket if necessary to the size you want. Fold under the edges and blanket stitch, using contrasting tapestry wool (yarn).

2 Position the zips (zippers) on the blanket and pin in place. Secure with running stitch, using contrasting tapestry wool (yarn).

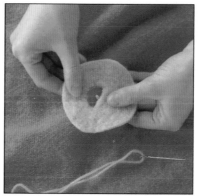

3 Cut out simple shapes, such as squares, circles and triangles, from coloured blanket or felt. Cut a slit in the centre of each shape for a button to go through. Stitch the buttons onto the blanket and fasten on the shapes.

4 Sew on pom-poms and shoelaces as more shapes to play with.

Fridge Magnets

There are several modelling mediums you could use in this project, such as polymer clay, which can be purchased from craft and hobby shops. Whichever material you use, it is important to follow the instructions on the packet.

YOU WILL NEED
modelling medium
rolling pin (optional)
modelling tools (optional)
acrylic paints, in
  assorted colours
paintbrush
magnets
non-toxic strong glue

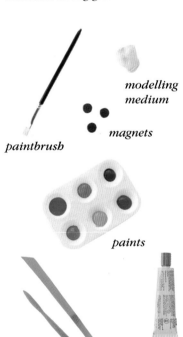

paintbrush

modelling medium

magnets

paints

strong glue

modelling tools

rolling pin

1 To make the teapot and the cups and saucers, mould each shape with your fingers, adding small pieces of the modelling medium for the details. If you are using polymer clay, you will need to roll it out first and cut out the shapes with modelling tools.

2 For the snail, roll out a length of modelling medium approximately 15 cm (6 in) long and coil it round. Add on small pieces for the antennae and tail.

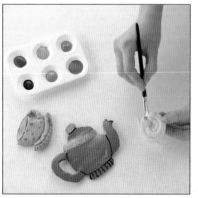

3 Paint the shapes and leave the paint to dry. If you are using polymer clay, you do not need to paint it.

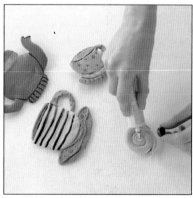

4 Glue a magnet onto the back of each shape with strong glue. Leave the glue to harden before placing the magnets on the fridge.

Bottle Maracas

Hold one of these in each hand and shake them in time to music – they make a great sound! For instructions on how to cover the bottles with papier-mâché, see the section at the beginning of the book.

YOU WILL NEED
FOR THE PAPIER-MÂCHÉ
newspaper
diluted PVA (white) glue
large bowl
FOR THE MARACAS
2 small, empty plastic bottles
emulsion (latex) paints, in
  assorted colours
paintbrush
buttons
non-toxic strong glue
A4 (11¾ x 8½ in) sheet of
  paper
100 g (4 oz) lentils or other
  dried pulses (legumes)
2 pieces of balsa wood, each
  - 12 cm (4¾ in) long
craft knife
coloured electrical tape

1 Make sure the bottles are clean and dry. Cover both bottles with two layers of papier-mâché.

2 When the papier-mâché is dry, paint the bottles all over in a base colour or two. Leave to dry.

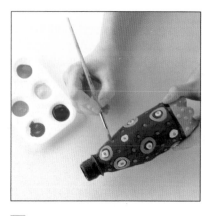

3 Paint colourful patterns on top of the base colour. Leave the paint to dry.

buttons
paints
PVA *(white) glue*
electrical tape
newspaper
paintbrush
lentils
strong glue
balsa wood
craft knife
plastic bottle

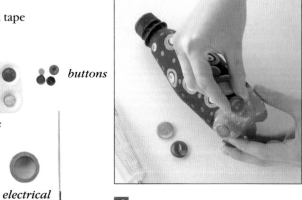

4 Glue buttons round the bottom of the bottles with strong glue. Leave to dry.

5 Roll the sheet of paper into a cone and fit into the top of one of the bottles. Pour half the lentils or pulses (legumes) into the bottle. Repeat for the second bottle.

6 ! Ask an adult to shave one end of the pieces of balsa wood with a craft knife until they fit snugly into the bottles.

7 Glue the balsa wood into the bottles with strong glue. When dry, wind coloured tape round the handles, and paint the ends of the handles.

Felt Picture Book

The great thing about this colourful book is that you don't have to worry about the pages getting torn or crumpled. Make up a bedtime story to go with the pictures, or invent your own story and pictures.

YOU WILL NEED
tracing paper
pencil
paper
scissors
scraps of felt, for the pictures
5 pieces of felt, 6 cm (2½ in) square, in different colours
fabric glue and brush
6.5 cm (2¾ in) strip of felt, for the spine
embroidery thread
needle

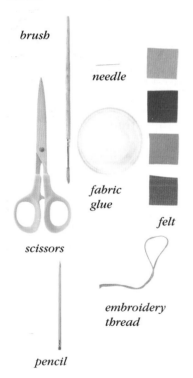

brush

needle

fabric glue

felt

scissors

embroidery thread

pencil

1 Trace the templates at the back of the book onto paper and cut out. Lay the paper shapes on scraps of different coloured felt and cut out.

2 Position the felt shapes on the felt squares to make the pictures. Glue in place. Leave the glue to dry.

3 Place the felt squares on top of each other, with the pictures facing upwards. Place a plain felt square on top. Cut the felt spine to the length of the book, fold in half and glue round the edge, trapping the pages inside. Leave to dry.

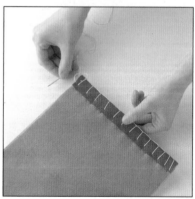

4 Finally, to secure the spine, stitch through all the layers with embroidery thread, using a contrasting colour and neat blanket stitch.

Skipping Rope

The simplest toys provide the most fun, and you can play skipping games for hours. Adjust the length of the rope as necessary.

YOU WILL NEED
34 cm (13½ in) coloured plastic
 tubing
craft knife
sandpaper
approximately 2 m (2¼ yd)
 smooth coloured rope
lighter

plastic tubing

coloured rope

craft knife

sandpaper

1 ! Ask an adult to help you cut the plastic tubing in half, using a craft knife. Smooth the edges with sandpaper.

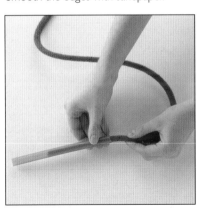

2 Thread each end of the rope through the tube.

3 Check the length of the rope then knot the ends securely.

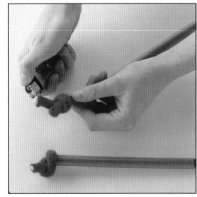

4 ! Burn the ends of the rope to prevent them from fraying if the rope is plastic.

Character Skittles

Plastic bottles make excellent skittles, especially if you paint them to look like people. You can play the game indoors as well as outside if you use a soft ball.

YOU WILL NEED
clean, empty plastic bottles
fretsaw
newspaper
diluted PVA (white) glue
large bowl
paper baubles (balls)
non-toxic strong glue
acrylic paints, in assorted colours
paintbrush
ribbons, in various colours and
  patterns

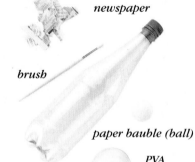

newspaper

brush

paper bauble (ball)

plastic bottle

PVA (white) glue

ribbon

paints

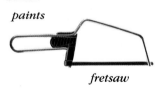

fretsaw

strong glue

1 ! Remove the labels from the bottles by soaking them in water. Saw off the top of each bottle as shown.

2 Cover the bottles in papier-mâché. Leave to dry.

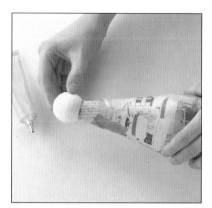

3 Glue a paper bauble on top of each bottle, using strong glue.

4 Paint the bottles and the bauble faces with a base coat. Leave the paint to dry.

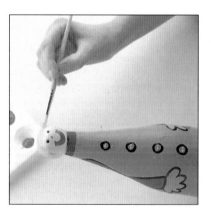

5 Give each skittle a different character by painting different-coloured hair and clothes. Leave to dry.

6 Tie a piece of ribbon in a bow round the neck of each skittle.

Felt Game

This popular game, known as Noughts and Crosses (Tic-tac-toe), is ideal for train or car trips. The felt shapes are attached to the board with Velcro so they can't fall off. Instead of adhesive felt, you can cut out the shapes from ordinary felt and stick them on with fabric glue.

YOU WILL NEED
30 x 30 cm (12 x 12 in)
  thick card (cardboard)
2 squares of adhesive felt,
  32 x 32 cm (13 x 13 in)
  and 30 x 30 cm (12 x 12 in)
adhesive felt, in 3 contrasting
  colours
tracing paper
pencil
ruler
scissors
thin card (posterboard)
9 Velcro spots
fabric glue and brush

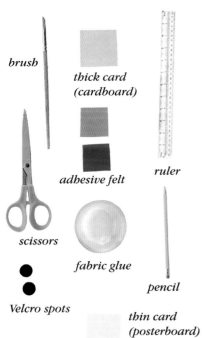

brush

*thick card
(cardboard)*

adhesive felt

ruler

scissors

fabric glue

pencil

Velcro spots

*thin card
(posterboard)*

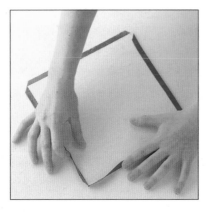

1 Position the 32 cm (13 in) square of felt in the centre of the thick card (posterboard). Stick down, folding the edges over to the back.

2 Stick the 30 cm (12 in) square of felt to cover the back of the card.

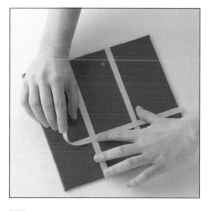

3 Cut four narrow strips of contrast-coloured felt 2 x 32 cm (¾ x 13 in). Stick them across the board to make nine equal squares.

4 Trace the templates from the back of the book onto card (posterboard). Cut out four of each shape. Cover each shape with felt on both sides. Use a different colour for the noughts (0s) and the crosses (Xs).

5 Cut out the felt shapes, leaving the card (posterboard) inside.

6 Glue the furry side of the Velcro spots onto the centre of the noughts and crosses. Glue the looped side in the centre of the squares on the board.

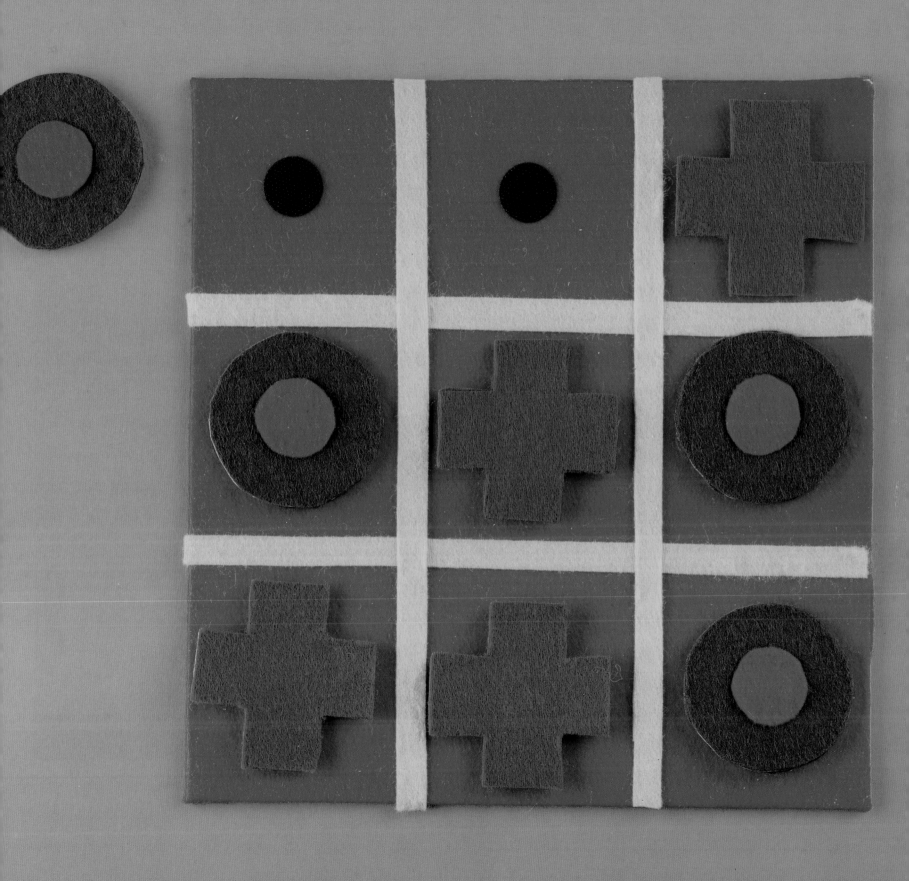

Magnetic Fish

See how many goldfish you can catch – the highest score wins the game. To make a fishing rod, tie a piece of coloured string to a magnet. Tie the other end to a garden stick or cane.

YOU WILL NEED
tracing paper
pencil
paper
thin card (posterboard)
scissors
paints, in assorted colours
paintbrush
coloured metal paper clips
shallow box
magnet

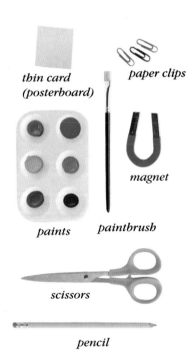

thin card (posterboard)

paper clips

paints   *paintbrush*

magnet

scissors

pencil

1 Trace the fish template at the back of the book onto paper. Draw round the shape five or six times on card (posterboard) and cut out.

2 Paint the fish. Leave to dry then paint a different number on each fish.

3 Attach a paper clip to the mouth of each fish.

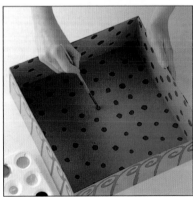

4 Paint the box blue and leave to dry. Using a darker blue, paint wavy lines round the edge to represent water.

Dog Jigsaw

It is very easy to make your own simple, large-scale jigsaw. A template for the dog is supplied, but you could also make a jigsaw of your own pet or another favourite animal, or choose a completely different shape.

YOU WILL NEED
graph paper
pencil
card (posterboard)
craft knife
acrylic paints, in assorted colours
paintbrush
ruler
about 20 self-adhesive Velcro
  spots
45 x 35 cm (18 x 14 in)
  piece of thick card (cardboard)
40 x 30 cm (16 x 12 in)
  piece of adhesive-backed felt

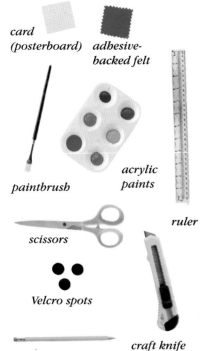

card
(posterboard) adhesive-
backed felt

paintbrush acrylic
paints

ruler

scissors

Velcro spots

pencil craft knife

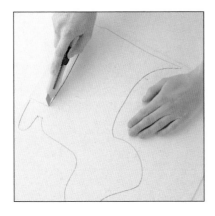

1 ! Enlarge the template at the back of the book to 36 cm (14 in) long. Draw round the shape onto card (posterboard). Cut out with a craft knife.

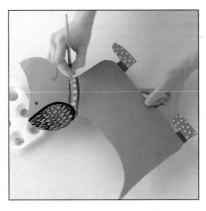

2 Paint the dog as illustrated, or use your own colours. Leave the paint to dry.

3 ! Using a ruler, divide the dog into four or five simple pieces. Ask an adult to help you cut along the lines with the craft knife. Stick three or four Velcro spots on the back of each piece.

4 Make the base by placing the thick card (cardboard) in the middle of the felt. Fold over the edges and stick down.

Toy Clock

Recycle your breakfast cereal packet to make a friendly clock, as a fun way of learning how to tell the time. Paint the clock face in sunny daytime colours, and surround it with a night sky painted with stars.

YOU WILL NEED
card (cardboard)
pencil
scissors
emulsion (latex) paint, in
  assorted colours
paintbrush
craft knife
paper fastener
cereal box
blue and yellow adhesive plastic
double-sided tape

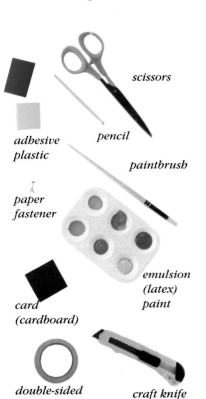

scissors

adhesive plastic

pencil

paintbrush

paper fastener

emulsion (latex) paint

card (cardboard)

double-sided tape

craft knife

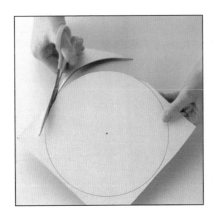

1 Draw round a small plate on to card (cardboard) and cut out. Find the centre of the circle and carefully pierce a hole using the tip of the scissors.

2 Paint the card circle in a sunny colour and leave to dry. Paint the numerals in contrasting colours with an inner circle of twelve dots. Leave to dry.

3 Draw two clock hands in the shape of arrows, one longer than the other, on to card and cut out. Paint and attach the arms to the clock with a paper fastener.

4 Cover the cereal box with blue adhesive plastic and smooth down, trying to avoid air bubbles.

5 Stick the clock face on to the box with double-sided tape. Cut out stars from yellow adhesive plastic and stick on to the sides of the box.

6 Stick more stars on the front of the clock round the face.

Dog and Bone Mobile

This witty mobile is great fun. As it swings around in the breeze, the Scottie dog chases the bone and the cat chases the fish! Trace the shapes from the templates supplied, cut them out of card (cardboard) and paint them in bright colours. Hang the rods up before tying on the shapes, as it will be easier to balance them.

! SAFETY NOTE

Ask an adult to drill, saw and cut with a craft knife for you.

YOU WILL NEED
2 x 45 cm (18 in) pieces of
   dowel, 5 mm (³⁄₁₆ in) diameter
saw
sandpaper
drill
craft knife
poster paints, in assorted colours
paintbrush
cord
sticky tape (optional)
tracing paper
pencil
card (cardboard)
scissors
single-hole punch
thread, in assorted colours

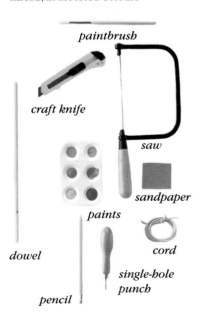

paintbrush

craft knife

saw

sandpaper

paints

dowel

cord

single-hole
punch

pencil

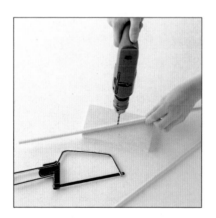

1 ! Cut the dowel to size and smooth the ends with sandpaper. Drill a hole in the centre of each dowel rod.

4 Trace the mobile templates at the back of the book and transfer them to card (cardboard). Cut out the shapes. Punch a hole on each shape where marked on the templates.

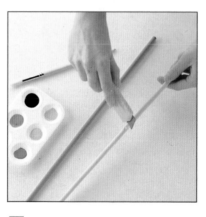

2 ! Using a craft knife, shave a 'V' shape round the hole on one of the dowel rods. This will help the rods to sit comfortably at right angles to each other. Paint each rod using a different colour. Leave to dry.

5 Paint the shapes on both sides.

3 Thread a piece of cord through the holes and tie in a knot either side of the dowel rods. If you have trouble threading the cord through the holes, wrap a piece of sticky tape tightly round the end.

6 Hang up the dowel rods and tie on each shape, using a different-coloured thread.

Flower Power Cushion

This checkerboard patchwork cushion is decorated with bright, sunny flowers, just right for small fingers to hold on to. The flowers are attached with Velcro so you can move them about to make a different design.

YOU WILL NEED
tracing paper
pencil
paper
scissors
scraps of felt in assorted
  colours, for the flowers
embroidery threads, in assorted
  colours
needle
16 cm (6½ in) Velcro
4 pieces of felt, each 22 cm
  (8½ in) square, in different colours
pins
stuffing (batting)
2 pieces of fabric, each 40 x 30 cm
  (16 x 12 in), for the cushion back
40 cm (16 in) square cushion pad
zip (zipper) (optional)

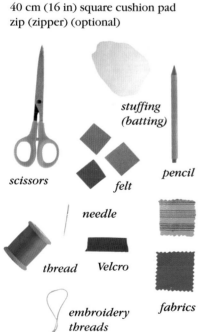

stuffing
(batting)

scissors

felt

pencil

needle

thread   Velcro

embroidery
threads

fabrics

1 Trace the flower template at the back of the book. Draw round it four times on different colours of felt. Cut out four circles for the flower centres in contrast colours, and embroider with French knots.

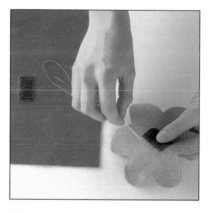

2 Cut the Velcro into four equal pieces. Stitch one half of each piece to the back of each flower. Stitch the other half to the centre of each of the felt squares.

3 Position the flower centres on top of the flowers, trapping a small ball of stuffing (batting) in between. Pin in place then stitch round the flower centres in running stitch.

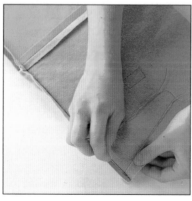

4 For the patchwork, place two of the felt squares together. Hand or machine stitch, leaving a 1 cm (½ in) seam allowance. Join the other two squares the same way, then stitch the two sets of squares together to make a large square.

5 Place the two pieces of fabric for the cushion back on the felt, right sides together. Pin then stitch round all four sides, leaving a 1 cm (½ in) seam allowance. Fold back the raw edges of the back pieces and attach in the seam.

6 Turn the cushion cover right side out and insert the cushion pad. Stitch the opening or insert a zip (zipper). Attach the flowers onto the front, using the Velcro.

Toy Bag

This bag is a real star! It is big enough to store plenty of toys in at home or if you are going out for the day. Position the star so that it will be in the centre of one side of the bag when the fabric is folded in half.

YOU WILL NEED
tracing paper
pencil
paper
scissors
scraps of fabric, for the star
fabric glue and brush
needle
matching sewing threads
52 x 110 cm (20½ x 43 in)
  hardwearing fabric, for the bag
pins
1 m (1 yd) coloured tape
1.5 m (1½ yd) ribbon or cord
safety pin

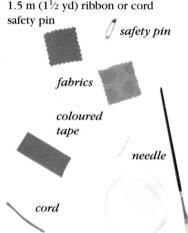

safety pin

fabrics

coloured tape

needle

cord

fabric glue and brush

pencil

scissors

thread

1 Trace the star template at the back of the book onto paper. Place on the reverse side of a piece of fabric and cut out. Cut out spots in a contrasting colour and glue them on to the right side of the star. Stitch the star onto the right side of the bag fabric.

2 With right sides facing, fold the bag fabric in half to make a square. Hand or machine stitch along three sides, leaving a 1 cm (½ in) seam allowance.

3 Fold over the open side by 5 cm (2 in), then stitch round the top of the bag. Turn the bag right side out.

4 Starting at a side seam, pin the tape round the outside of the bag 3 cm (1¼ in) from the top. Fold in the raw ends then stitch along either side of the tape. Attach a safety pin to the end of the ribbon or cord and thread it through the tape. Tie the ends in a knot.

Paper Fastener Puppet

It's amazing what you can do with basic, everyday equipment such as paper fasteners. Here they are used to joint the limbs of this smartly dressed puppet, so that you can make him wave and dance. Hang him up on the back of a bedroom door or on the wall.

YOU WILL NEED
tracing paper
pencil
card (posterboard)
scissors
paints, in assorted colours
paintbrush
4 paper fasteners
electrical tape
embroidery thread

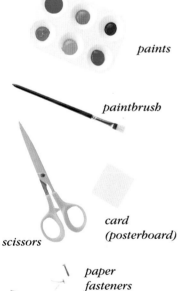

paints

paintbrush

scissors

*card
(posterboard)*

*paper
fasteners*

pencil

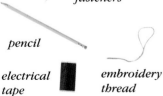

*electrical
tape*

*embroidery
thread*

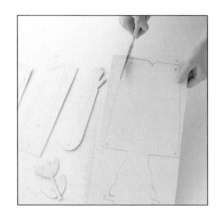

1 Trace the puppet templates from the back of the book. You will need two arms and two legs. Draw round the shapes onto card (posterboard) and cut out using scissors.

2 Paint the shapes in background colours and leave to dry. Then carefully paint the details of the man's checked suit and his face.

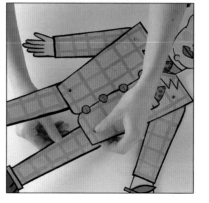

3 Ask an adult to help you make holes on the arms and legs, as shown on the templates. Make four holes on the body, as shown. Attach the limbs to the body with the paper fasteners.

4 Using electrical tape, stick a double length of embroidery thread behind the top of the puppet's head so that you can hang him up.

Big Foot Stilts

Children will love walking about on these giant feet! If possible, ask the child for whom the stilts are intended to stand on the cans so that you can measure the length of rope needed.

YOU WILL NEED
2 large, empty cans, the same
  size
plasticine
bradawl
spray paint
enamel paint, in contrasting
  colour
paintbrush
sticky stars
rope

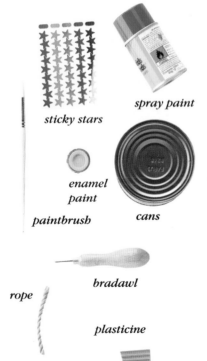

sticky stars

spray paint

enamel paint

paintbrush   cans

rope

bradawl

plasticine

1 ! Remove the labels from the cans. Place a ball of softened plasticine on either side of the top of each can. Ask an adult to pierce a hole through the plasticine with a bradawl then remove the plasticine.

2 Place the cans on a well-protected surface, preferably outdoors. Spray with spray paint and leave to dry. Spray on a second coat if necessary.

3 Paint the top of the cans with enamel paint. Leave to dry.

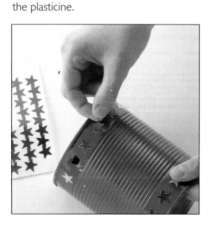

4 Decorate the cans with sticky stars.

5 Stand on the cans. Measure the length of rope needed to suit your height then thread through the holes on each can. Tie the ends together in a knot.

6 ! Burn the ends of rope to prevent them from fraying

Mexican Clay Doll

This doll is made in the traditional Mexican way, with the arms and legs tied to the body with threads. It is very fragile so this toy is best kept on a shelf as an ornament.

YOU WILL NEED
self-hardening clay
modelling tools
acrylic paints, in assorted colours
paintbrush
strong embroidery thread

self-hardening clay　*embroidery thread*

acrylic paints

paintbrush

modelling tools

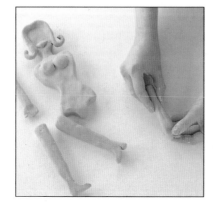

1 Shape the body, arms and legs out of the clay. The arms and legs should be the same size. Lay the pieces on a board or other flat surface.

2 Using a modelling tool, pierce a hole at the top of each limb and at each corner of the body. Leave to dry in a warm place overnight, or as directed on the packet.

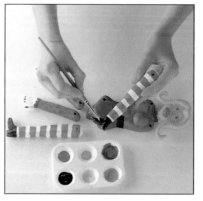

3 When the pieces have fully hardened, paint them in bright colours. Leave the paint to dry.

4 Tie the arms and legs to the body with lengths of thread, leaving enough slack for them to move freely.

Star Board Game

Make your own painted board for this fun game, then make a set of star playing pieces to match using any small pastry cutter shape. Play the game the same way as traditional draughts (checkers).

YOU WILL NEED
52 x 52 cm (20 x 20 in) MDF (fiberboard)
metal ruler
pencil
emulsion (latex) or acrylic paints, in 2 contrasting colours
paintbrush
masking tape (optional)
varnish and brush
polymer clay, in 2 colours to match board
rolling pin
small star pastry cutter

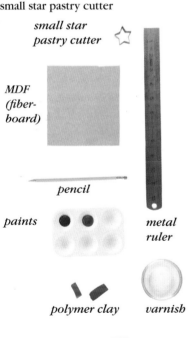

small star pastry cutter

MDF (fiber-board)

pencil

paints

metal ruler

polymer clay

varnish

paintbrush

masking tape

1 Using a metal ruler, divide the MDF (fiberboard) into 64 squares, each measuring 6.5 x 6.5 cm (2½ x 2½ in).

2 Paint alternate squares in the first colour. To help paint straight lines, you can mark out the squares with masking tape and remove it when the paint is dry.

3 Paint the remaining squares with the second colour. When dry, apply a coat of varnish.

4 For the pieces, roll the polymer clay approximately 5 mm (¼ in) thick. Using the pastry cutter, cut out twelve shapes from each colour. Bake the pieces following the manufacturer's instructions, and allow to cool.

Sunny Flower Blackboard

This novel blackboard should make sums and spelling more fun! Make it as large as you like, to fit your wall. If you have an electric jigsaw you can use it to cut out the flower shape, otherwise use a coping saw.

YOU WILL NEED
MDF (fiberboard)
pencil
string
saw
sandpaper
emulsion (latex) paints, in
  assorted colours
paintbrush
blackboard paint
bradawl
2 screw eyes
screwdriver

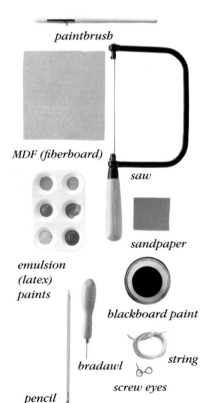

paintbrush

MDF (fiberboard)

saw

sandpaper

emulsion (latex) paints

blackboard paint

bradawl

string

screw eyes

pencil

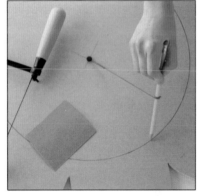

1 ! Draw the flower on the MDF (fiberboard) and ask an adult to cut it out. For the centre, use a pencil and string to draw a circle or draw round a plate. Smooth the edges with sandpaper.

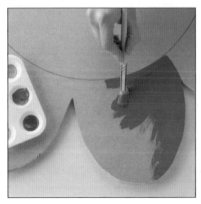

2 Paint each petal a different colour, leave to dry then paint a second coat. Leave to dry.

3 Paint the centre of the flower with two coats of blackboard paint. Leave to dry.

4 ! Turn the flower over. Mark two points, one on each side, and make small holes with a bradawl. Screw the screw eyes into the holes until they are tight. Tie a piece of string securely to each screw eye, allowing some slack for hanging.

Glove Puppets

Make a different puppet for each hand, so they can perform together. If your hands are a different size to the template, simply draw round the hand and add a generous seam allowance.

YOU WILL NEED
tracing paper
pencil
paper
scissors
felt, blanket or wool fabric
blue and red embroidery threads
tapestry needle
knitting wool (yarn)
buttons

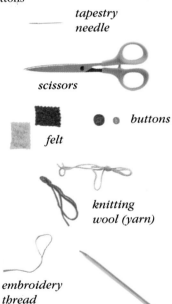

tapestry needle

scissors

buttons

felt

knitting wool (yarn)

embroidery thread

pencil

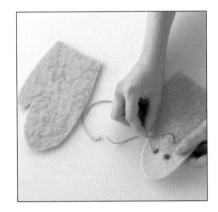

1 Trace the glove template from the back of the book onto paper and cut out. Draw round it onto the felt or fabric and cut out two glove shapes. Embroider blue eyes and a red mouth on one shape.

2 Place the two shapes together, wrong sides together, and stitch round the edge in running stitch. Leave the bottom edge open.

3 For the hair, stitch short lengths of knitting wool (yarn) through the top of the glove and knot.

4 Finally stitch a row of buttons down the centre front.

Decoupage Toy Box

Jazz up an old, or boring, toy box with a splash of paint and some fun cut-outs. Decoupage is very cheap and simple to do – you simply cut out shapes from wrapping paper and paste them on. A layer of varnish means the paper shapes will not rub off and the finished decoration is very hardwearing.

YOU WILL NEED
wooden toy box
sandpaper
emulsion (latex) paint, in
  several colours
paintbrush
wrapping paper
scissors
PVA (white) glue and brush
varnish and brush

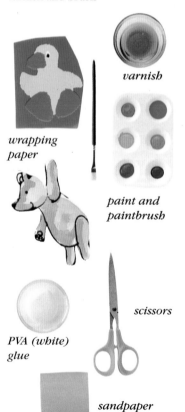

wrapping paper

varnish

paint and paintbrush

PVA (white) glue

scissors

sandpaper

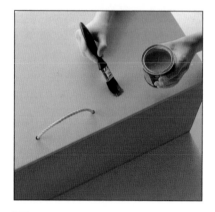

1 First sand down the toy box. Paint the box with emulsion (latex) paint, using a different colour for each side. Leave the paint to dry then apply a second coat.

2 When the paint is dry, cut out shapes from the wrapping paper.

3 Arrange the paper shapes on the box to make a good design. Using the PVA (white) glue, paste them in place.

4 When the glue is dry, varnish the box and fill with toys.

Monster Feet

Disguise your hands with these colourful monster feet! They're great fun for parties and, as they cover only the backs of your hands, you will still be able to eat and drink a monstrous amount!

YOU WILL NEED
heavy coloured paper
pencil
scissors
thin paper in contrasting colours
non-toxic paper glue
paper clips (optional)

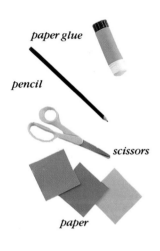

paper glue

pencil

scissors

paper

1 Draw a five-toed monster foot on the heavy paper. Cut it out and use it as a template to make a second foot. Remember to cut an extension of paper from each ankle to form a fastening band.

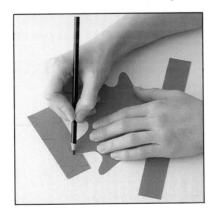

2 Place the monster feet on thin coloured paper. Draw around the tip of each toe and cut out the shapes to make toenails. Stick each toenail to its corresponding toe.

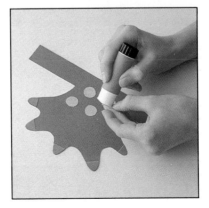

3 Cut out polka dots from a third coloured paper. Stick these in position on the fronts of the feet.

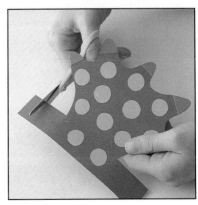

4 Wrap the fastening bands around your wrists and ask a friend to mark the point where they overlap. Trim if necessary and cut notches to form a fastening, or attach with paper clips.

Squeaky Floor Cushion

Make a large, comfortable cushion for sitting or lying on the floor but watch out – this joke cushion has a squeaker hidden underneath each of the coloured spots! The back of the cushion is made in two pieces so that you can insert a cushion pad.

YOU WILL NEED
scraps of fabric
scissors
6 squeakers
needle and matching sewing
  threads
paper
pencil
mug or tumbler
felt, in 6 different colours
62 cm (25 in) square of plain-
  coloured fabric, for the front
2 pieces of fabric 62 x 40 cm
  (25 x 16 in), for the back
60 cm (24 in) square cushion pad

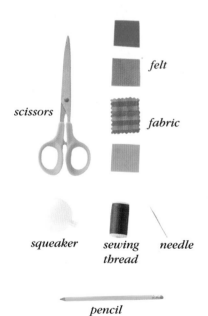

scissors

felt

fabric

squeaker *sewing thread* *needle*

pencil

1 Cut out twelve 6 cm (2½ in) squares of fabric. Stitch the squares together in pairs round three sides. Insert a squeaker inside each square then stitch up the openings.

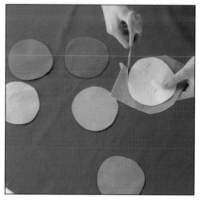

2 Draw round a mug or tumbler to make a round paper template. Place the template on the felt and cut out six circles.

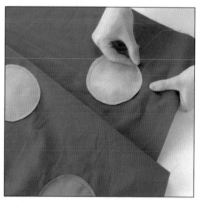

3 Arrange the felt circles on the square of plain fabric to make a nice design. Place a fabric-covered squeaker under each circle then stitch round the edge.

4 Turn under a double hem along one long edge of each piece of fabric for the cushion back. Hand stitch in place, or ask an adult to help you machine stitch.

5 With right sides facing, lay the two back pieces on top of the cushion front so that they overlap slightly. Hand or machine stitch round all four sides.

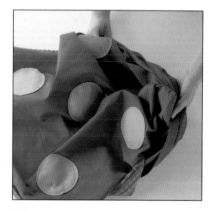

6 Turn the cushion cover right side out and insert the cushion pad.

Nature Fun

There are so many things to discover when you go
exploring in the countryside, whether in a wood, a
riverbank or at the seaside. You can do the fieldwork
projects outdoors, and bring some plants or animals
home to study in an aquarium or picture frame.

Parts of a Tree

Trees are the giants of the plant world. See if you can find these different parts of a tree.

2 **Twigs:** In winter, twigs and branches can help you to identify a tree. From the top, these twigs are: birch, ash, apple, oak and willow.

3 **Trunk bark and roots:** We do not often see a tree's roots. These willow trees are growing by a pond. Can you see the fine, hairy rootlets?

1 **Leaves:** These come in many shapes and sizes. Some have toothed edges. Others are divided up into many smaller leaflets. Pine leaves are like needles.

4 **Flowers:** Some trees have flowers with petals. But many have green or yellow catkins and do not look like flowers at all.

5 **Fruit:** There is a great variety of tree fruits and seeds. Fruit and nuts are spread by animals who try to eat them. Other seeds have wings that spin through the air like helicopters.

6 **Cones:** Pines are usually evergreen. Most do not lose their leaves in winter. Their leaves are like needles. Their fruit are seeds which are carried in pine cones.

7 Deciduous trees like the walnut opposite lose their leaves in winter. Every autumn the green leaves change colour to yellow, brown or red. They shrivel and fall from the tree. Can you see them on the ground?

How Tall is a Tree?

Field guides and other books often tell us the height of a tree. But how do we actually measure it?

YOU WILL NEED
pencil
stick
tape measure or ruler
notebook

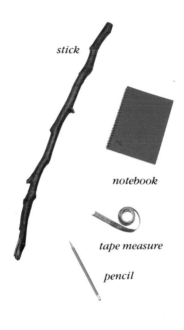

stick

notebook

tape measure

pencil

1 Stand in front of the tree. Hold out a pencil at arm's length so that you can see it and the tree at the same time. Ask a friend to stand at the bottom of the tree.

2 Line the pencil up so that the top of it is in line with the top of the tree. Move your thumb down the pencil until it is level with the bottom of the tree.

4 Mark the place where your friend is standing with a stick. Measure the distance from the stick to the tree. This distance is the same as the height of the tree. Record your findings in your notebook.

3 Turn the pencil so that it is horizontal, still keeping your thumb level with the bottom of the tree. Ask your friend to walk away from the trunk. Call and tell her to stop when she is level with the top of the pencil.

How Big and How Old is a Tree?

Some trees are very old. We can measure how big and old a tree is very easily.

YOU WILL NEED
rope
tape measure or ruler
notebook
pencil

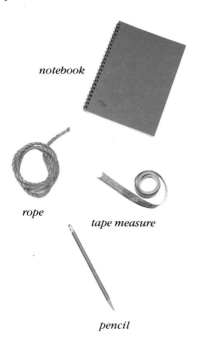

notebook

rope

tape measure

pencil

1 How big is a tree? Take a piece of rope to measure the tree trunk. Put it around the tree and keep your finger on the place where the rope overlaps. A large oak tree like this one could be several hundred years old.

2 Lay the rope out straight on the ground and measure to the place you have marked with your finger. This will equal the distance around the outside of the trunk (the girth).

3 How old is a tree? The tree rings on a log can tell us its age. The tree grows a new ring every year.

4 Count the rings and you will discover the age of the log. If the tree has one hundred and fifty rings then the log is one hundred and fifty years old. Record your findings in your notebook with a pencil.

NATURE TIP

Next time you go for a walk look at the trees. How many really old trees can you find? These will be the tallest and/or those with the thickest trunks.

Growing a Tree

Trees are easy to grow at home. Collect some acorns, seeds or nuts in autumn and grow yourself a forest!

YOU WILL NEED
flowerpot
potting soil
acorn or other tree fruit such as nuts
    or seeds
plastic bag
rubber band
saucer
small trowel

flowerpot

potting soil

acorns

small trowel

plastic bag

rubber band

1 Fill the flowerpot with potting soil.

2 Push an acorn, nut or seed into the soil. Cover with more soil.

3 Water the flowerpot with just enough water to make the potting soil moist. Put the flowerpot into the plastic bag and seal the top with a rubber band. Leave on a windowsill until the acorn or seeds sprout. Be patient, this could take several weeks or even months.

4 Once the seeds have sprouted, remove the flowerpot from the plastic bag. Stand it in a saucer to catch any water that drains from the bottom. Keep the seedling on a windowsill and remember to water it regularly.

5 As your tree grows you will eventually need to repot it into a larger flowerpot.

6 When the young tree (or sapling) is 50–100 cm (18–39 in) tall, plant it outside in a place where it can grow into a large tree.

7 Look at the picture on the right. Can you see three stages in the life of an oak tree? The children are holding a seedling and a young sapling. Behind them is a young oak tree. Eventually this small tree will grow into an old giant of a tree – just like the one that was measured earlier.

Keeping Caterpillars

This is a nice clean way to keep caterpillars.
Eventually they will turn into pupae and then
into beautiful butterflies and moths.

YOU WILL NEED
collecting pot
plastic bottle
scissors
paper towels
large jar
sticky tape
gauze or netting
rubber band or string

plastic bottle

collecting pot

gauze

scissors

sticky tape

rubber band

1 Look for some caterpillars living on cabbages and other plants. Put them in a collecting pot. At the same time, collect some leaves from the plants that you found the caterpillars living on.

2 Cut the bottom from the plastic bottle with a pair of scissors.

3 Take a bunch of leaves and foliage that you found the caterpillars on. Wrap a piece of paper towel around the stalks of the leaves.

4 Put the leaves inside the bottle and push the stalks through the neck so that the tissue forms a plug.

5 Stand the bottle neck-down in a jar of water. Make sure that the plant stalks are standing in the water. Tape the bottle to the jar if it is wobbly and does not stand firmly.

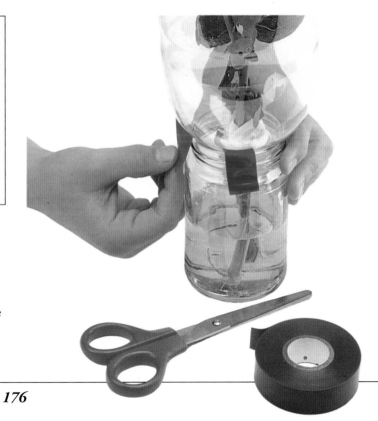

NATURE TIP

Every few days, clean out the bottle, wash it, dry it, and give the caterpillars fresh plants to eat. Eventually the caterpillars will pupate. They will turn into sausage-shaped pupae. You can keep them until the butterflies or moths emerge, and then you must release them outside.

6 Put the caterpillars inside the bottle. Cover the top with a piece of gauze. Hold it in place with a rubber band or tie with string. Feed your caterpillars regularly.

Plaster Casts

Animals often leave their footprints in soft mud and sand. Make plaster casts of them to keep a permanent record. You can paint them when the plaster is dry.

YOU WILL NEED
strip of card (cardboard)
paperclip
plaster of Paris
water
bucket or plastic tub
spoon
small trowel
old brush or toothbrush (optional)

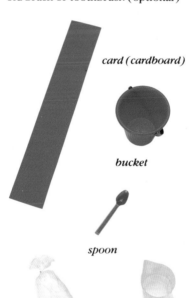

card (cardboard)

bucket

spoon

water

plaster of Paris

paperclips

1 Look for animal footprints in mud and sand.

2 Select the clearest footprint.

3 Put the card (cardboard) around the print and secure with a paperclip. Push the card down slightly into the mud.

4 Next, mix the plaster of Paris. Put a small amount of water into the bucket. Add plaster powder and stir well.

5 Pour the plaster into the mould and leave to set.

6 Once set, use a small trowel to dig up the plaster and print. Clean off the soil and sand. You may need to use an old brush or toothbrush to clean into all the small cracks.

Keeping Slugs and Snails

Slugs and snails can be kept in a tank. Here, you can learn how to make them a comfortable home.

YOU WILL NEED
gravel
small tank or large plastic
   ice cream container
soil
moss and grass
small stones, pieces of bark and
   dried leaves
gauze or netting
string
scissors

small tank

gauze

string

soil

gravel

moss

stone, bark and dried leaves

1 Put a layer of gravel in the bottom of the tank or container.

2 Cover the gravel with a layer of soil.

NATURE TIP

Keep your snails in a cool place. Feed them on a small amount of breakfast cereal (not too sugary), and small pieces of fruit and vegetables. Add fresh grass and leaves when needed.

3 Plant pieces of moss and grass in the soil. Add stones, bark and the dried leaves. Water the tank just enough to moisten the soil.

4 Put in a few slugs or snails and cover the tank with a piece of gauze or netting. Tie it down with string or replace the lid. Make sure that it has plenty of air holes.

Feeding Winter Birds

Choose some of these ideas to feed birds in winter.

YOU WILL NEED

Choose food from the following:
dried bird food
dried seed heads such as corn cobs,
  millet and sunflower
peanuts
bread and cake crumbs
coconut
lard or other hard fat
chopped bacon rind

bowl of water
peanut feeder
string
scissors
spoon
supermarket packaging such as plastic
  pots or nets

peanut feeder

lard

plastic pot

chopped rind

corn cob

dried bird food

peanuts

bread

string

1 Dried food is the easiest to put out. Give the birds grain, sunflower seeds, peanuts (but not in spring), bread and cake crumbs. Do not forget to also give them a bowl of water to drink.

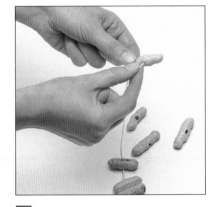

2 Hanging food allows birds to perch on the food. Hang strings of peanuts, half a coconut, a dried sweet corn cob, millet or other seed heads from the screw-eyes on your bird feeder. You can also hang these foods from the branches of nearby trees. Put loose peanuts in a peanut feeder, if feeding in the winter.

3 Birdy cake is a rich food for cold winter weather. Soften lard or a similar hard fat in a warm place. Mash in mixed grains, crumbs, bread, chopped bacon and rinds. Mix well.

4 Press into supermarket packaging such as plastic pots and nets. Set until hard in a refrigerator. When set, tip the birdy cake from the pots and put on a bird table or hang the nets beneath it.

Pond and River Dipping

Beneath the surface of the water lives a rich and varied animal and plant life. Dip into the world of a pond or river using a fishing or plankton net and discover the creatures that live there.

YOU WILL NEED
ice cream container or bucket
fishing and/or plankton net
shallow white dishes, made by cutting
   the top from an ice cream container
paintbrush
jam jar or tank
notebook
pencil

net

jam jar

pencil

notebook

ice cream container

paintbrush

I Fill an ice cream container or bucket with pond water. You will then have something to put your animals in as soon as you catch them.

2 Sweep the fishing or plankton net through the weeds.

3 Pour the water from the plankton net into an ice cream container or bucket by pushing the jar up through the net. Pull the net back and pour the water out.

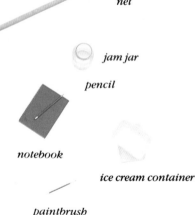

4 You will soon catch many different animals. Here are two types of pond snail – a round Ramshorn Snail and a pointed Greater Pond Snail.

5 Carefully pick out the animals you have just caught with a paintbrush and place them into a clean shallow dish or ice cream container, of water. You will have caught a lot of rubbish such as dead leaves, and the clean water will help you see the animals more clearly.

!SAFETY TIP

Take care around water, no matter how shallow it seems.

6 You can also put them into a large jam jar, or small tank. Identify the species you have found and make notes in your notebook. Visit different ponds, lakes, and rivers. Do you find the same species living in different places?

Making a Freshwater Aquarium

Pond animals can be kept easily in an aquarium. Watch the busy lives of your pond animals.

YOU WILL NEED
aquarium gravel
bucket
large tank
newspaper
waterplants
stones or rocks
seashells (optional)
fish or other creatures collected from
    a pond or river

rock

aquarium gravel

newspaper

tank

1 Wash the gravel in a bucket. Keep stirring it under running water. You must do this thoroughly to remove dirt from the stones which will make the water in your tank cloudy.

2 Put the gravel in the bottom of the tank. Once you have filled the tank with water it will be too heavy to move – so decide where you want to keep it now. Do not place the tank in bright sunshine or the water will get too hot and your animals will die.

3 Put the newspaper over the top of the gravel. Slowly pour the water on to of the paper. This prevents the water from becoming too cloudy.

4 The water will be slightly cloudy, so leave the tank to clear for several days.

5 Add some waterplants and the rocks. Put the roots of the plants under the rocks to stop them from floating up to the surface. If you use any seashells, make sure that they have been well washed in fresh water to remove any salt that they may contain.

6 Put in the animals that you have collected from a pond or river. If you are going to have fish in the aquarium, only choose small ones or else they will eat all of your pond animals.

Beachcombing at the Seaside

We all like to go to the seaside. Be a nature detective on the beach and see what treasures you can find.

YOU WILL NEED
bucket
plastic bags
notebook
pencil

pencil

notebook

plastic bags

bucket

1 Look for animals under seaweed and rocks where they stay nice and damp. Cuttlefish, crab and urchin shells, feathers and other animals are often washed up. You will find them at the highest place reached by the tide, known as the strandline.

2 You will find a variety of shells all over the beach.

3 Look for unusual stones and pebble sculptures, fossils and minerals. The holes in this large stone were drilled by rock-boring clams. Can you see the Indian's head? This is a real stone that was just picked up on a beach.

4 Who lives under the sand? Look for worm holes and dig down to find the worm beneath. Collect animals and shells and put them in a bucket or plastic bags. Make notes in your notebook, and release living creatures afterwards.

! 5 A lot of garbage is washed up onto the beach. Ropes, plastic and driftwood are harmless, but fishing tackle, bottles and canisters can be dangerous. Take care and do not touch. Some can contain dangerous chemicals.

Rock Pools

Many animals such as shrimps, crabs and baby fish live in rock pools. Here they find a safe place to wait until the tide comes in again.

YOU WILL NEED
fishing net
bucket
plastic bags
notebook
pencil

fishing net

bucket

pencil

notebook

plastic bags

! SAFETY TIP
Take care on slippery rocks. Do not get cut off by incoming tides.

1 When the tide goes out, animals on the beach must close up or hide and wait until the water returns. In the rock pool however, the animals can continue to swim and feed.

2 Some animals such as limpets and anemones attach themselves to rocks. They can move, but only very slowly.

3 Sweep a fishing net through the sandy bottom of the pool. You may catch shrimps, crabs and tiny fish that lie buried in the sand.

! 4 Be careful if you find a crab. Do not handle it roughly because you may damage its legs. You can pick it up safely by holding it across the back of its shell. This way it cannot nip you!

5 Lift up rocks carefully. Many animals live underneath them. Always replace rocks gently so that you do not damage the microhabitat and the animals underneath.

6 Collect animals in a bucket or plastic bag. Identify them and make notes in your notebook. In this bucket there are hermit crabs, shore crabs, periwinkles and a sea anemone. Do not forget to release them into the water afterwards.

Potpourri

Potpourri has been used for centuries to make rooms and stored linen smell nice and fresh.

YOU WILL NEED
fresh flowers
fresh herbs, such as lavender and
  rosemary
scissors
string
foil dish or tray
bowl
spices, such as nutmeg, cinnamon
  sticks and cloves (optional)
airtight jars or bags

lavender

fresh flowers

cinnamon sticks

fresh herbs

foil dish

string

scissors

1 Pick the flowers and herbs. This plant is lavender.

2 Cut the herbs and tie them into bunches. This plant is rosemary.

3 Hang the bunches of herbs up in a warm place to dry.

4 Put fresh rose petals, small flowers, flower buds, herb leaves and herb flowers onto a foil dish or tray. Put them somewhere warm such as an airing cupboard or near a radiator to dry.

5 When the herbs and flowers are completely dry, strip the leaves from the herb bunches. Put them into a bowl with the dried petals and flowerheads.

6 Add the spices (if using) and mix well. If you wish, you can also add a few drops of perfumed oil. Mix well. Store in airtight jars or bags. To use, place in a shallow dish or basket so that the scent of the flowers, herbs and spices can escape into the air.

Make your own Garden

Create your own indoor garden paradise within a
cardboard box. If you use moss from the garden you
may need to replace it after a few days if it dries out.

YOU WILL NEED
scissors
ruler
cardboard box
brown paint
paintbrush
small mirror
magazine pictures
bits and pieces from the garden such
    as moss, earth, gravel, ivy and twigs
shells
plasticine

shells

leaves

gravel

moss

ivy

plasticine

magazine picture

1 With a pair of scissors, cut the card-board box so that it is just 4 cm (1 ½ in) deep and paint it brown. Allow to dry.

2 For the pond, place the mirror in the bottom of the box.

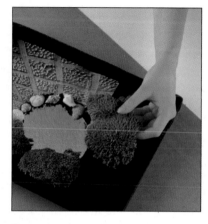

3 For the garden, arrange the magazine pictures, moss and shells inside the box.

4 For the trees, stick the twigs into a piece of plasticine and place them among the moss and shells.

5 Scatter the gravel and earth to cover any bare patches.

6 Finish off the garden by decorating it with pieces of ivy.

Making a Terrarium

Ferns grow in damp places among rocks and in woodlands. You can make yourself an indoor garden by growing them in a large jar or bottle.

YOU WILL NEED
gravel
large plastic jar or bottle with lid or stopper
charcoal
potting soil
spoon taped to a long stick
ferns and other plants

plastic jar

plants

spoon taped to a stick

gravel

charcoal

potting soil

1 Put a layer of gravel in the bottom of the jar or bottle.

2 Put a layer of charcoal on top.

3 Put in a layer of potting soil. Smooth and level the soil with the long-handled spoon.

4 Again using the long-handled spoon, plant the ferns and other plants.

5 Gently add enough water to moisten the soil.

6 Replace the lid or stopper on the jar or bottle. The moisture is kept inside the jar so the plants rarely need watering.

Growing Curly Beans

Here is a simple plant experiment that you can easily do at home.

YOU WILL NEED
paper towels
jam jar
bean or pea seeds such as French
(string), runner or mung beans

paper towels

jam jar

bean seeds

NATURE TIP

Bean shoots will always try to grow upwards and towards the light. Look at the large picture on this page. The beans top left are normal beans, growing straight up. The other two jars contain curly beans.

1 Fold a piece of paper towel in half, roll it up and put inside the jam jar.

2 Put several bean seeds between the paper and the side of the jam jar. Pour water into the bottom of the jam jar to a depth of approximately 2 cm (¾ in).

3 When the beans have sprouted a long shoot, turn the jam jar on its side.

4 Put the jam jar on a windowsill and turn the shoot away from the light. Keep turning the jam jar so that the shoot is turned away from the light. You will soon grow curly beans.

Colouring Celery and Flowers

This experiment works almost like magic! You can change white flowers and celery to almost any colour you like.

YOU WILL NEED
jam jar
brightly coloured water-soluble
    ink or dye
stalk of celery with leaves
white flowers such as carnations,
    chrysanthemums or daisies

water-soluble ink

celery

flowers

jam jar

1 Half-fill the jam jar with water.

2 Add some ink or dye.

! NATURE TIP

If you have difficulty making this experiment work, try again with another type or colour of dye. Remember, you will not be able to eat the celery once it has been dyed!

3 Stand some celery or flowers in the dye or ink solution.

4 You can make celery or flowers that are half one colour and half another. Split the celery or flower stalk lengthwise and put half in a jam jar of one coloured dye and the other half-stalk in the second jar containing a different colour.

Growing a Pineapple

We all see pineapple in the supermarket. Did you know that you can often use one to grow your own pineapple plant?

YOU WILL NEED
flowerpot
potting soil
fresh pineapple
plastic bag

flowerpot

plastic bag

pineapple

potting soil

1 Fill the flowerpot with potting soil.

2 Twist the top from the pineapple. (You may need an adult to help you with this.)

3 Remove the lower leaves from the stalk. Plant the stalk in the potting soil.

4 Water and place the flowerpot in a plastic bag. Leave in a warm sunny place. Remove the bag when the roots have started to grow. Water your pineapple regularly. Some may eventually produce fruit if kept in a warm greenhouse. Most just make nice houseplants.

Growing Exotic Plants from Seed

Other exotic plants can be grown from the seeds and pips that we find inside fruit.

YOU WILL NEED
fresh fruit
sieve
knife
paper towel
flowerpot
potting soil
plastic bag

paper towel

knife

flowerpot

plastic bag

potting soil

sieve

fresh fruit

1 Eat the fruit but save the seeds. Wash the seeds in the sieve. Ask an adult to help you to remove any flesh with a sharp knife. Dry the seeds on a piece of paper towel.

2 Fill the flowerpot with potting soil. Plant the seeds in the soil. Cover them with more potting soil.

3 Water, and put the flowerpot in a plastic bag. Keep in a warm place. Some seeds will sprout quickly, others may take longer. Remove the bag when the sprouts first appear. Keep the flowerpot on a windowsill. Transplant into larger flowerpots as the plants grow larger. The plants in the picture above were grown from supermarket fruit. On the left is a lemon, and on the right a tree tomato.

Autumn Leaves

Every autumn deciduous trees lose their leaves.
A tiny layer of cells grow across each leaf stalk like a
wall, and the leaf shrivels, dies and falls off. As the leaf
dies, it changes colour to yellow, brown, orange, red
or purple. Collect fallen leaves and make a collage
with them.

YOU WILL NEED
autumn leaves
newspaper
book
large envelope
PVA (white) glue
card (cardboard) or paper

newspaper

book   *PVA (white) glue*

large envelope

card (cardboard)

autumn leaves

1 Collect as many different autumn leaves as you can.

2 Place the leaves between the folds of a newspaper. Lightly press them by putting a book on top.

3 You can store the flat leaves in an envelope until you need them.

4 Glue the leaves onto a piece of card (cardboard).

5 Make a collection of different types of leaf or use them to make a collage, picture or to decorate greetings cards.

Gardening Fun

Being a gardener is great fun, especially if you grow
plants like sunflowers and strawberries which are very
easy to look after. Learn how to make a bottle garden,
how to press flowers and how to have plenty of
worms in your garden!

Equipment

You don't need lots of fancy equipment and you don't need all these tools to start gardening. For many projects just a trowel and hand fork will do, but as you get more enthusiastic, some of these tools will be very useful.

Bamboo canes
Canes are for staking plants, making a compost bin and a wigwam for climbing plants.

Broom
Gardening can be rather like housework because there is always a lot of tidying up to do.

Buckets
Good for collecting weeds and carrying soil, hand tools or even water.

Potting compost (soil)
This is used for potting house plants. It will feed your plants the nutrients they need.

Fork
For loosening the soil, and adding compost and manure.

Gardening gloves
Use these to protect your hands from thorns and stinging nettles, and to keep them clean. Try to find a pair that fits properly, if they are too big they can be difficult to work in.

Hand fork
For carefully loosening the soil between plants in small flower beds and for window boxes.

Hoe
For weeding. It slices like a knife under the roots of weeds which then shrivel up and die.

Penknife
Often useful instead of scissors.

Rake
For making a level surface.

Scissors
Used mainly for cutting garden twine, but useful for snipping off all sorts of things.

Secateurs (clippers)
For cutting off plant stems and small branches.

Seed tray
Seed trays are used for sowing seeds and growing seedlings.

Spade
For turning over the soil by digging and for making holes for planting trees and shrubs.

Trowel
A mini spade for making small holes and digging up big weeds.

Twine
This is gardening string for tying plants, and for marking out a straight line.

Watering can
A very important piece of equipment as without water plants die quickly. Immediately after planting always water thoroughly with the sprinkler for a gentle rain-like shower.

Wheelbarrow
For carting all sorts of things round the garden.

Wire
Useful for holding plants against walls and fences. Little pieces are used for pegging down.

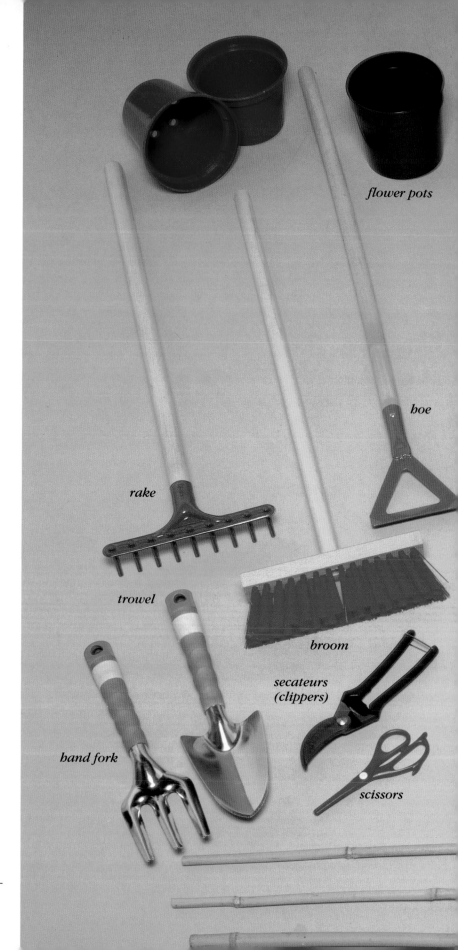

flower pots

hoe

rake

trowel

broom

secateurs (clippers)

hand fork

scissors

seed tray

spade

wheelbarrow

wire

fork

gloves

buckets

compost

twine

penknife

watering can

bamboo canes

Glossary

Bulb
Some plants have an underground part that is specially adapted for storing food and protecting the start of a shoot. A dry bulb is a resting plant, as soon as it has some water and something to grow in, roots will grow from the bottom and a shoot from the top.

Cloche (bell jar)
This is a cover that is put over tender plants to protect them from the weather. The simplest one is the top half of a plastic bottle (with the top removed so that air can get in).

Compost
There are different sorts of compost. Potting compost (soil) is used to grow plants in, and also for seed sowing. It is better than soil because it is carefully made to a recipe that makes sure it holds air, water and plant food. Buy peat-free compost if you can, to protect threatened peat bogs. Garden compost is made from recycled vegetable and fruit peelings and tea leaves and garden clippings. All the ingredients are heaped together in a compost bin where after a few months they turn into rich compost that is full of goodness, perfect for digging into beds.

Cutting
A cutting is a piece of a plant stem, usually the tip, that when planted will make its own roots and grow into another plant.

Drainage
Water, whether it is rain or from a watering can, is used by plants as it passes through the soil. The water that doesn't get used must be able to escape from the soil, or drain away, otherwise the plant's roots become water-logged and the plant dies. Flower pots must always have holes in the bottom, and garden soil should be forked over occasionally to help any excess water drain away.

Earthing up
When you are growing potatoes you need to cover up the first shoots with soil or potting compost. This is called earthing up and it encourages the stems to make more potatoes and stops light getting to them. Light turns potatoes green which is slightly poisonous.

Fertile
A fertile soil is one that is in good condition and holds lots of food for plants.

Fertilizer
Fertilizer is food for plants. There are many different sorts in granules, powders or liquids. It will say on the packet which type of plant it is for. Buy organic fertilizer whenever you can, chemical ones can be toxic.

Flower
The flower is the part of a plant from which the fruit or seed will develop. They are usually brightly-coloured to attract the insects which pollinate them.

Germination
When a seed starts to grow, it germinates by growing leaves and stems.

Leaf
Leaves are used by plants to catch food. Green leaves trap sunlight and carbon dioxide from the air and turn it into sugars for energy to grow. In return, they give back oxygen to the air which all animals need.

Manure
Manure is made from the straw bedding of horses or cattle, it has all their droppings mixed in with it. It isn't smelly at all, because the animals only eat grass which decomposes naturally and is full of goodness. Manure is forked into flower beds and put in the bottom of planting holes and is an excellent fertilizer.

Pinching out
Pinching out is removing the top pair of leaves from the stem tip; this makes a plant grow bushy rather than tall and thin.

Pollen
The fine, yellow dust which you see inside a flower is called pollen. It is usually collected by bees from the stamens – which are the male part of the flower – and carried to the female part of another flower (the stigma), this is called pollination.

Pricking out (thinning)
When seeds germinate they are usually growing close together and need to be moved into a bigger pot where they have more room to grow. This is normally done when they have three or four leaves, it is called pricking out (thinning).

Rootball
This is the area immediately around the base of the plant where there are lots of feeding roots. It gets bigger as the plant grows.

Runner
Some plants, like strawberries, make long stems that creep over the soil. When they find an empty spot, the stem will make roots and eventually grow into a new plant.

Secateurs (clippers)
Tough gardeners' scissors that can be used for cutting thick plant stems.

Seed
Seeds are like tiny time-capsules, they can rest for years, carrying a minute package of information and energy which will grow into a new plant when water and soil are added.

Seed bed
A seed bed is a piece of soil that has been prepared for planting seeds, with a firm, level surface.

Seed drill
A seed drill is a groove in the soil into which seeds are sown.

Shrub
A shrub is a bush that will live for many years.

Soil
The soil is the top layer of earth in which plants grow. It is made from tiny particles of rocks, which have been worn down over millions of years, mixed with minute bits of dead plants.

Sowing
When you put seeds into the soil to grow you are sowing them. You can sow seeds directly into the soil, or into seed trays to keep on your windowsill. Remember to water thoroughly whenever you sow some seeds.

Stake
A stake is a stout, strong stick that is used to support a plant and stop it falling over or growing the wrong way.

Stem
The part of the plant that is above the ground and carries the leaves and flowers is called the stem.

Weed
A weed is any plant that is growing somewhere you don't want it to be. They are usually plants that grow very fast and if you leave them, they take over.

Bugs: the good, the bad and the ugly

Bugs can be gardeners' friends as well as enemies, so it is important to recognize the good guys like ladybird and lacewing larvae, as well as the baddies.

Here are some of the most common and important bugs which you will find in your garden. Encourage the insects which are on your side to stay by creating the right environment for them. Don't be frightened of them! They're much smaller than you and each one has an important role to play in the life of a garden.

Examine your garden for these insects and find out who lives where.

THE GOOD

Butterfly and bee tub.

Bees
Without bees we would have hardly any fruit or vegetables because they play the vital role of pollinating the flowers.

Beetles
Beetles scurry around at night feeding on the small insects and slugs that feed on your plants.

Lacewings
These pretty insects have see-through lacy wings, and the larvae feed on plant-eating greenflies (aphids).

Ladybirds
Both the ladybird itself and its larvae feed greedily on greenfly (aphids) and help to keep them under control.

Encourage lacewings to stay in your garden by making them somewhere to live.

THE BAD

Caterpillars
Caterpillars feed hungrily on all sorts of plants. If they are on your cabbages, you might want to get rid of them. However, many caterpillars are fascinating to watch and they do turn into beautiful moths and butterflies.

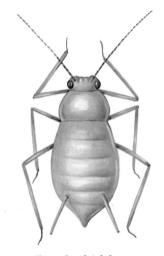

Greenflies (aphids)
Greenflies (aphids) have pointed mouths with which they pierce the leaves and stems of plants and suck out the sap. The plants then become misshapen and weak.

A blast of water will help to reduce the numbers – soapy water is best. The trouble with a lot of chemical sprays is that they kill all the good guys too, who would normally help to keep the greenflies (aphids) under control.

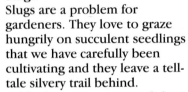

Slugs
Slugs are a problem for gardeners. They love to graze hungrily on succulent seedlings that we have carefully been cultivating and they leave a tell-tale silvery trail behind.

The best way to control them is to go out at night when they are feeding, pick them off and drop them in a pot of salty water. Or buy some slug pellets.

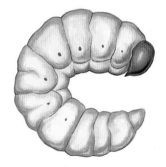

Vine weevil
This is a baddie, no doubt about it! The adult weevil lives a secretive life feeding on the leaves of plants, but it is their larvae that do the real damage.

They feed off the roots of plants, usually of those growing in pots and containers although they can sometimes be found in flower beds too.

Plants being attacked start to wilt, then topple over as soon as you touch them because they have no roots left. If you find any, immediately throw away all the compost or soil that the affected plant was growing in.

THE UGLY

Lily beetle
Lily beetles are often left alone because they are a pretty bright red colour. Their larvae, however, are one of the ugliest things around. They are covered in a horrible jelly-like mucus which protects them.

Both the adult beetles and the larvae feed on lily leaves and stems and can quickly strip a plant so watch out for them!

A Bag of Potatoes

Home-grown potatoes taste ten times better than bought ones, and nothing could be easier to grow. Start them off early in the year using potatoes either from your vegetable rack at home, or, better still, using special seed potatoes from a garden centre. When the plant starts flowering the potatoes are ready for harvesting. This is about 10-12 weeks after planting.

YOU WILL NEED
seed potatoes
egg box
strong, dark coloured plastic bag
potting compost (soil)
sharp object to make holes in bag

1 To help your potatoes get off to a speedy start, put them in an egg box with the end that has the most eyes pointing upwards. This is where the baby shoots will grow from. Place the box on a cool but light windowsill and leave for a few weeks until the first signs of life appear – little fat green leaves.

2 Fill the plastic bag one-third full of potting compost (soil), and make a few holes with a screwdriver in the bottom so that excess water can drain through.

potting compost (soil)

screwdriver

egg box

seed potatoes

plastic bag

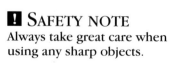

watering can

3 Plant 2 or 3 potatoes in the bag, with their shoots pointing upwards.

4 Cover them over with potting compost (soil) so you end up with the bag half full. Give the bag a good water and put it outside, in a sheltered place where it will not get caught by a frost.

bucket

5 After several weeks when the shoots are between 15 and 30 cm (6 and 12 in) tall, add more compost (soil) so the bag is completely full. This is called earthing up and it encourages the stems to make more potatoes as well as stopping light getting to them.

DID YOU KNOW?
Sunlight makes potatoes go green and green potatoes are poisonous to eat – enough to give you an upset tummy.

Good Enough to Eat!

You don't need a large garden to grow fruit and vegetables – it is possible to grow some in just a window box. Strawberries and bush or trailing types of tomatoes are small enough, so are radishes and lettuces.

YOU WILL NEED
window box
potting compost (soil)
tomato plants
strawberry plants
radish seeds
lettuce seeds
nasturtium seeds

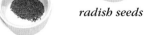

window box

strawberry plants

potting compost (soil)

tomato plants

nasturtium seeds

lettuce seeds

radish seeds

DID YOU KNOW?
Nasturtium leaves and flowers are edible, with a hot, peppery taste. They look lovely on a plate of salad.

GARDENER'S TIP
To get a plant out of a pot, turn it upside down with the stem between your fingers. With the other hand, firmly squeeze the bottom of the pot to loosen it.

1 Fill the window box with potting compost (soil) to just below the rim.

2 Plant the tomatoes in the back corners of the window box.

3 Plant the strawberries about 30 cm (12 in) away from the tomatoes.

4 Sow radish and lettuce seeds 1 cm (½ in) apart The radishes will come first, then the lettuces can have the space.

5 Sow some nasturtium seeds in the corners so that they can grow up and trail over the edge. Water thoroughly.

The Tallest Sunflower

Sunflowers are one of the speediest plants to grow in your garden. In just 6 months they outstrip everything else and can easily grow up to 3 metres (10 ft) tall.

They need some sort of support to stop them blowing over in windy weather. Plant them against a wall or fence that you can tie them to, or use a tall bamboo cane.

YOU WILL NEED
small flower pot
potting compost (soil)
sunflower seeds
watering can
a very tall bamboo cane – at least 2 m (6 ft)
string

flower pots

sunflower seeds

potting compost (soil)

bamboo canes

string

1 Fill the flower pots with compost (soil) and sow 2 or 3 seeds about 1 cm (½ in) deep. Water them in using a watering can with a sprinkler on the end.

2 When the seeds have germinated, pull out all but the strongest seedling in each pot.

3 Keep the pots on a sunny window sill until the seedlings have grown and the weather is warm, then plant outside.

4 Put the cane in the soil and tie it loosely to the plant. Measure the height of the plant when the flower appears.

Lovely Lilies

Few flowers have as much going for them as lilies. They are exotic, colourful and often heavily scented. They are also easy to grow and are perfect for planting in pots. Be sure to buy only fat, healthy bulbs with thick, fleshy roots.

YOU WILL NEED
pebbles
large flower pot
potting compost (soil)
3 lily bulbs

potting compost (soil)

flower pot

pebbles

lily bulbs

1 Put a layer of pebbles in the bottom of a large flower pot so that water can drain away easily.

2 Fill the pot half full with potting compost (soil).

GARDENER'S TIP
When the flowers die cut them off. Let the leaves die and in autumn (fall) replant the bulbs into fresh compost and they will grow all over again!

3 Plant the lily bulbs, taking great care of the roots, and spacing the bulbs evenly in the pot.

4 Cover with compost (soil), finishing a little way below the rim of the pot, then water them well.

Blooming Old Boots

Don't these look great? It is a blooming wonderful way to recycle an old pair of boots, the bigger the better. It just goes to show that almost anything can be used to grow plants in as long as it has a few holes in the bottom for drainage. Try an old football, a sports bag, or even an old hat, for plant containers with lots of character.

! SAFETY NOTE
Always take great care when using any sharp objects.

YOU WILL NEED
knife
old pair of working boots
potting compost (soil)
selection of bedding plants
watering can

knife

bedding plants

watering can

potting compost (soil)

old boot

1 Using a knife very carefully (in fact you will probably need help), make some holes in between the stitching of the sole for drainage. Even better if there are holes there naturally!

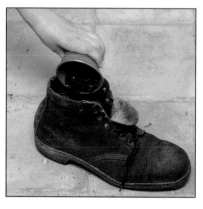

2 Fill the boots with potting compost (soil), pushing it down right into the toe.

3 Plant flowers that can cope with hot, dry places like geraniums and verbenas which will trail over the edge.

5 The boot needs watering every day in the summer, and blooms even better if you mix some plant food in to the water once a week.

4 Squeeze in a pansy with a contrasting flower colour, and a trailing lobelia plant. Lobelia grows in the smallest of spaces and will delicately tumble over the edge.

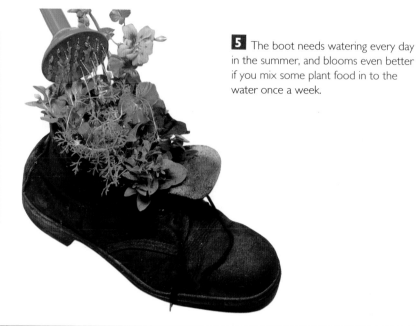

Sprouting Seeds

How do you grow fresh vegetables at any time of the year without having a garden? Sprouting seeds. They grow quickly, are very good for you and taste delicious too, so who could ask for more? These bean sprouts are grown from mung beans, but other dried seeds like chickpeas (garbanzo beans) and whole lentils work well too. For the quickest results try tiny alfalfa seeds. All these are easy to buy from any health food shop and many supermarkets.

YOU WILL NEED
flat-bottomed dish
cotton wool or kitchen paper towel
mung beans
newspaper

newspaper

mung beans

flat-bottomed dish

cotton wool

3 Wash the beans again and spread them evenly over the damp bottom of the dish.

1 Wash the beans and soak them overnight in cold water.

2 Next morning, cover a flat-bottomed dish with a layer of cotton wool, or several sheets of kitchen paper towels, and water.

4 Cover the dish with newspaper to keep out light and put it in a warm place. The beans will soon sprout and be ready to eat in 6-9 days. Don't let them grow too long, they should be plump and about 2.5 cm (1 in) long for the best taste.

VARIATION

Another way of sprouting larger seeds is to put a large spoonful of dry seeds such as chickpeas (garbanzo beans) into a wide-necked jar and cover with a small piece of muslin (cheesecloth), secured by an elastic band. Fill the jar with water and swish the seeds around a bit, then pour the water out. Do this at least once every day (twice if you can) to stop them going bad. They will take between 2-7 days to sprout, depending on what type you are growing.

DID YOU KNOW?

To cook bean sprouts, wash them, then boil in a pan of salted water for 2 minutes. Drain, and serve with butter and a few drops of soy sauce.

Grow Spaghetti

Yes, it's true! This type of marrow (summer squash) is packed with vegetable spaghetti. It only needs cooking to spill out its treasures. Bake it in the oven, or boil it until soft, add some butter and give it a twirl.

GARDENER'S TIP
If more than one seedling germinates, leave the strongest looking one in the pot and pull out the others.

YOU WILL NEED
small flower pot
potting compost (soil)
spaghetti marrow seeds
hand fork
manure or garden compost
trowel
hand fork

flower pots

spaghetti marrow seeds

potting compost (soil)

DID YOU KNOW?
All marrows (squashes) have separate male and female flowers and to get fruit they need to be pollinated. It is easy to tell which flower is which because the female one always has a swelling at the bottom beneath the petals.

1 Fill a small flower pot with potting compost (soil) and make it level. Plant 3 seeds, pushing them in about 1 cm (½ in) deep.

4 When the plant flowers, play the part of a bee by picking off a male flower and dusting the yellow pollen onto the middle of the female one to pollinate it.

2 Prepare the soil well, by forking over and adding some manure or garden compost.

3 When the young plant has 3 or 4 fully grown leaves and the weather is nice and warm, plant it outside in the prepared spot.

5 They are very greedy plants for both water and food. When the first flowers appear, start to add some fertilizer to its water once a week. Choose a fertilizer made especially for flowers and fruit and you will be rewarded with plates piled with vegetable spaghetti.

Wigwam Runners

Runner beans are climbing plants and need something to run up, so a wigwam is just the thing. This looks just as good in a flower bed as in a vegetable garden. The flowers are pretty and are followed by long, tasty beans which, if you pick them every few days, will grow all summer.

YOU WILL NEED
fork
manure or garden compost
5 x 2 m (6 ft) bamboo canes
garden string
runner bean seeds

garden string

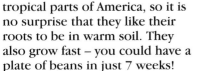

runner bean seeds

bamboo canes

compost

DID YOU KNOW?
Runner beans came from the tropical parts of America, so it is no surprise that they like their roots to be in warm soil. They also grow fast – you could have a plate of beans in just 7 weeks!

1 At the end of spring, when the days are warm and there are no more frosts, fork over a patch of soil. Add a bucketful of manure or well-rotted garden compost and mix it in well.

2 Push 5 long bamboo canes into the ground, in a circle measuring roughly 1 m (3 ft) across the middle.

3 Gather the canes together at the top and tie with a piece of string to make a wigwam shape.

4 Plant a seed about 3 cm (1¼ in) deep on both sides of each cane. Water thoroughly. They will soon germinate and start to run up the canes. When they reach the top, pinch out the top few centimetres (inches) of the stem.

Turn Detective

Watch out! Be careful where you step. There is a fascinating, hidden world going on unnoticed right beneath your feet. Take time to look and you will be amazed what there is to discover on a mini safari in a garden.

YOU WILL NEED
string
2 bamboo canes or sticks
magnifying glass
notebook and pencil

string

bamboo canes

pencil

magnifying glass

notebook

1 Tie a piece of string about 1.5 m (5 ft) long to 2 bamboo canes or sticks.

2 Peg this down across some long grass or a woodland edge.

3 Creep along the line of string very slowly, centimetre by centimetre, (inch by inch) with your nose to the ground looking through a magnifying glass.

4 Try to identify what you find with the help of nature books, or start a nature diary to make notes in.

Cunning Cuttings

Early in the year, fresh young shoots are bursting with energy and can be cut off and persuaded to make roots. Try taking cuttings of lots of different plants – some are easier than others but you won't know until you try.

YOU WILL NEED
small shallow flower pot
potting compost (soil)
penknife or scissors
fuchsia
plastic bag
piece of string

fuchsia

flower pot

potting compost (soil)

watering can

piece of string

penknife

plastic bag

DID YOU KNOW?

The plastic bag helps to keep the air moist around the leaves, while the cuttings make roots to grow on their own.

❗ SAFETY NOTE

Always take great care when using any sharp objects.

1 Fill a small shallow flower pot either with ordinary (regular) potting compost (soil) or, even better, one that is specially mixed for cuttings.

3 Gently take off the lower pair of leaves, being careful not to tear the stem.

2 Using a penknife or scissors, cut off a shoot tip which is at least 5 cm (2 in) long and which has three sets of leaves

4 Make a hole in the compost (soil) and put the cutting in. Then press the compost (soil) lightly against the stem. Fill the pot with a few more cuttings, spacing them about 3 cm (1½ in) apart.

GARDENER'S TIP

If you don't have any potting compost (soil), it is often possible to root cuttings in a glass of water. After a couple of weeks in one pot the cuttings will need more space and should be gently moved to pots of their own.

from the fuchsia. Then make a clean, straight cut just below where a pair of leaves joins the stem.

5 Give the pot a good watering then put it in a plastic bag and tie the top together with string. Place on a light windowsill and watch a new plant grow!

Desert Garden

If you like dreaming of hot, sunny places and plants that are not too much trouble, then cacti and succulents are the plants for you. Keep this desert garden on a sunny windowsill and water it well during the summer but hardly at all in the winter. With this winter rest, a cactus might surprise you with a dazzling display of flowers.

YOU WILL NEED
clay flower pot
pebbles
special cacti compost (soil) or
 potting compost (soil), grit and
sand
rocks
cacti and succulent plants
strips of folded newspaper
gravel

potting compost (soil)

cacti and succulent plants

newspaper

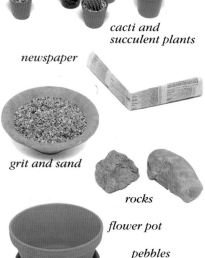

grit and sand

rocks

flower pot

pebbles

1 Find a container that is not too deep but quite wide at the top – it must have holes for drainage. Put a handful of pebbles in the bottom. Fill the pot with special cacti compost (soil) or mix your own, using equal quantities of potting compost (soil), grit and sand.

2 Position one or two large rocks in the container.

3 Pick the cacti up with strips of folded newspaper to protect yourself from getting pricked, and plant them around the rocks.

4 Cover the surface with gravel. During the spring and summer water like ordinary houseplants, but during the winter water about once a month when the compost (soil) is very dry.

Pot of Herbs

A handful of herbs adds the finishing touch to all sorts of dishes. You can keep this pot anywhere in the garden, on a balcony or even on a window sill, to give you lovely, fresh snippets just when you want them. Put in a silver and a golden thyme because thyme is one of the best herbs for pots, not growing too large and great for soups and sauces.

YOU WILL NEED
large pot
pebbles
potting compost (soil)
selection of herbs such as curry plant, marjoram, parsley, chives and thyme

herbs

large pot

potting compost (soil)

pebbles

1 Put a good handful of pebbles in the bottom of the pot so water can drain out easily (herbs don't like soggy feet).

GARDENER'S TIP
Larger herbs like mint, rosemary and fennel, are great for the first year, but in the second they will outgrow the pot and swamp anything else in it, so it is really best to give them a pot each. Remember to keep all your herbs well watered but not too soggy.

2 Fill the pot almost full with potting compost (soil). The curry plant is the tallest, so plant that in the middle.

3 Plant the marjoram towards the back because it is the next biggest.

4 Work around the pot planting chives, parsley and thyme. You can start using the herbs as soon as you like!

Minty Tea

Sprigs of mint look and taste great in cool summer drinks and mint tea is delicious either hot or cold at any time of the year.

YOU WILL NEED
mint leaves
teapot
boiling water
sugar or honey to taste

mint leaves

1 Pick a large handful of mint leaves.

2 Tear the leaves into little pieces.

teapot

! SAFETY NOTE
Always take great care when pouring boiling water.

4 Pour on boiling water and leave to steep for 5 minutes before pouring out to drink immediately, or leave until cool and then chill in the refrigerator. Add a little sugar or honey for a special treat.

GARDENER'S TIP
Mint grows very quickly by long running stems that creep through the soil making new plants along their length. Cut one of these off and plant it in a large pot.

3 Put the leaves into the teapot.

Long-lasting Lavender

Need something to make your room smell nice?
Here is just the thing – some good old-fashioned
English lavender. Fill bowls with dried lavender
or make muslin (cheesecloth) bags to put among
your clothes.

YOU WILL NEED
scissors
fresh lavender
raffia
sheet of paper
small bowl

scissors

raffia

paper

bowl

lavender

1 Cut whole stalks of lavender when
the flowers are showing colour, but are
not fully opened.

2 Tie them in small, loose bundles with
a bit of raffia.

! SAFETY NOTE
Always take great care when
using any sharp objects.

3 Hang them upside down in a warm,
dry place for a few days.

4 When the flowers are completely
dry, rub them free of the stalks onto a
sheet of paper. Tip the lavender flowers
into a small bowl.

Press Them Pretty

With a flower press you can keep colourful, summer flowers to cheer you up on a winter's day. A flower press is very easy to make out of things you might just throw away.

YOU WILL NEED
card (cardboard)
scissors
pretty gift wrap
sticky tape
corrugated cardboard
newspaper
flowers
ribbon

ribbon

gift wrap

card (cardboard)

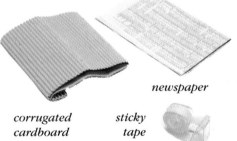

corrugated cardboard

sticky tape

newspaper

1 Cut out two matching pieces of card (cardboard) any size you like, and cover them with pretty gift wrap, using sticky tape.

2 Cut out two matching pieces of corrugated cardboard to fit. Because it is crinkled, it lets in the air which slowly dries the flowers.

! **SAFETY NOTE**
Always take great care when using any sharp objects.

3 Build the press in layers starting with a piece of card (cardboard), then a piece of corrugated cardboard and finally some thick layers of newspaper cut to fit. Lay the flowers on top. Cover with more newspaper and the second sheet of corrugated cardboard.

4 Put the remaining piece of card (cardboard) on top, then tie two pieces of ribbon tightly around, finishing them off with a bow. Keep the press in a warm, airy place for about a week. Your pressed flowers can then be made into birthday cards or pretty pictures.

Scare Them Off!

Fed up with those pesky pigeons stealing your precious plants? Give them a fright by making a scarecrow out of odds and ends that you find lying around. Model it on someone you know and give them a shock too!

YOU WILL NEED

2 sticks – one 1.85 m (6ft) long, the
  other 1.25 m (4 ft) long
nails
hammer
spade
old pillowcase
permanent marker pen
straw for stuffing
thick string
safety pins
old clothes

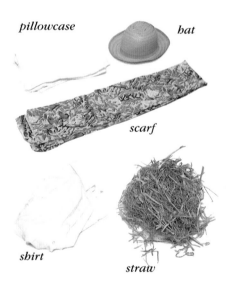

pillowcase *hat*

scarf

shirt *straw*

1 Put the longer stick on the ground and lay the shorter one across it about 30 cm (12 in) from the top. Nail them together with a couple of nails so that the frame is good and strong. Dig a 30 cm (12 in) hole, plant the frame and fill up the hole with soil.

2 Using a marker pen, draw a face on the pillowcase with the open end down. Then bring the top corners together and tie. Fill the pillowcase with straw.

3 Put the head over the top of the frame so that the stick goes up into the straw. Tie the open end of the pillowcase tightly around the stick with a piece of string. Pin the hat to the head with safety pins.

4 Tie the trouser bottoms up and fill them with straw.

5 Attach the trousers to the frame by running string through the back belt loop and around the stick.

6 Put the shirt on so the ends of the short stick go through the armholes and fill it with straw. Now you have a permanent guest in your garden!

! SAFETY NOTE
Always take great care when using a hammer.

Monkey Nuts

Most of us like eating peanuts, but it is surprising how little most people know about the plant that they come from. In fact peanuts are not really nuts at all, but are related to peas and beans. The plant is quite small and lives for just one season. Its flowers bend down to the ground after they have been pollinated, and plant themselves in the soil where the fruit or "nuts" develop.

YOU WILL NEED
large flower pot – at least 12 cm
 (5 in) in diameter
potting compost (soil)
peanuts in their shells (unsalted)
cling film (plastic wrap)

potting compost (soil)

peanuts

cling film (plastic wrap)

flower pot

1 Fill a large pot with potting compost (soil) and press down lightly to make the surface level. Crack the peanuts across the middle with your fingers.

2 Plant the peanuts on their sides, putting in about 7-8 spaced evenly apart.

3 Cover them with about 2 cm (³/₄ in) of potting compost (soil) and water them well.

4 Cover the whole pot with cling film (plastic wrap) to keep them warm and moist and encourage them to grow. Remove the cling film (plastic wrap) when they have germinated, which should take about 2 weeks.

GARDENER'S TIP
Peanuts which have been roasted will not grow. Peanut plants will only produce fruit in very hot countries.

Name It

Every time you sow some seeds, don't forget to stick a label in the pot. Many seedlings look the same, so if you don't label them you could end up with monster sunflowers in a window box!

YOU WILL NEED
large plastic yogurt pot
scissors
ruler
ballpoint pen

yogurt pot

ballpoint pen

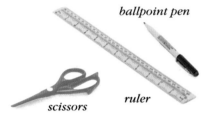

ruler

scissors

1 Cut lengthways down the side of a large yogurt pot, then carefully cut out the bottom.

2 Open the side out flat and cut off the rim. Using a ruler and ballpoint pen, draw lines about 2 cm (³/₄ in) apart.

! SAFETY NOTE
Always take great care when using any sharp objects.

3 Cut along the lines with the scissors.

4 Cut a tapered point at one end to stick into the pot or soil. Now your labels are ready to write on.

Glass Gardening

Welcome to the world of glass gardens, plants that live within a jar. This is a mini tropical rainforest, it does not need much watering because the water is recycled. Jars and bowls of almost all shapes and sizes can be transformed into a glass garden, so see what you can find. A large sweet (candy) jar does a first class job but I bet you don't get a chance to empty one of those very often!

YOU WILL NEED
gravel
glass bowl
charcoal
potting compost (soil)
selection of small houseplants
spoon and fork attached to
 pieces of cane to make
 long-handled tools for planting
plate or lid

potting compost (soil)

plate

glass bowl

charcoal

houseplants

fork

gravel

spoon

1 Put a generous layer of gravel in the bottom of the container.

2 Mix two handfuls of charcoal into the potting compost (soil), then fill the container one-third full.

3 Start to plant delicate plants that are normally quite difficult to grow indoors. This is a silver fern.

4 Then add an aluminium plant and a small African violet.

5 A polka-dot plant and some creeping moss completes the planting. Now give it a thoroughly good drink to start the water cycle off.

6 Put a plate or lid on top to close the glass garden.

GARDENER'S TIP

By moving the top on and off, you can control the atmosphere inside. If water is running continuously down the sides, it is probably too wet, so take off the lid for a few days to let it dry out. Slight fogging collecting on the glass means the conditions are perfect – if there is no fogging, the conditions could be too dry and you will need to do some hand watering.

DID YOU KNOW?

Water in a glass jar is recycled in much the same way as it is in the earth's atmosphere. Inside the jar water evaporates from the surface of the soil and from the plants themselves, but rather than rising to form high clouds in the atmosphere, it collects on the inside of the glass and runs down the sides (like rain), and as the plants are watered the cycle is complete.

Rock It

Part of the fascination of rock gardens is that it is possible to create a small piece of hillside or mountain in your own garden. Play around with the rocks until you are happy with their position and keep standing back a few paces to get a proper picture of the overall effect.

YOU WILL NEED
spade
gardening gloves
rocks
garden soil
trowel
alpine plants
grit

rocks

garden soil

grit

trowel

gardening gloves

alpine plants

1 Wearing gardening gloves, put the biggest rock in a hole that is deep enough to bury the bottom third. Lean the rock back slightly and press in firmly.

2 Arrange the next two biggest rocks either side of the first. Fill in the gaps with some garden soil. Use lots of soil so that a mound begins to form.

3 Put two or three more rocks on the next level, making sure they are secure. Then fill in with more soil.

4 Place a final rock on the top, making sure it is still one-third buried.

5 Plant a collection of alpine plants among the rocks, putting a small handful of grit in the bottom of each planting hole – the soil on a hillside is much quicker draining than most garden soils and alpine plants don't like wet feet.

6 Cover the soil around the plants with a layer of grit, which gives it a natural finish and stops any water sitting in puddles around the plants.

Crazy Grass-head

Crazy grass-heads make great mates to have lounging around on your windowsill. Grow a head of long, wild green hair for a cool dude, or keep it trimmed regularly and looking neat and tidy. They cost practically nothing to make and are very original presents for your friends, if you can bear to give them away.

GARDENER'S TIP

The bottom of the sock sucks up water from the paper cup. Never let it go thirsty or the hair will wilt! Keep it on a windowsill that gets plenty of daylight.

YOU WILL NEED
old sock or pair of tights
 (panty hose)
scissors
grass seed
potting compost (soil)
cotton thread
elastic band
pieces of felt
fabric glue
paper cup

sock

felt

scissors

string

cotton thread

grass seed

fabric glue

paper cup

potting compost (soil)

1 Cut off the foot of a thin, old sock or a pair of thickish tights (panty hose), with about 10 cm (4 in) of the leg.

2 Put a generous handful of grass seed in the end of the toe and press it down in a thick layer.

⚠ SAFETY NOTE

Always take great care when using any sharp objects.

3 Fill up the toe with potting compost (soil) pressing down each handful firmly, so you end up with a good-sized head that is quite solid. It can be any size you want but the bigger the better.

4 Knot the end like a balloon, or tie it firmly with string or strong cotton thread. Make the nose by pulling out a wedge in the middle and fixing an elastic band around the bottom.

5 Cut out the eyes, mouth and even a beard or moustache from the felt. Stick them in place using fabric glue. Leave to dry overnight. Next morning sit the head on top of a paper cup filled with water.

Wonderful Worms

Worms are truly wonderful creatures that we often take for granted. They keep the soil healthy by making channels for air and water and by eating plant remains. A wormery is an excellent way of making potting compost from kitchen scraps. It is on a smaller scale than a compost bin and provides a richer material which can be used for potting up plants. The type of worms that live most happily in a wormery are not earthworms which you find in the soil, but tiger worms which you can buy from most fishing tackle shops.

YOU WILL NEED
hand drill
small dustbin (trash can)
gravel
newspaper
potting compost (soil)
tiger worms
vegetable peelings

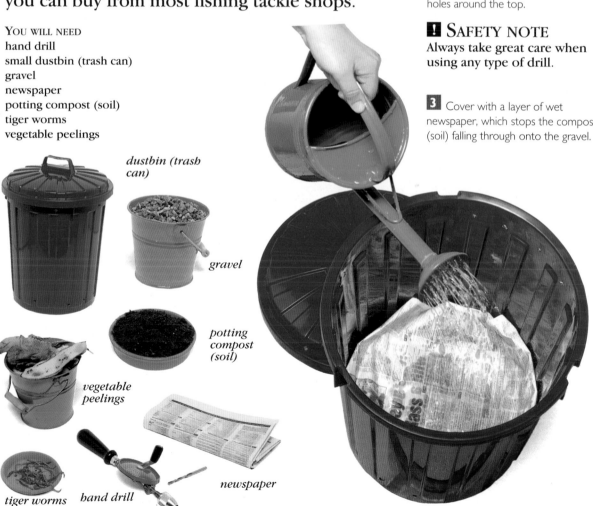

dustbin (trash can)

gravel

potting compost (soil)

vegetable peelings

tiger worms   *hand drill*   *newspaper*

1 Drill two rows of drainage holes 2.5 cm (1 in) up from the bottom of a small dustbin (trash can), plus a row of air holes around the top.

! SAFETY NOTE
Always take great care when using any type of drill.

3 Cover with a layer of wet newspaper, which stops the compost (soil) falling through onto the gravel.

2 Put a 10 cm (4in) layer of gravel in the bottom.

4 Then add a 10 cm (4in) layer of potting compost (soil).

5 Now add a good handful of tiger worms, use gloves if you like!

6 Add a thin layer of vegetable peelings and cover everything with a thick layer of newspaper. It will take a couple of weeks for the worms to settle into their new home. Don't add more vegetable peelings until the worms have started to work on the previous batch and only add a thin layer at a time.

DID YOU KNOW?

Worms' favourite foods are banana skins, tea-bags, carrot and potato peelings, and all greens. They are not very keen on orange or lemon skins so it is best to leave them out.

Face Painting Fun

Everyone loves face paints and this chapter shows you how to get a really professional look. Try your new skill out for your next fancy dress party. Whether you want to be a wild animal or a spooky vampire, there are lots of faces to choose from.

Materials

There is an enormous range of face painting materials available at a range of different prices. Toy and novelty shops often stock a range of face paints, as well as theatrical suppliers.

Child's make-up kit
This is a good starter kit. It includes a bright range of coloured face paints, sponges, brushes, and a well for water. It is available from most toy shops.

Cleansing towels
These are ideal for removing the last traces of face paint.

Cold cream cleanser
Even though most water-based face paints come off with soap and water, you can also use a cream cleanser with soft tissues or cotton wool.

Cotton buds
These are used to apply and remove make-up around the eye.

Eyebrow brush
This is used for combing eyebrows and eyelashes.

Fake blood
This is great for special effects and can be purchased from theatrical and novelty shops.

Glitter gel
This comes in a range of colours and gives a sparkly finish. It can be purchased from costume shops.

Make-up brushes
These come in a range of sizes and shapes. It is a good idea to have different types to use for different effects. Wide brushes either have a flat or rounded edge and are used for large areas of modelling or for applying blusher, highlights or all-over powder. Medium brushes with a rounded edge are useful for modelling colour, while narrow brushes, either flat or pointed, are used for outlining and painting fine details and lips.

Make-up fixative
This is available from professional theatrical shops. It fixes the make-up, therefore making it last longer. Make sure the model's eyes are closed when spraying it.

Make-up palette
This provides a range of solid, vibrant colours that give very good effects. You can mix colours together if the set you have doesn't provide the range of colours you require.

Make-up (eye-liner) pencils
These are used for drawing fine details on the face. They can also be used for outlining your basic design, if necessary.

Make-up pots
These are purchased from specialist theatrical shops. They are more expensive but are excellent quality and come in a wonderful range of colours.

Plastic palette
Use as a surface for mixing face paints together to achieve more subtle colours.

Soft tissue
Use with a dab of cold cream cleanser to remove make-up or for wiping off excess make-up from your brush.

Sponges
Covered sponges such as powder puffs are used for applying dry powders. Cellulose or latex sponges can be used slightly damp to give an even colour. Stipple sponges are made from soft plastic and are used for creating textured effects such as beard growth, animal skins and other effects.

Temple white
This is available from theatrical shops and is applied to the hair to give an aged effect.

Wax make-up crayons
If you do not mind a less professional finish, these are a good, inexpensive option. They give a less solid colour and the result is less long-lasting but they are often formulated for young children to use themselves.

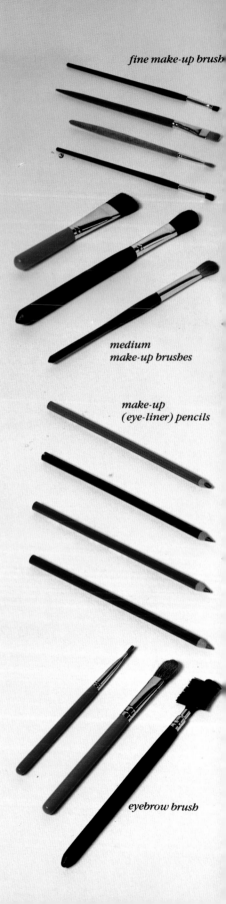

fine make-up brush

medium make-up brushes

make-up (eye-liner) pencils

eyebrow brush

make-up fixative

cleansing towels

child's make-up kit

cold cream cleanser

fake blood

make-up palette

make-up pots

temple white

cotton buds

sponges

plastic palette

soft tissue

wax make-up crayons

glitter gel

wide make-up brushes

Applying a Base

An evenly applied, well-modelled base is the foundation for successful face-painting effects. Experiment with different colours, blended directly onto the face, to change the model's appearance.

YOU WILL NEED
make-up sponge
water-based face paints

1 Using a damp sponge, begin to apply the base colour over the face. To avoid streaks or patchiness, make sure the sponge is not too wet.

2 Make sure the base is applied evenly over the face and fill in any patchy areas.

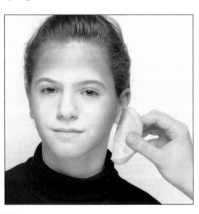

3 Using a contrasting colour, sponge around the edge of the face.

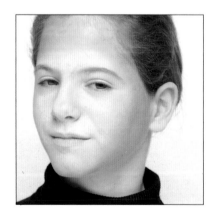

4 Blend the colours together for an even finish. Always make sure the base colours are dry before you start to decorate the face with other colours.

Shading

Shading can change the shape of your model's face dramatically.

YOU WILL NEED
powder face paints
soft make-up brush

1 When shading under the model's eyes, ask her to look up so that the area becomes smooth and easy to work on. This also stops the model from blinking as you work.

2 To exaggerate the shape of the model's face, shade each cheekbone with blusher or dark powder face paint.

3 To shade the whole face, use a large soft brush.

Painting Lips

YOU WILL NEED
fine lipstick brush
water-based face paints

1 Using a fine lipstick brush, paint the lips. Ask the model to close her mouth as this makes the muscles firmer and easier to outline. Then ask the model to open her mouth to fill in the corners. You may need to wait a few seconds to allow the make-up to dry before going on to the next stage.

2 Rest your hand on the model's chin, on a piece of tissue or a powder puff. This will help you to paint an even outline around the lips. You might want to experiment with using a different colour for the outline, or extending the line beyond the natural curve of the model's mouth to create a different shape.

Ageing the Face

You can make even the young look very old with this technique.

YOU WILL NEED
water-based face paints
fine make-up brush
wide make-up brush

1 To find where wrinkles occur naturally, ask the model to frown. This will show where lines will occur with age. Apply fine lines of make-up in these areas. Ask the model to smile, and apply a fine line starting at either side of the nose, down the fold of the cheek.

2 Ask your model to purse her lips, and apply fine lines around the mouth, within the natural folds.

3 Finish by giving a light dusting of a lighter coloured base with a wide brush on the cheeks and temples.

Removing Make-up

Most face paints will come off with soap and water. If soap is too drying, or if some colours persist, you may want to remove make-up as follows.

YOU WILL NEED
cold cream cleanser
cotton wool ball or soft tissues

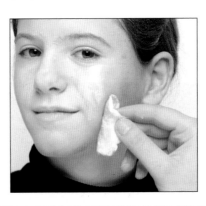

1 Pour the cream onto a damp cotton wool ball or tissue and gently rub the make-up off the face. Use a clean tissue or your fingers to apply more cold cream cleanser.

2 If desired, give a final cleanse with soap and water, and dry by patting the face with a soft towel.

Making a Tail

This tail was made to go with the spotted dog outfit. You can make a tail for a cat or tiger in the same way.

YOU WILL NEED
old pair of children's black tights
scissors
newspaper
elastic
needle and thread
felt
fabric glue

newspaper

fabric glue

scissors

tights

1 Cut one leg off the pair of tights. Scrunch up balls of newspaper and fill up the leg until it is quite firm.

2 Tie a knot at the end of the leg.

3 Measure your waist so you know how much elastic you need. Sew the elastic in a loop onto the knotted end of the tail.

4 This tail is for the spotted dog so it has been decorated with spots of felt glued on with fabric glue. You could always paint on a different design using fabric paints.

Making Ears

These ears add a cuddly touch to any of the animal outfits. You can adjust the size of the ears and choose material to suit the animal.

YOU WILL NEED
hairband
tape measure
fake fur
scissors
needle and thread
felt
fabric glue (optional)
template for ears
cardboard
pencil

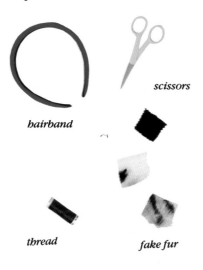

hairband *scissors*

thread *fake fur*

1 Measure the length of the hairband with a tape measure. Cut out a piece of fur to fit, allowing an extra 2 cm/1 in at each end for folding over. Sew the fur onto the hairband as shown.

2 Cut out a piece of felt to fit the inside of the hairband and sew or glue it on.

3 Trace the appropriate template from the back of the book onto a piece of cardboard and draw around the cardboard on the reverse side of the fur. You will need two pieces of fur for each ear. Place the two pieces of fur together with the right sides facing and sew round, leaving a gap to turn the right sides out.

4 Sew the ears onto the hairband, making sure they are in the correct position.

Cat

Use the instructions given previously in this chapter to make a pair of black furry ears. Dress up in a black catsuit and you will be the most glamorous, sleek pussy cat in town.

YOU WILL NEED
make-up sponge
water-based face paints
medium make-up brush
fine make-up brush
thick make-up brush
blusher

medium make-up brush

fine make-up brush

thick make-up brush

make-up sponge

water-based face paints

1 Using a damp sponge, apply a white base over the whole face. Using a medium brush, paint a border of black spikes around the edge of the face. You might find it easier to paint the outline first and then fill it in.

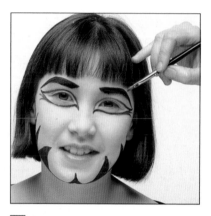

2 Paint a black outline around the eyes as shown and paint over the eyebrows.

3 Making sure the model's eyes are closed, fill in the eyelids and inside the black outline with a bright colour. This is a very delicate part of the face, so take care, and do not apply make-up too close to the eyelashes. Paint above the eyes.

4 Using a fine brush, paint a heart shape on the tip of the nose and a thin line joining the nose to the chin, avoiding the mouth.

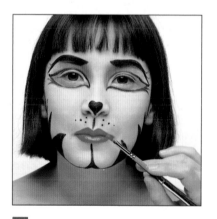

5 Paint the lips a bright colour and paint black whisker spots under the nose.

6 Using a thick brush, dust each cheek with blusher.

Mouse

Use the template and the instructions provided earlier to make a pair of furry mouse ears. Beware of cats and owls when you are wearing this costume as one of their favourite meals is little mice!

YOU WILL NEED
make-up sponge
water-based face paints
black make-up (eye-liner) pencil
medium make-up brush
thick make-up brush
pink blusher
fine make-up brush

make-up sponge

*water-based
face paints*

fine make-up brush

medium make-up brush

thick make-up brush

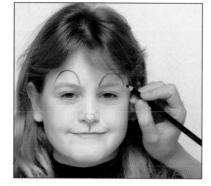

1 Using a damp sponge, apply a base coat of white over the face. With a black make-up (eye-liner) pencil, mark a pair of eyebrows above the model's own. Draw the outline of a heart on the tip of the nose and draw a line joining the nose to the mouth.

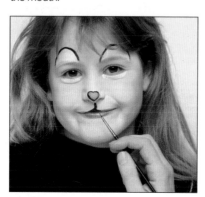

2 Using a medium brush, paint the area under the drawn eyebrows white. Apply more white underneath the model's eyes. Paint the heart pink and the outlines of the eyebrows and the heart black. Paint a line that joins the nose to the mouth and continue the line onto the centre of the top lip, forming a triangle.

3 Using a thick brush, dust pink blusher onto each cheek.

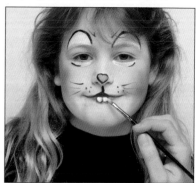

4 Using a fine brush, paint the black outline of the teeth over the bottom lip. Fill in the teeth white. Paint on a few black whisker spots and whiskers.

Panda

If you only have a few face paints, this is the perfect project for you. It is good for beginners as it is simple to do. Use the template and the instructions provided earlier to make a pair of furry ears to match.

YOU WILL NEED
black make-up (eye-liner) pencil
make-up sponge
water-based face paints
medium make-up brush
fine make-up brush

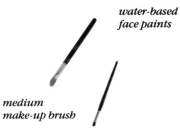

make-up sponge

water-based face paints

medium make-up brush

fine make-up brush

1 Using a black make-up (eye-liner) pencil, gently draw an outline around each eye as shown. Draw an outline across the tip of the nose.

2 Using a damp sponge, apply a white base over the face, avoiding the areas you have just marked with the pencil.

3 Using a medium brush, paint the eyes and the tip of the nose black. Using a fine brush, paint a line joining the nose to the mouth and paint the lips. Paint small whisker spots either side of the mouth. Add black lines between the eyebrows.

Tiger

For a complete look, dress up in an outfit made from fake tiger fur and use the instructions at the beginning of this chapter to make a pair of matching furry ears.

YOU WILL NEED
make-up sponge
water-based face paints
medium make-up brush
fine make-up brush

medium make-up brush

fine make-up brush

make-up sponge

water-based face paints

1 Using a damp sponge, apply the base colour over the face.

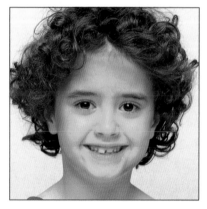

2 Rinse the sponge, then stipple a darker shade of paint around the edge of the face as shown.

3 Sponge the chin and the area above the mouth white. Using a medium brush, paint the area around the eyes white as shown. You might find it easier to paint the outline first and then fill it in.

4 Using a medium brush, paint on the black markings around each eye, as shown, making sure each side is the same.

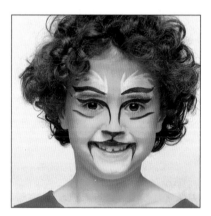

5 Using a fine brush, paint the tip of the nose black and paint a thin black line from the centre of the nose to the top lip. Paint the top lip black and extend the line at each corner of the mouth, stopping half-way down the chin.

6 For the rest of the markings, paint brushstrokes of colour across the face. To keep the design symmetrical, finish one side of the face first and then copy the design onto the other side.

Spotted Dog

This funny dog's outfit is easy to make. Simply cut out circles of felt and stick them onto a pair of leggings and a T-shirt using fabric glue. Use the template and the instructions provided earlier to make a pair of spotted ears and a tail to match.

YOU WILL NEED
make-up sponge
water-based face paints
fine make-up brush
medium make-up brush

make-up sponge

water-based face paints

fine make-up brush

medium make-up brush

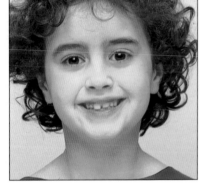

1 Using a damp sponge, apply a white base colour over the face. Gently sponge a slightly darker shade around the eyes.

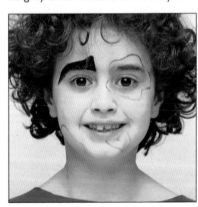

2 Paint one eyebrow black and, using a fine make-up brush, paint a wiggly outline around the other eye to make a patch. Paint another patch outline on the side of the face. Paint the outline for a droopy tongue below the bottom lip.

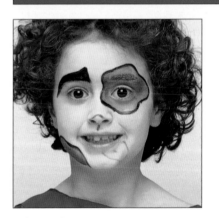

3 Using a medium brush fill in the patches grey and outline them in black. Draw the outline for the nose and a line joining the nose to the mouth.

4 Fill in the tongue red and outline in black. Paint a short black line along the centre of the tongue. Fill in the tip of the nose pink and add a thick black line where the nose joins the mouth. Paint the centre of the top lip black. Paint black whisker spots under the nose.

Rabbit

This adorable little bunny is dressed all in white. As well as using the instructions provided earlier to make a pair of furry ears, you could also make a fluffy tail from cotton wool and stick it onto the T-shirt.

YOU WILL NEED
make-up sponge
water-based face paints
black make-up (eye-liner) pencil
medium make-up brush
pink blusher (optional)
fine make-up brush

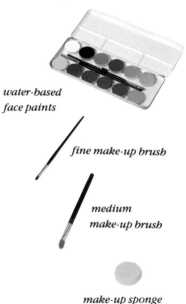

water-based
face paints

fine make-up brush

medium
make-up brush

make-up sponge

1 Using a damp sponge, apply a white base over the face.

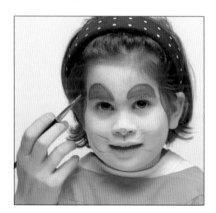

2 Using a black make-up (eye-liner) pencil draw a heart on the tip of the nose, a circular outline above each eyebrow, a line joining the nose to the mouth and a circle on each cheek. Using a medium brush, fill in the marked area above the eyebrows grey.

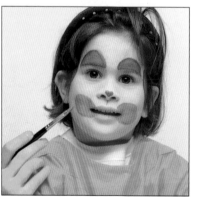

3 Paint the heart at the tip of the nose red and paint the cheeks pink with water-based face paints or pink blusher.

4 Using a fine brush, draw the outline of the teeth over the bottom lip and fill them in with white make-up. Using a medium brush, paint the line joining the nose to the mouth black. Paint black whiskers above each eyebrow and on each cheek.

Bumble Bee

Buzz around in this striped outfit. Why not paint a pair of tights or leggings in the same style?

YOU WILL NEED
yellow T-shirt
newspaper
black fabric paint
paintbrush
paints
hairband
paper baubles (balls)
scissors
milliner's wire
needle and thread
black felt
glue
black cardboard
pencil
needle and thread

FOR THE FACE
make-up sponge
water-based face paints
medium make-up brush

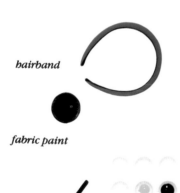

hairband

fabric paint

paints

medium make-up brush

glue

1 Place the T-shirt on a flat, well-covered surface. Fill the T-shirt with flat pieces of newspaper. Paint black lines across the T-shirt and on the arms and leave the paint to dry. Turn the T-shirt over to the other side and continue painting the lines.

2 For the antennae, first paint the hairband black and leave the paint to dry. Paint the paper baubles (balls) yellow and, when the paint has dried, paint a black line around each one.

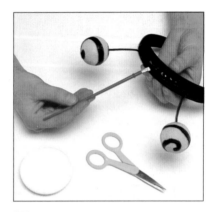

3 Cut a length of wire, approximately 45 cm/18 in long. Bend the wire to fit the hairband, making sure each piece of wire that will support the bauble is the same length. Sew the wire onto the hairband and glue a strip of black felt over the wire for extra support. Secure the baubles onto the ends of the wire.

4 Fold a piece of black cardboard in half and draw the shape of a wing, so that, when it is cut out and the paper is opened out, you will have two identical wings that are joined together. Sew the wings along the fold onto the back of the T-shirt.

5 For the face, use a damp sponge to apply a yellow base. Using a medium brush, paint a black line on the eyelids and under each eye. Paint a black spot on the tip of the nose.

Dinosaur

Dress up as a prehistoric monster in this spiky camouflaged outfit.

YOU WILL NEED
green fabric or felt
scissors
green polo neck (turtleneck) or
   T-shirt
fabric glue
needle and thread
fire resistant stuffing (batting)
hairband
green paint
paintbrush
glue

FOR THE FACE
make-up sponge
water-based face paints
stipple sponge
medium make-up brush

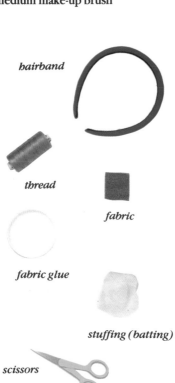

hairband

thread

fabric

fabric glue

stuffing (batting)

scissors

1 To make the costume, cut out lots of triangles, more or less the same size, from a piece of old green fabric or felt. You could use different coloured green fabrics if you don't have enough of one kind.

2 Starting at the bottom of the shirt, glue on the fabric spikes so that they overlap each other. Leave a circle in the centre of the shirt empty.

3 For each spike on the spine, you will need to cut out two triangles. Sew the two triangles together with right sides facing. Turn the triangles right side out and fill with stuffing (batting) to make a spike shape. Sew a running stitch around the bottom edge of the spike and pull gently. This will draw up the threads and close the spike. Tie a knot.

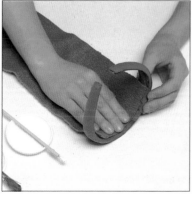

4 Paint the hairband green and leave it to dry. Cut a strip of green fabric approximately 10 cm/4 in wide and however long you wish it to be. Using glue, secure the strip onto the inside of the hairband and leave to dry.

5 Sew the spikes onto the strip of fabric attached to the hairband.

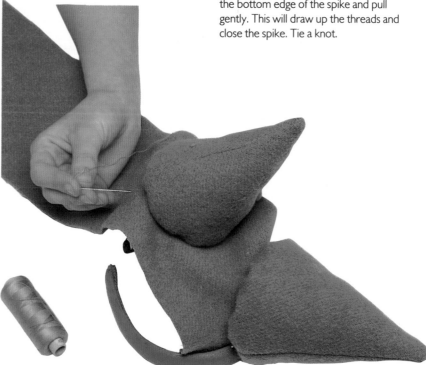

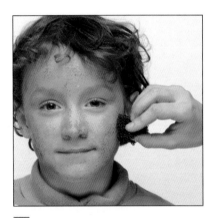

6 For the face, use a damp sponge to apply the base colour over the face. Using a stipple sponge, dab a darker shade over the base colour.

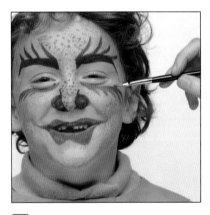

7 Using a medium brush, decorate the face. Paint on wild eyebrows, exaggerated nostrils, spots, big lips and markings under each eye.

Clown

Bounce around in this jolly outfit and entertain your friends and family. Decorate a hat and an old pair of shoes to match the colourful costume.

YOU WILL NEED
6 self-covering buttons
scraps of fabric
template for clown button
pencil
coloured felt
scissors
needle and thread
old shirt
old pair of trousers (pants)
fabric glue
milliner's wire
broad ribbon
fabric for the bow tie
narrow ribbon

FOR THE FACE
make-up sponge
water-based face paints
black make-up (eye-liner) pencil
medium make-up brush
fine make-up brush
thick make-up brush

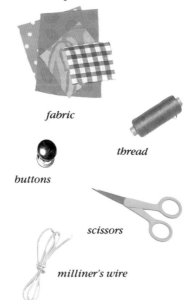

fabric

thread

buttons

scissors

milliner's wire

1 To make the costume, cover each button in a different scrap of fabric. Using the template, draw and cut out a flower shape from a piece of felt and snip a hole in the centre of it. Fix the flower onto the back of the button and secure on the back. Sew the buttons onto the shirt and trousers (pants).

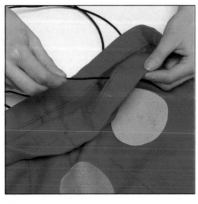

2 Cut out large dots of felt and stick them onto the trousers with fabric glue. Thread a piece of milliner's wire through the waistband. Twist the two ends of the wire together to secure them.

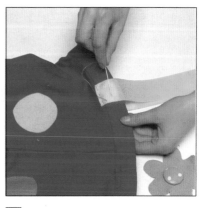

3 Sew two separate lengths of ribbon onto the waist of the trousers to make a pair of braces (suspenders). Sew a covered button onto each brace.

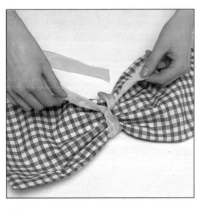

4 To make the bow tie, sew two rectangular pieces of fabric together with the right sides facing, leaving a gap. Turn right side out and stitch the gap. Tie a piece of ribbon around the centre of the rectangle and tie a knot. Tie around the clown's neck under the shirt collar.

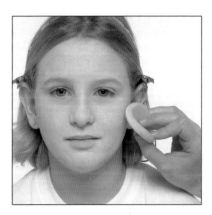

5 For the face, use a damp sponge to apply a smooth white base.

6 Using a black make-up (eye-liner) pencil, draw the outline of a clown's mouth. Draw a pair of eyebrows above the model's own and gently mark an area around each eye as shown.

7 Using a medium brush, paint the area around each eye with lots of colour and paint over the drawn eyebrows with a thick black line.

8 Using a fine brush, paint the mouth red, and outline the shape of the mouth in black. Using a thick brush, colour the cheeks a rosy red.

Witch

This young witch looks like she's got a few tricks up her sleeve. She is wearing a cloak made from an old piece of fabric and long black nails.

YOU WILL NEED
tape measure
black fabric for hat
iron-on interfacing (optional)
pencil
scissors
needle and thread
raffia or straw

FOR THE FACE
make-up sponge
water-based face paints
lipstick brush
fine make-up brush
thick make-up brush

black fabric

thread

raffia

iron-on interfacing

scissors

1 To make the hat, measure the width of your head so that you know how wide to make the rim of the hat. If the fabric you are using needs to be stiffened, iron a piece of interfacing onto the reverse side. Ask an adult to help you. Draw and cut out a triangle with a curved base, making sure the rim measures the width of your head with a small allowance for sewing the fabric together.

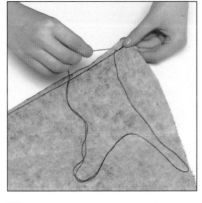

2 With the right sides facing, fold the triangle in half to form a tall cone and sew along the side.

3 Make bundles of raffia or straw and tie a knot in the centre of each bundle. Sew each bundle around the rim of the hat leaving a gap at the front. The more bundles you sew on, the wilder the wig will be. Turn the hat the right way out.

4 For the face, use a damp sponge to dab the base colours over the face.

5 Using a lipstick brush, paint on a pair of wild, black eyebrows. Paint a black line on each eyelid just above the eyelashes. Paint a line of red just under each eye and a black curve below it.

6 Add ageing lines with a fine brush Build more colour onto the cheeks using a thick make-up brush. Paint the lips red, exaggerating the top lip.

Vampire

Dress all in black for this costume. Don't be surprised if you frighten your friends and family with your haunted face.

YOU WILL NEED
make-up sponge
water-based face paints
medium make-up brush
fine make-up brush
black make-up (eyeliner) pencil
  (optional)
red make-up (eyeliner) pencil
fake blood (optional)

water-based face paints

fake blood

fine make-up brush

medium make-up brush

1 Using a damp sponge, apply a base colour on the face. Rinse the sponge, then dab a slightly darker shade on the forehead, blending it with the base colour.

2 Using a medium brush, paint a triangle in the centre of the forehead, one on either side of the face at the cheekbones and a small one at the bottom of the chin. You might find it easier to draw the outline for each shape first, to make sure they are symmetrical, and then fill them in.

3 Using a fine brush paint a pair of jagged eyebrows over the model's own. Again, you may find it easier to draw the outline first.

4 Paint the eyelids white and the area up to the eyebrows grey. Use the red make-up pencil to colour the area under the eyes.

5 Exaggerate the points on the top lip and colour the lips black.

6 Paint the outline of long, pointed fangs under the bottom lip and fill them in with yellow. Dab fake blood or red make-up at the points of the fangs and at the corners of the eyes.

Zombie

You could dress in black to make this character look even more creepy.

YOU WILL NEED
make-up sponge
water-based face paints
thick make-up brush
medium make-up brush
fine make-up brush
fake blood (optional)

make-up sponge

water-based face paints

fine make-up brush

thick make-up brush

medium make-up brush

fake blood

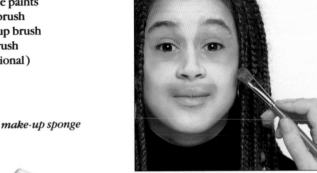

1 Using a damp sponge, apply the base colour over the face, avoiding the area surrounding the eye. Use a thick brush to dust a darker colour on the forehead, around each eye and around the mouth, to create a bruised effect.

2 Using a medium brush, fill in the area surrounding the eye with a darker colour, then paint dark lines under the eyes and on the eyebrows.

3 Paint the lips a light colour and use a fine brush to paint on dark lines, making the lips look as if they are cracked. Using fake blood or red make-up, paint the corners of the mouth to look as if they are bleeding.

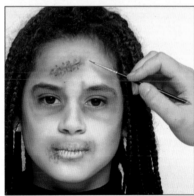

4 Use a fine brush to paint the scar on the forehead.

Gremlin

This mischievous creature is all dressed in green. Cover a green T-shirt with a piece of fur and wear a pair of green tights.

YOU WILL NEED
tape measure
hairband
fake fur
scissors
needle and thread
glue
felt
pencil

FOR THE FACE
water-based face paints
medium make-up brush

water-based face paints

medium make-up brush

1 Measure the length of the hairband and cut the fake fur to fit. Sew the fur onto the hairband, then sew or glue a strip of felt to the inside.

2 Cut out two pieces of fur for each ear, in the shape of softly rounded triangles. Make sure that the base of the triangles match the curve of the hairband. With right sides facing, sew the two ear pieces together. Turn right side out and stitch onto the hairband.

3 For the face, apply green areas with feathery brush strokes.

4 Paint a brown spot at the end of the nose and paint the lips the same colour, enlarging the top lip so that it meets the tip of the nose.

Spectacular Sea-face

Pretend you've just popped up from the ocean bed with this wonderful design of starfish and seaweed.

YOU WILL NEED
coloured face paints
tinsel wig (optional)

face paints

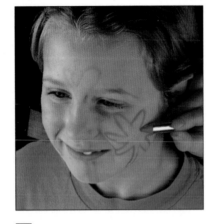

1 Paint the outlines of the sea-shapes such as fish, seaweed and starfish onto your face.

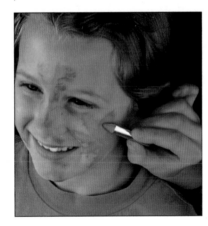

2 Colour in the starfish and seaweed.

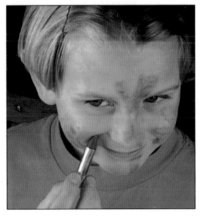

3 Fill in the fish with bright colours. Add a mixture of details to them.

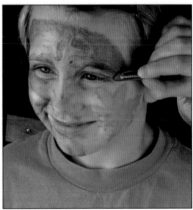

4 Carefully colour in around the shapes so that your whole face is covered with face paints. Put on the tinsel wig, if using.

Monkey

For the complete monkey outfit make a pair of furry ears and wear brown clothes. You could even make a brown tail.

YOU WILL NEED
make-up sponge
water-based face paints
fine make-up brush
medium make-up brush

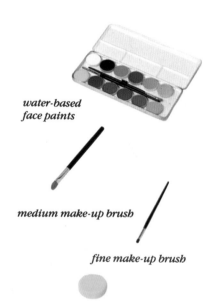

water-based face paints

medium make-up brush

fine make-up brush

make-up sponge

1 Using a damp sponge, apply a yellow base colour over the face.

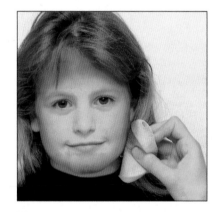

2 Rinse the sponge, then dab a few darker shades around the edge of the face, blending them in with the base.

3 Paint the outline of the monkey's mouth using a fine brush. Use a medium brush to fill in the marked area with black.

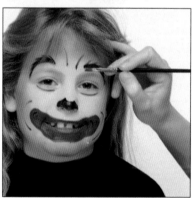

4 Paint the tip of the nose black and paint on a pair of eyebrows above the model's own. Using a fine brush, paint a few lines in between the eyebrows, under each eye and at each side of the mouth.

Owl

In this design, large yellow owl eyes are painted onto your eyelids, so when your eyes are closed, it looks as though they are wide open.

YOU WILL NEED
thick make-up brush
water-based face paints
medium make-up brush
fine make-up brush
hair spray
hair clips

medium make-up brush

thick make-up brush

water-based face paints

1 Using a thick brush, paint a white area around each eye, leaving bare the area immediately surrounding the eye.

2 Paint the rest of the face brown, except for the mouth, the upper lip and the tip of the nose.

3 Using a medium brush, apply red to the tip of the nose, the upper lip and the mouth.

4 Making sure the brush is not too wet, gently paint yellow on the eyelids and around the eye. Do not apply too close to the eyelashes. Using a fine brush, paint a black stripe across the top of each eyelid and a short stripe down the centre. Paint a black line around the red nose and mouth area and black streaks around the eye area.

5 Add feathery streaks around the eye area in yellow and white.

6 Brush the hair off the face into feathery tufts and secure it with hair spray and hair clips.

Frankenstein's Monster

Practise your monster's walk when you wear this costume. This will really scare your friends.

YOU WILL NEED
make-up sponge
water-based face paints
thick make-up brush
medium make-up brush
fine make-up brush
black swimming hat (bathing cap)

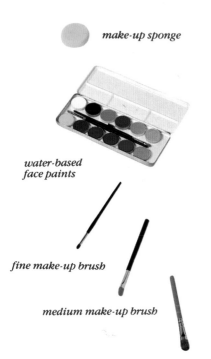

make-up sponge

water-based face paints

fine make-up brush

medium make-up brush

thick make-up brush

1 Using a damp sponge, apply the base colour over the face. Rinse the sponge, then apply a darker shade, avoiding the mouth and the nose area. Finally, shade the cheekbones with a third colour.

2 Using a medium brush, paint the eyebrows black and darken the eyelids and the area under each eye.

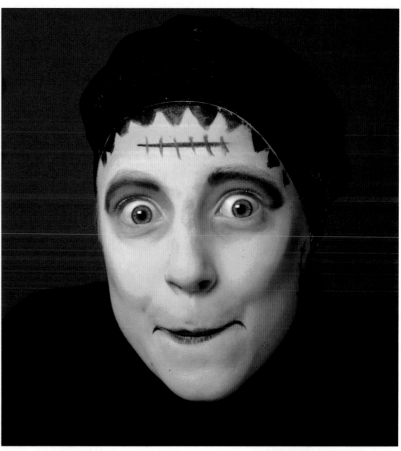

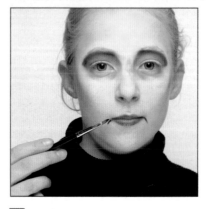

3 Paint the lips black and, using a fine brush, paint fine black lines at either side of the mouth.

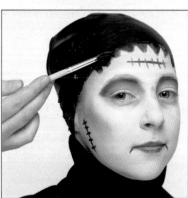

4 Using a fine brush, paint a black scar on the forehead and on one side of the face. Put on a black swimming hat (bathing cap), making sure you hide most of the hair. Where the hat meets the forehead paint a jagged hair line.

Purple Monster

If you want to be a really gruesome monster, wear a set of rotten-looking plastic teeth. They can be bought from toy or joke shops.

YOU WILL NEED
make-up sponge
water-based face paints
fine make-up brush
medium make-up brush

water-based face paints

make-up sponge

fine make-up brush

medium make-up brush

1 Using a damp sponge, apply the base colour over the face. Dab a darker shade around the edge of the face and on the forehead, blending it with the base colour.

2 Using a fine brush, paint a pair of eyebrows slightly above the model's own. Paint the tip of the nose and paint on a droopy moustache just above the model's mouth. You might find it easier to sketch an outline for the shapes first and then fill them in.

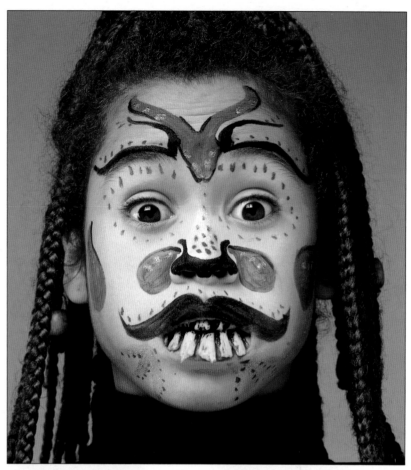

3 Use a medium brush to paint on other shapes. Paint the shapes on one side of the face first and then paint the other side. This will help you to make sure the design is symmetrical. Paint the lips the same colour.

4 Decorate the face with silver and purple spots and other details.

Lion

The wilder your hair is the fiercer you will look. Try roaring and snarling in a mirror to see what different expressions you can make, but don't frighten your friends or family too much.
Complete the look by making a pair of furry ears.

YOU WILL NEED
make-up sponge
water-based face paints
natural sea sponge
medium make-up brush
fine make-up brush or make-up (eye-liner) pencil
lipstick brush
thick make-up brush

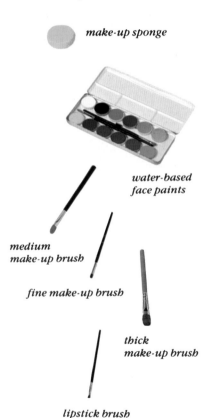

make-up sponge

water-based face paints

medium make-up brush

fine make-up brush

thick make-up brush

lipstick brush

1 Using a damp sponge, apply the base colour over the face.

2 Using a natural sponge, dab a darker shade around the edge of the face as shown.

3 Using a medium brush, apply white make-up over each eyebrow to form an almost circular shape. Colour the area around the mouth and chin white.

4 Study the picture carefully so that you know where to paint the markings on the face. You might find it easier to outline some of them with a fine brush or make-up (eye-liner) pencil first and then fill them in. Only paint the top lip at this stage.

5 Paint the bottom lip red.

6 Using a thick brush, dust the nose and centre of the forehead with a shade of brown.

Martian

Try decorating an old pair of tights or leggings in a similar style to the T-shirt and give an old pair of shoes a "space lift" with paint and glitter.

YOU WILL NEED
4 paper baubles (balls)
hairband
paints
paintbrush
glue
glitter
glitter glue
sequins
ribbon or elastic
T-shirt
felt
scissors
fabric glue
fabric paints

FOR THE FACE
make-up sponge
water-based face paints
stipple sponge
medium make-up brush
glitter gel
lipstick brush

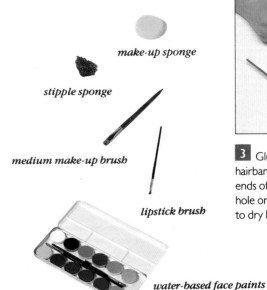

make-up sponge

stipple sponge

medium make-up brush

lipstick brush

water-based face paints

1 To make the costume, paint the baubles (balls) and the hairband and leave them to dry. Using contrasting colours, paint spots on the baubles.

2 Paint areas of the baubles with glue and dip them into the glitter. Use glitter glue to make exciting shapes and patterns and glue on a few sequins. Try to create a different pattern on each bauble.

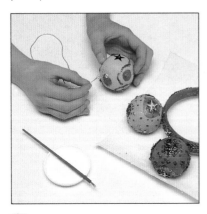

3 Glue three baubles onto the hairband. For the necklace, glue the two ends of the ribbon or elastic into a small hole on the fourth bauble. Allow the glue to dry before trying on the accessories.

4 To decorate the T-shirt, cut out two spiral shapes from coloured felt and using fabric glue, stick them onto the T-shirt. Decorate the spirals with fabric paints and glitter glue.

5 For the face, use a damp sponge to apply the base colour. Using a stipple sponge, dab a slightly darker shade over the base colour to add texture.

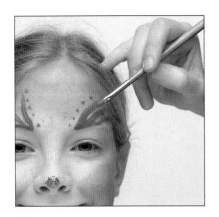

6 Using a medium brush, paint on a pair of wiggly eyebrows as shown. Using glitter gel in a contrasting colour, paint a spot on the tip of the nose.

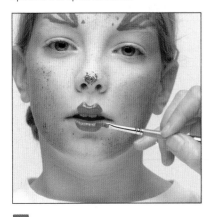

7 Using a lipstick brush, paint a tiny mouth as shown, avoiding the corners of the mouth.

Dressing-up Fun

There are plenty of good ideas here for a fancy dress
party. The only problem is deciding who you want to
be. Once you have chosen a costume or headdress,
why not paint your face to match using the techniques
described in the last chapter?

Materials

These are a selection of useful materials. If you can't find exactly the same ones, see if there is anything else you could substitute.

Baubles (balls)
These can be used to decorate headdresses and other accessories. Only use baubles made from plastic or paper.

Braid
This comes in a range of styles and widths and can be used to decorate clothes and accessories.

Buttons
Interesting buttons can be used as decoration.

Coloured sticky tape
This strong tape can be used for fastening heavy materials. It also can be used for decoration.

Coloured paper
Heavy paper can be used for making hats and headdresses.

Covered elastic cord
This can be purchased from department stores and comes in different colours and strengths. It can be attached to hats to make them easier to wear.

Crepe and tissue paper
These can be used for decoration. They are quite fragile and are best suited to costumes that will only need to be worn once or twice.

Feathers
These can be bought from sewing shops and can be used to decorate hats and accessories.

Felt
This comes in a range of colours. It is easy to cut and won't fray.

Garden canes
These have many uses. Decorate one and turn it into a fairy's wand, or use several as the stems on a fun bunch of paper flowers.

Glitter
This can be glued on as decoration. If there is any left be sure to pour it back into the tube to use again.

Hairbands
These can be decorated to make a headdress or covered in fur to make a pair of ears.

Hessian (burlap)
This heavy cloth is perfect for costumes. When cut, the cloth may be frayed to make a fringe.

Metal kitchen scourers
These are made of soft metal and are used in the kitchen to clean pots and pans but they also make fun decorations.

Milliner's wire
This is covered with thread and is therefore safer to use than ordinary wire. You should still take care with the sharp ends, and cover them with tape.

Netting
This fabric is perfect for making light, airy skirts and wings. It is available in a wide range of colours from fabric shops.

Newspaper
Save old newspaper and use to protect surfaces when you are working or to make papier mâché.

Paintbrushes
Use a range of different sizes to apply paint and glue.

Paints
Use non-toxic paints to add details. If you don't have exactly the colour you want, try mixing paints together to make new ones.

Poppers (snaps)
These are quicker to add to a costume than buttons and buttonholes.

Ribbons
These come in a range of colours and patterns and can be used for making bows as decoration.

Safety pins
These can be taped onto the back of badges or used to help thread elastic through a waistband.

Sewing thread
Some of the costumes require basic sewing techniques. It is a good idea to match your sewing thread to your main material.

String
String can be used as a single fastener on an outfit, or can be used for hanging pendants.

Supermarket packaging
Boxes, egg cartons, and plastic and foil containers can all be used to make and decorate costumes.

Tin foil
This can be cut up or crumpled to create different decorative effects.

Tinsel
Save spare tinsel from the Christmas tree and use it to create sparkly accessories and details.

Wool
This can be used for making wigs and plaits (braids).

feathers

egg carton

bauble (ball)

metal kitchen scourer

netting

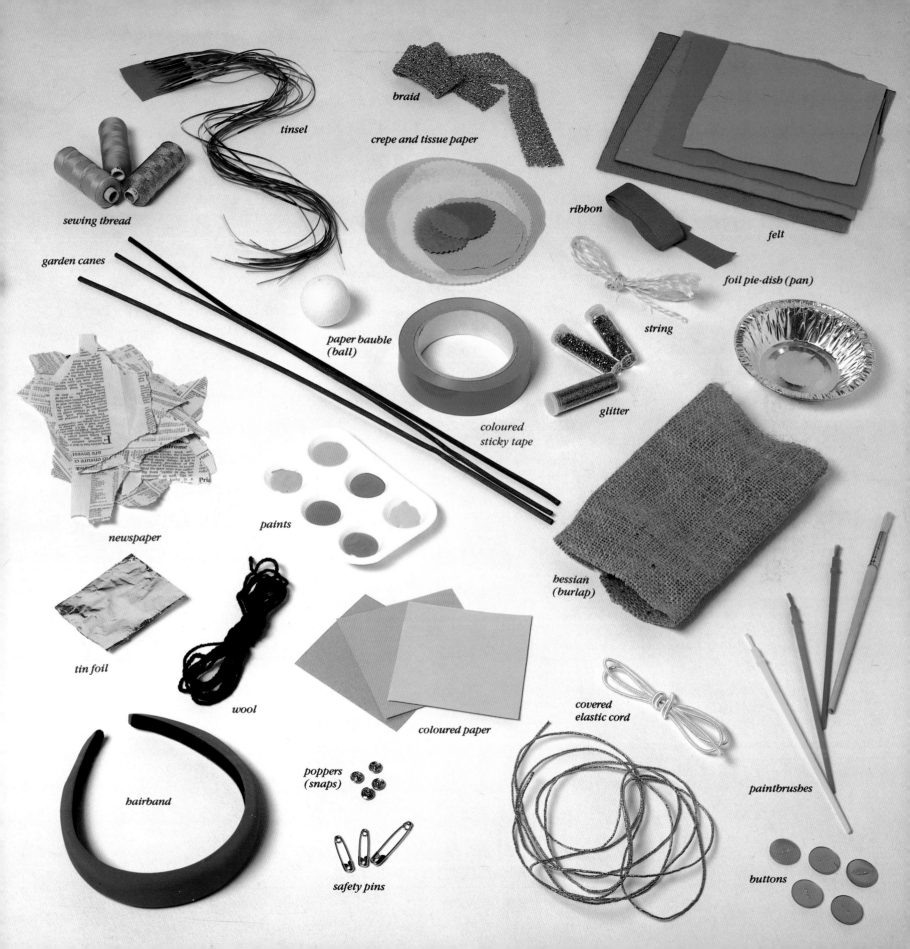

tinsel

braid

crepe and tissue paper

ribbon

felt

sewing thread

garden canes

foil pie-dish (pan)

string

paper bauble
(ball)

glitter

coloured
sticky tape

newspaper

paints

bessian
(burlap)

tin foil

wool

coloured paper

covered
elastic cord

paintbrushes

hairband

poppers
(snaps)

safety pins

buttons

Making a Waistband

Elasticated waistbands make all costumes easy to put on and take off.

YOU WILL NEED
needle and thread or sewing machine
safety pin
elastic

1 Fold over the waist and sew a line of stitches to make a tube. Leave a gap to thread the elastic through.

2 Attach a safety pin to the end of the elastic and thread it through the tube until it comes out the other end.

3 Pull the two ends of elastic to gather the waist to the right size and tie a knot. Sew up the opening in the tube.

Covering a Button

By covering buttons you can choose your own fabric to match the outfit. The clown costume includes lots of colourful buttons.

YOU WILL NEED
fabric
scissors
self-covering button
needle and thread

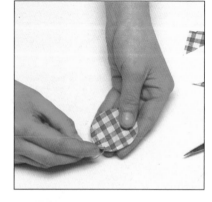

1 Cut out a circle of fabric twice as wide as the button. Sew a line of running stitches around the edge of circle.

2 Open the button and place the front on the circle of fabric. Pull the threads to gather them up around the button.

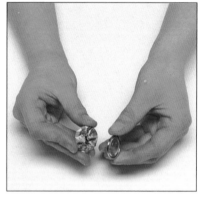

3 Place the back on the button.

Decorative Stitches

These stitches can add a finishing touch to an outfit, whether adding colourful details in thread, or sewing on fabric shapes.

You will need
needle and thread

1 Running stitch is useful for sewing on patches and other shapes. You can make the stitches as long or as short as you like.

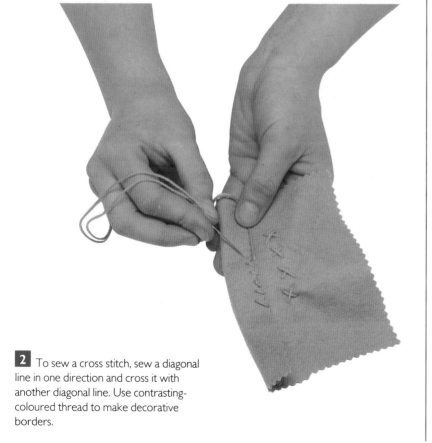

2 To sew a cross stitch, sew a diagonal line in one direction and cross it with another diagonal line. Use contrasting-coloured thread to make decorative borders.

Making your own Pantaloons

Decorate the pantaloons according to the character required. These basic pantaloons can be used for the genie costume.

You will need
2 metres/2 yards fabric
pattern, enlarged from the template section
scissors
needle and thread or sewing machine
safety pin
elastic

1 Fold the fabric in half, with the right sides facing, and place the pattern on the fold of the fabric. Cut out two identical pieces. Keep each piece of the pantaloon folded in half with the right sides facing and sew along the inside leg with a 5 mm/¼ in seam allowance.

2 Turn one leg piece right side out and place it inside the other leg, matching up the raw edges. Stitch the two pieces together. Turn the legs right side out. Fold over the waist of the pantaloons and sew a double line of stitching to make a tube for the elastic to go through. Leave a gap to thread the elastic through. Do the same around the bottom of each pantaloon leg.

3 Attach the safety pin to one end of the elastic and tie a knot at the end. Thread the elastic through the tube. Do the same with each pantaloon leg. Sew up the gaps in the tubes.

Ballerina

Show off your ballet steps in this pretty tutu. Make it the same colour as your ballet leotard.

YOU WILL NEED
2 metres/2 yards coloured netting
needle, thread and pins
tape measure
wide ribbon for the waistband
narrow ribbon for the bows
scissors
matching leotard and tights

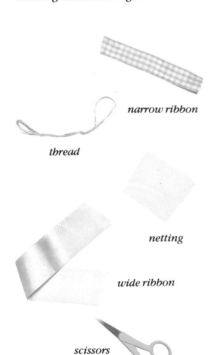

narrow ribbon

thread

netting

wide ribbon

scissors

1 Fold the netting over lengthwise and sew a line of running stitch along the folded edge. Measure your ballerina's waist. For a short tutu, fold over again, and secure with running stitches. Pull the thread gently to gather the netting to fit the waist and tie a knot or sew a few stitches to secure the gathers.

2 Pin the wide ribbon onto the gathered netting and then sew it on.

3 Using the narrower ribbon, tie approximately six small bows. Sew five bows onto the waistband.

4 To finish the costume, sew the last bow onto the leotard.

Fairy

Dress up in this sparkling outfit and make a special wish. For a magical effect, wear a white leotard and pin some tinsel in your hair.

YOU WILL NEED
2 metres/2 yards netting
needle and thread
scissors
tinsel
1.5 metres/1½ yards white fabric
milliner's wire
silver elastic cord
garden cane
silver paint
paintbrush
silver paper or cardboard
adhesive tape
glue
white leotard and tights

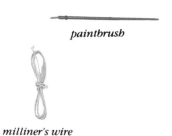

paintbrush

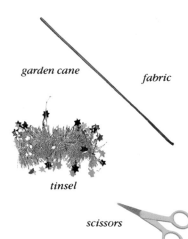

milliner's wire

garden cane

fabric

tinsel

scissors

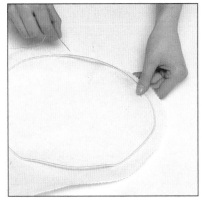

1 To make the tutu, follow the instructions for the ballerina tutu, folding the netting lengthwise once only for a longer skirt. Instead of decorating the waistband with ribbon, sew on a piece of tinsel. Cut out two pieces of white fabric for the wings, in a figure-of-eight shape. On the wrong side of one of the pieces of fabric, sew a separate length of wire around each wing.

2 Place the other piece of fabric on top of the first, making sure the wrong sides are facing. Sew around the edge to secure the two pieces together.

3 Sew a loop of elastic cord onto each wing, near the centre. These will slip over the arms to support the wings on the body.

4 To make the wand, first paint a garden cane silver and leave it to dry. Cut out two silver stars and fasten the silver stick onto the reverse side of one of the stars with a piece of adhesive tape. Glue the stars together.

Scarecrow

If you don't have any suitable old clothes of your own, visit a second-hand clothes shop or rummage through piles of clothes at a local flea market. The older the clothes are the better the costume will be.

YOU WILL NEED
raffia
old felt hat
scissors
plastic toy mouse
glue
needle and thread
old clothes, such as a jacket and
    trousers (pants)
scraps of fabric
orange cardboard
orange paint
paintbrush
elastic cord

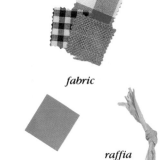

fabric

cardboard

raffia

scissors

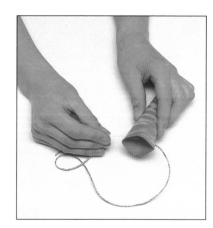

paint

1 Tie a few strands of raffia around the hat. Cut a fringe into the rim of the hat with a pair of scissors. Glue a plastic mouse on the top of the hat.

2 Tie bundles of raffia in a knot and sew the bundles around the inside rim of the hat, leaving a gap at the front.

3 Cut ragged edges on the jacket and the trousers (pants).

4 Cut scraps of fabric into squares and rectangles and sew them onto the jacket and the trousers.

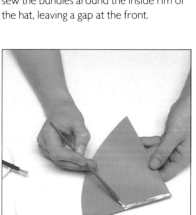

5 To make the nose, cut a piece of orange cardboard into a cone shape. Roll the cardboard into a cone and glue it together.

6 Paint orange lines around the cone and leave them to dry. Make a small hole on either side of the cone and thread a piece of elastic cord through that will fit around your head. Tie a knot at each end of the elastic.

Gypsy

Wear your brightest clothes to go with the accessories and make up your own gypsy dance.

YOU WILL NEED
cardboard
scissors
newspaper
PVA (white) glue
bowl
water
paints
paintbrush
glitter
sequins
fabric for the head scarf and shawl
needle and thread or sewing machine
braid
pom-poms

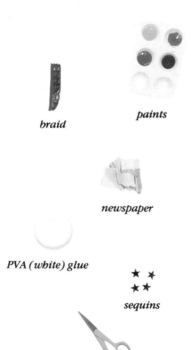

braid

paints

newspaper

PVA (white) glue

sequins

scissors

1 Cut a strip of cardboard to fit comfortably around your wrist and approximately 5 cm/2 in wide. Bend the cardboard to make a bracelet and glue it in place.

2 Scrunch up small balls of newspaper and glue them onto the bracelet. Cover the bangle in three layers of papier mâché as described in the introduction, and leave it to dry thoroughly in a warm place.

3 Paint the bangle using lots of colours and leave the paint to dry.

4 Paint dabs of glue on the bangle and sprinkle on the glitter. Glue a few sequins on for extra sparkle and decoration. Leave the glue to dry before trying on the bracelet.

5 For the head scarf, sew two triangular pieces of fabric together with the right sides facing. Leave a gap and turn right side out. Sew up the gap.

6 Sew a strip of braid along the longest side of the scarf. Make a larger, but similar, scarf to go around the neck and sew pom-poms along the sides.

Cowboy

Find a hat and a toy gun to complete this costume.
Round up your friends and have fun.

YOU WILL NEED
tape measure
felt for the waistcoat (vest)
scissors
needle and thread or sewing machine
templates for pocket
pins
fabric glue
template for sheriff badge
pencil
cardboard
tin foil or silver paint
paintbrush
safety pin
strong adhesive tape

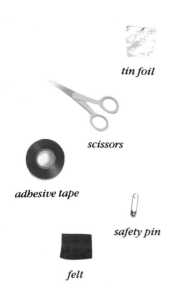

tin foil

scissors

adhesive tape

safety pin

felt

1 For the waistcoat (vest), measure from the nape of your neck to the length required, and cut two squares of felt to this size. Cut one piece in half lengthways for the two front pieces. With the right sides facing, sew the two front pieces to the back along the shoulders. Sew the sides together leaving gaps for the arms.

2 Turn the waistcoat right side out. Use the template to cut out two pockets from felt. Pin them in position on the front. Use the template to cut out two pieces of fabric in a contrasting colour to decorate the top of each pocket and glue them on with fabric glue. Sew the pockets onto the waistcoat using brightly coloured thread.

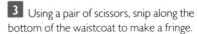

3 Using a pair of scissors, snip along the bottom of the waistcoat to make a fringe.

4 To make the badge, draw around the template and cut out a piece of cardboard. Cover it in tin foil or paint it silver. Decorate the badge with a silver 'S' in the centre and silver spots on the tip of each point. Fasten a safety pin onto the reverse of the badge with a piece of tape.

Knight

Have a pretend battle with your friends in this shiny suit of armour.

YOU WILL NEED
cardboard
scissors
tin foil
black felt
glue
coloured foil paper
template for helmet
pencil
silver paint
paintbrush
template for body shield
hole puncher
ribbon

paint

glue

scissors

coloured foil paper

tin foil

1 Cut a piece of cardboard in the shape of a sword. Cover the blade in silver foil. Cut two pieces of felt to fit the handle of the sword and glue them on. Decorate the handle with diamond shapes cut out of foil paper.

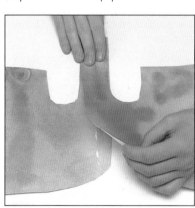

2 To make the helmet, use the template to draw and cut two equal pieces of cardboard. Paint these silver and leave to dry. Glue the two pieces together as shown in the picture.

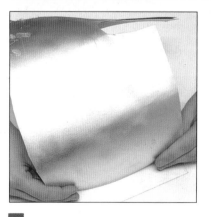

3 When the glue has dried, fold the helmet so that it curves and glue the sides together. Hold the helmet together while the glue dries. To make the body shield you will need to draw round the shape, then flip it to complete the other half. Do this for the front and back pieces and cut them out.

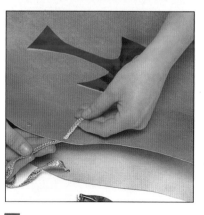

4 Paint the two pieces silver. When the paint has dried, glue the two pieces together at the shoulder seam. Cut a foil paper cross and glue it onto the front of the shield. Punch a hole on either side of the body shield and thread a piece of ribbon through. Tie a knot to secure.

Robot

The fun part of this project is collecting all the bits and pieces to recycle. Ask your friends and family to help you collect interesting boxes, cartons and packages.

YOU WILL NEED
2 cardboard boxes
pencil
scissors
silver spray paint
cartons and containers made of
    cardboard and clear plastic
glue
3 Christmas baubles (balls)
foil pie-dishes (pans)
masking tape
pair of old shoes
2 metal kitchen scourers
tin foil

foil pie-dish
(pan)

Christmas
bauble (ball)

metal kitchen
scourer

egg carton

glue

silver spray

scissors

1 To make the helmet you will need a cardboard box that fits comfortably over your head. Draw a square on one side of the box and cut it out.

2 Ask an adult to help spray the box silver. You should do this outdoors or in a very airy room where the surfaces are well covered and protected. When the paint has dried, glue a clear plastic carton over the square hole. Punch a few holes in the carton to let air through.

3 Decorate the box by gluing on Christmas baubles (balls) and foil pie-dishes (pans).

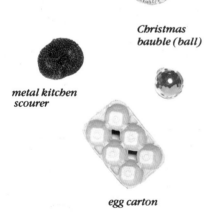

4 For the body of the robot, you will need a large cardboard box. Draw and cut out a hole on the top of the box for your head and one on either side for your arms. Secure the edges of the holes with masking tape.

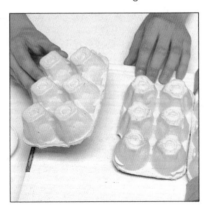

5 Decorate the robot body by gluing on all the boxes and containers you have been collecting. When the glue has dried, spray the box silver, following the same instructions as in step 2. Leave the paint to dry thoroughly before you try on the costume.

6 Spray a pair of old shoes silver and decorate them with a metal kitchen scourer or anything shiny. Finally, when you are dressed in your costume, ask a friend to wrap your arms and legs in tin foil to finish.

Wizard

Wave the magic wand and conjure up some secret spells. Look in flea markets for a piece of material to make the cape.

YOU WILL NEED
tape measure
fabric for hat
fabric interfacing (optional)
scissors
needle and thread
silver fabric
fabric glue
templates for wizard's pendant
pencil
cardboard
tin foil
silver ribbon
double-sided adhesive tape
garden cane
paint
paintbrush
tinsel

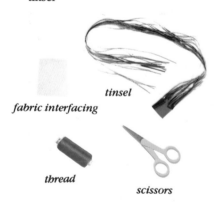

tinsel

fabric interfacing

thread

scissors

1 Measure the width of your head with a tape measure so that you know how wide to make the rim of the hat. If the fabric you are using needs to be stiffened, iron a piece of interfacing onto the reverse side. Ask an adult to help you. Draw and cut out a triangle with a curved base, making sure the rim measures the width of your head with a small allowance for sewing together. Hem the bottom and, with right sides facing, fold the triangle in half to make a tall cone. Sew along the side. Turn the hat the right side out and decorate with silver fabric stars, stuck on with fabric glue.

2 To make the pendant, use the template to cut out a cardboard star. Cut two circles of cardboard of the same size to make the backing. Cover both circles and the star with tin foil. Attach the ribbon to the back of the card circles with a piece of adhesive tape.

3 Roll up strips of foil and place them on the reverse of one of the foil circles. Glue the other circle on top to trap the foil strips and secure them in place.

4 To make the wand, first paint a garden cane and leave it to dry. Stick a piece of shiny tinsel around one end of the stick with adhesive tape.

Native American

You can buy the feathers for this costume from most good fabric shops. You can make the skirt from felt with an elastic waistband.

YOU WILL NEED
tape measure
wide ribbon
scissors
feathers
felt
fabric glue
needle and embroidery threads
wool
narrow ribbon

FOR THE FACE
water-based face paints
medium make-up brush

feather

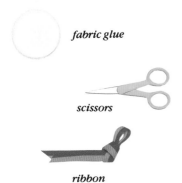

thread

felt

fabric glue

scissors

ribbon

1 Measure around your head with a tape measure, allowing a 5 cm/2 in overlap and cut the wide ribbon to this length. Arrange the feathers in the centre of the ribbon on the reverse side. Cut a strip of felt the same width as the ribbon and glue it onto the feathers. This will help to secure them in place.

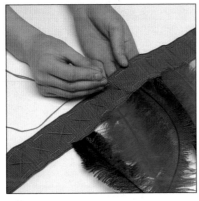

2 Sew a few lines of decorative stitching along the ribbon, using colourful embroidery threads. With the right sides facing, sew the two ends of the ribbon together.

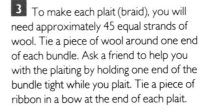

3 To make each plait (braid), you will need approximately 45 equal strands of wool. Tie a piece of wool around one end of each bundle. Ask a friend to help you with the plaiting by holding one end of the bundle tight while you plait. Tie a piece of ribbon in a bow at the end of each plait.

4 Sew or glue the plaits onto the inside of the headdress, so that they lie either side of your face. For the face, use bright colours to paint three zig-zag lines on each cheek.

Prince

To make a sword, follow the instructions given for the knight's costume. The cloak was made from a piece of fabric found at a flea market and was decorated with a piece of tinsel to match the crown.

YOU WILL NEED
tape measure
pencil
scissors
cardboard
silver paint
paintbrush
coloured foil paper
glue
glitter
tinsel
fabric for cloak
safety pins

coloured foil paper

scissors

glitter

glue

tinsel

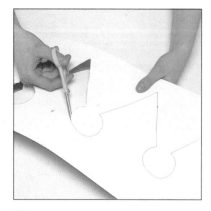

1 Measure around your head with a tape measure so that you know approximately how big to make the crown. Draw and cut out the crown from a piece of cardboard.

2 Paint the cardboard silver and leave the paint to dry thoroughly. Cut shapes out of coloured foil paper and glue them onto the crown. Paint dots of glue onto the shapes and sprinkle on some glitter.

3 Glue a piece of tinsel around the rim of the crown and leave the glue to dry.

4 Glue the two ends of the crown together to fit on your head and leave the glue to dry before you try the crown on. Pin the fabric to your shoulders to make a cloak.

Princess

If you have always dreamed of being a beautiful young princess, and imagined living in a castle, dress up in this costume and maybe your dream will come true.

YOU WILL NEED
tape measure
fabric for hat
fabric interfacing (optional)
pencil
scissors
needle and thread
chiffon fabric
wool
narrow ribbon
braid

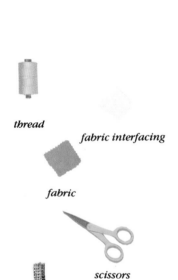

thread

fabric interfacing

fabric

scissors

braid

1 Measure the width of your head with a tape measure, so that you know how wide to make the rim of the hat. If the fabric you are using needs to be stiffened, iron a piece of interfacing onto the reverse side. Draw and cut out a triangle with a curved base, making sure the rim measures the width of your head, with an allowance for sewing together. Sew a hem around the rim of the triangle and, with the right sides facing, fold the triangle in half, trapping a piece of chiffon fabric at the point of the cone.

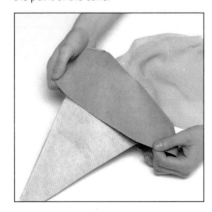

2 Sew the cone together and turn it right side out.

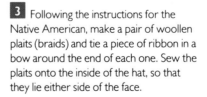

3 Following the instructions for the Native American, make a pair of woollen plaits (braids) and tie a piece of ribbon in a bow around the end of each one. Sew the plaits onto the inside of the hat, so that they lie either side of the face.

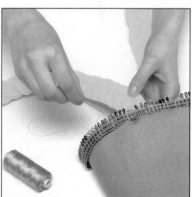

4 Sew a piece of braid around the rim of the hat, and arrange the chiffon fabric so that it trails down the side like a veil.

Hippy

Be loving and laid-back in this colourful flower-power
costume. Search local flea markets and second-hand
shops for bright clothes to wear with the accessories.
Go completely wild and paint a flower on your cheek.

YOU WILL NEED
template for flower pendant
pencil
scissors
cardboard
newspaper
PVA (white) glue
bowl
water
paints
paintbrush
hole puncher
ribbon
fabric or old scarf
scraps of coloured felt
needle and thread
buttons
tissue and crepe paper
garden canes

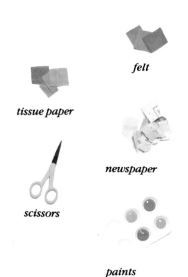

felt

tissue paper

newspaper

scissors

paints

 buttons

1 Use the template to draw around
and cut a piece of cardboard in the shape
of a flower. Scrunch up small balls of
newspaper and glue them in the centre of
the flower.

2 Cover the flower in three layers of
papier mâché as described in the
introduction and leave to dry thoroughly
in a warm place.

3 Paint the flower in lots of bright
colours and leave to dry. Using a hole
puncher, punch a hole in one of the petals
and thread a piece of ribbon through.

4 For the headband you will need a
band of bright fabric or an old scarf. Cut
out different shaped flowers from
coloured felt. Sew the flowers onto the
headband and sew a button onto the
centre of each flower.

5 To make a colourful bouquet of
flowers, first cut out lots of shapes in
tissue and crepe paper. Starting with the
largest petal at the bottom, layer the
petals on top of each other, piercing a
hole through them with the garden cane.

6 Roll a piece of tissue paper with glue
and place it in the centre of the flower on
the stick. Fan out the petals to finish off.

Genie

You can make your own baggy pantaloons by
following the instructions provided.

YOU WILL NEED
pair of shoes
glitter paint
paintbrush
glue
glittery braid
scraps of fabric
baggy trousers (pants) or pantaloons
scissors
fabric glue
fabric for the cummerbund
tape measure
needle and thread or sewing machine
fabric for the turban
feathers

FOR THE FACE
make-up sponge
water-based face paints
medium make-up brush

thread   *feather*

fabric

fabric glue

glittery braid

paintbrush

scissors

1 To make the costume, paint a pair of shoes a sparkling colour and leave to dry. Stick a piece of glittery braid around the side of each shoe.

2 Making use of scraps of fabric, cut out lots of stars and glue them onto a pair of baggy trousers (pants) or pantaloons using fabric glue.

3 Measure your waist for the cummerbund, allowing an extra 25 cm/10 in so you can tie the fabric at the back. Sew two pieces of fabric together to the required length with the right sides facing, leaving an opening at one end, and turn it right side out. Sew up the end.

4 Cut out some more stars from scraps of fabric and glue them onto the cummerbund with fabric glue.

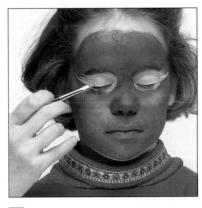

5 For the face, use a damp sponge to apply the base colour, avoiding the area around the eyes. Paint the area around the eyes a bright colour.

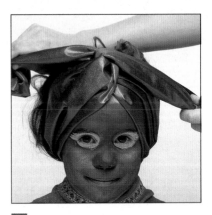

6 Tie the turban around the head, tying a knot on the top of the head. Tuck the loose fabric underneath the turban. Place a few colourful feathers on the top of the turban to decorate.

Butterfly

When you wear this pretty outfit, gently move your arms to make the wings flap.

YOU WILL NEED
2.5 m (2½ yd) milliner's wire
scissors
sticky tape
coloured netting
needle and embroidery thread
smaller pieces of different coloured
  netting
silver or gold elastic cord
hairband
2 paper baubles (balls)
paints
paintbrush
glue
glitter
felt

glue

hairband

paper bauble (ball)

glitter   *netting*

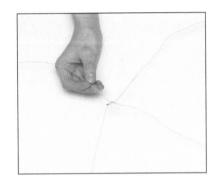

I Cut a piece of milliner's wire approximately 2 m/2 yd long. Bend the two ends together to make a big circle. For extra safety, secure the ends with a piece of sticky tape. Pinch the two sides of the wire circle together and twist. The wire should now resemble a figure-of-eight.

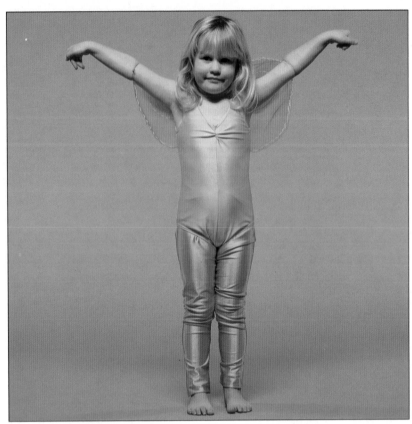

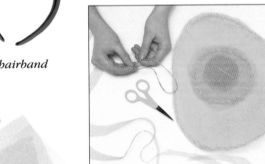

2 Place the wire frame between two pieces of coloured netting. Sew the netting onto the wire frame using a brightly coloured embroidery thread. Trim away any excess net. Cut out circles of different coloured netting and sew them onto each wing. To support the wings, thread a loop of elastic cord onto the outside of each wing for the arms to slip through.

3 Paint the hairband and each paper bauble (ball) a bright colour and leave them to dry thoroughly. Cut a short piece of wire and stick it into each bauble (ball). This will make covering it in glitter much easier. Paint the bauble (ball) with a coat of glue and dip it into the glitter. Leave the glue to dry.

4 Cut another length of wire for the antennae, measuring 45 cm/18 in. Bend the wire to fit the hairband, making sure each end of wire is the same length. Fasten the wire to the hairband with glue and glue on a piece of felt for support. Decorate the hairband with glitter. Secure the baubles (balls) onto the ends of the wire. Complete the costume by wearing a leotard and pair of tights.

Tattoo

Wow your friends with this fake tattoo! A butterfly is shown below but you can make any design you like.

YOU WILL NEED
coloured face paints

face paints

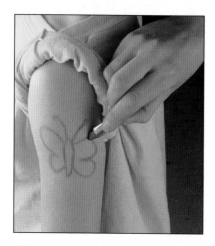

1 Paint the outline of a butterfly or your chosen design onto your arm.

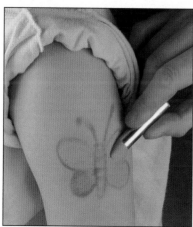

2 Carefully begin to colour it in.

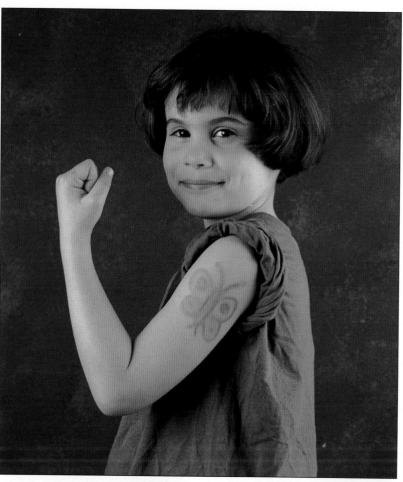

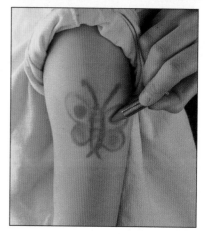

3 Try to make your design as beautiful as possible by drawing tiny patterns and other details.

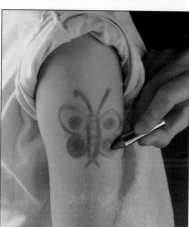

4 Complete your design. Face paints can smudge very easily, so look after your tattoo and don't let it rub against anything.

Ghost

Spook your friends in this fabulous disguise. See how long it takes before they guess who you are.

YOU WILL NEED
old white sheet
scissors
needle and thread or sewing machine
milliner's wire
black felt
fabric glue

white thread

felt

sheet

milliner's wire

fabric glue

scissors

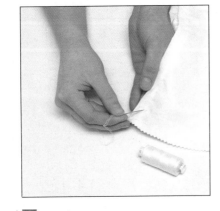

1 Cut two pieces of sheet in the shape of a dome, making sure the height of the dome is longer than your own height. Sew the two pieces together leaving an opening at the bottom. Sew another line of stitching parallel to the line you have sewn. This is to make a tube for the wire.

2 Thread the wire through the tube. Secure each end of the wire to the sheet with a few stitches.

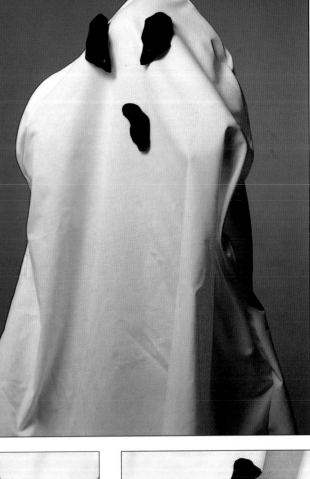

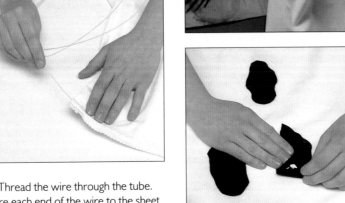

3 Cut out a mouth and pair of eyes from a piece of felt and glue them onto the sheet using fabric glue.

4 Cut small holes in the eyes and the mouth, so that you can see where you are going. Try the costume on and bend the wire to fit your body.

Egyptian Mummy

Make sure you wear a white T-shirt and a pair of white tights or leggings underneath the costume, just in case it starts to unravel!

YOU WILL NEED
old white sheet
scissors
needle and thread
white T-shirt and leggings or tights

FOR THE FACE
make-up sponge
water-based face paints

sheet

white thread

scissors

water-based face paints

make-up sponge

1 To make the costume, tear or cut strips of the sheet approximately 10 cm/4 in wide and as long as possible.

2 Sew the strips of fabric together to form one long strip.

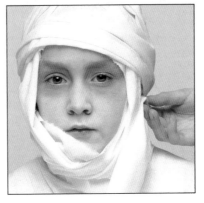

3 For the face, use a damp sponge to apply a white base. Rinse the sponge, then dab light purple around the eye sockets to give a ghoulish appearance. Then wrap the fabric round the head first, leaving the face open. Gradually wrap the fabric down the body.

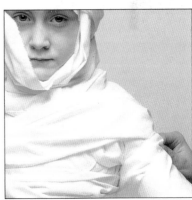

4 When you get to the hands, go back up the arm again, still wrapping the fabric around. Do the same with the legs. When you have wrapped the whole body, sew the end of the strip to part of the costume. To take the costume off, simply unravel the strip of fabric.

Astronaut

This space traveller looks all set for a journey to the stars and planets. Collect recycled containers to decorate the costume.

YOU WILL NEED
large balloon
newspaper
diluted PVA (white) glue
mixing bowl
pin
pencil
scissors
silver paint
paintbrush
foil pie dishes (pans)
tin foil
sticky tape
piece of foam rubber
plain T-shirt
cardboard containers, such as fruit
  cartons
old pair of gloves (optional)

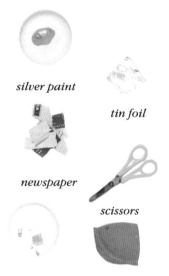

silver paint

tin foil

newspaper

scissors

PVA (white) glue

cardboard container

1 To make the helmet, blow up a large balloon and cover it with approximately 10 layers of papier-mâché. Leave to dry.

2 When the papier-mâché has dried, pop the balloon with a pin. Draw and cut out an opening for the face and remove the balloon.

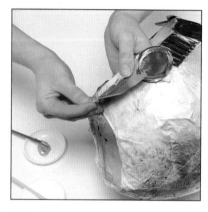

3 Paint the helmet silver and decorate with shapes cut from pie dishes (pans).

4 Make a microphone from a piece of rolled tin foil and tape it to the inside of the helmet. To make the helmet more comfortable to wear, glue a piece of foam rubber to the inside.

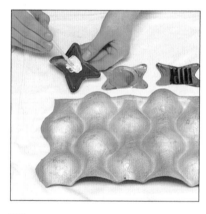

5 Decorate a plain T-shirt by gluing on containers and foil pie dishes (pans).

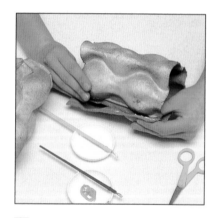

6 Make the arm and leg shields from cardboard containers. Fruit cartons have been used here. Paint the cartons silver and bend them to make a tube. Glue the edges together. If you have an old pair of gloves, paint them silver.

Sunflower

Dazzle your friends with this bright cheerful headdress. Wear yellow and green clothes to complete the costume.

YOU WILL NEED
pair of compasses
cardboard
scissors
ribbon
sticky tape
pencil
yellow paper
glue
black paint
paintbrush

FOR THE FACE
make-up sponge
water-based face paints
medium make-up brush

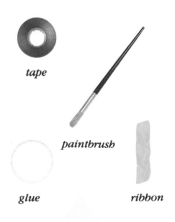

tape

paintbrush

glue   *ribbon*

paper

cardboard

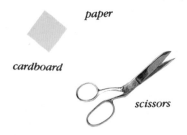

scissors

1 To make the costume, use a pair of compasses to draw and cut out a circle from a piece of cardboard. Draw and cut out a circle in the middle big enough for your face to show through.

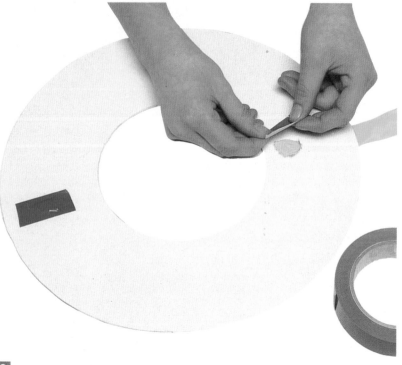

2 Make a slit either side of the circle and thread a piece of ribbon through. Secure the ribbon with a knot and a piece of sticky tape.

3 Draw a petal shape onto yellow paper, and use it as a template for the others. You will need about 42 petals for a full sunflower. Cut out the petals.

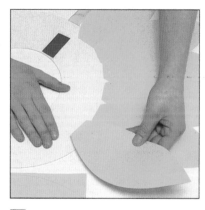

4 Starting at the edge of the cardboard circle, glue on the petals so that they overlap each other. When you have covered the outer edge start on the second row and finish off in the centre of the circle.

5 Paint black marks around the centre of the sunflower and leave the paint to dry. When you are ready to wear the flower, tie the ribbon around your head in a bow.

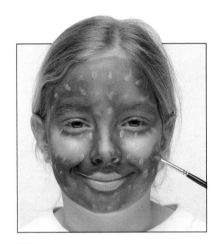

6 For the face, use a damp sponge to apply a brown base colour. Use a medium brush to paint yellow spots on the base colour. Paint the lips the same colour.

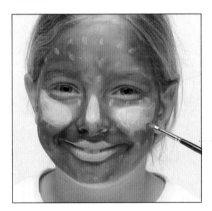

7 Paint yellow highlights under each eye and on the nose.

Pumpkin

You will certainly win the biggest pumpkin competition if you wear this outfit.

YOU WILL NEED
hairband
green paint
paintbrush
scissors
green fabric
needle and matching thread or
  sewing machine
stuffing (batting)
3 m (3 yd) orange fabric
fabric tape
milliner's wire
safety pin
elastic

hairband

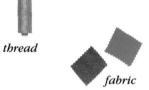

thread

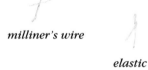

fabric

milliner's wire

elastic

scissors

1 To make the pumpkin stalk, first paint the hairband green and leave it to dry. Cut out two pieces of green fabric and sew them together with the right sides facing. Leave a gap and turn right sides out. Fill the stalk with stuffing (batting) and sew up the end. Sew the stalk onto the centre of the hairband.

2 To make the pumpkin body, first fold over the two long sides of the orange fabric and sew a line of stitches on each long side to make a 1.5 cm (⅝ in) tube for the elastic.

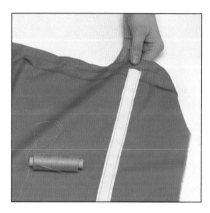

3 Sew lengths of fabric tape widthwise on the reverse side of the fabric. You will need to sew on approximately five lengths of tape, positioned equal distances apart.

4 Thread a length of milliner's wire through each fabric tape tube. Bend the ends over and sew them onto the tape.

5 With the right sides facing fold the fabric in half widthwise, and turn so that the tubes for the elastic are at the top and bottom. Sew the shorter sides together.

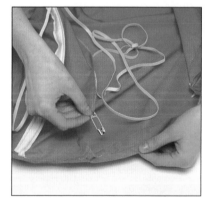

6 Attach a safety pin to the elastic and thread through the top and bottom tubes. Pull the end of the elastic to gather the fabric and tie a double knot. Before you try on the pumpkin costume, bend the wires so that they are curved, to make a full, round shape.

Skeleton

This is the perfect outfit for spooking your friends and family on Hallowe'en.

YOU WILL NEED
black leotard
white fabric paints
paintbrush
black leggings

FOR THE FACE
black make-up (eye-liner) pencil
water-based face paints
medium make-up brush

water-based face paints

medium make-up brush

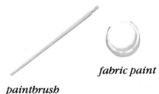

fabric paint

paintbrush

1 To make the costume, use white fabric paint to draw on the outline of the skeleton's body, making sure that the leotard is lying flat.

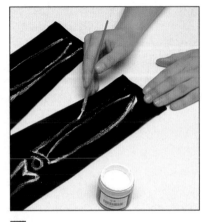

2 Paint the outline of the skeleton's legs on the front of the leggings.

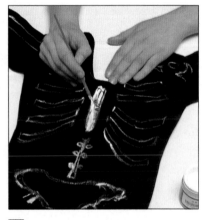

3 Fill in the outlined areas with white on both the leotard and leggings.

4 Using a black make-up (eye-liner) pencil, draw a circular outline around each eye, a small triangle above each nostril, and a large mouth shape around the model's own mouth. Draw an outline around the edge of the face.

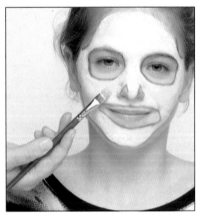

5 Using a medium brush, paint the face white, avoiding the shapes you have just drawn in pencil.

6 Paint the eyes, the triangles above the nostrils and the sides of the face black. Paint a thick black outline around the mouth and fill the mouth area in white. Divide the mouth into a set of ghostly teeth with black lines.

Carrot

For the complete outfit, dress up in an orange T-shirt and leggings and, if you have an old pair of shoes, paint them orange.

YOU WILL NEED
pencil
cardboard, in 2 shades of green
scissors
glue

FOR THE FACE
make-up sponge
water-based face paints

cardboard

glue

scissors

1 Draw lots of differently shaped leaves on green cardboard and cut them out.

2 Cut two strips of green cardboard 5 cm/2 in wide and long enough to fit around your head. Glue the leaves along one of the strips.

3 Glue the other strip on top of the first, sandwiching the base of the leaves between the two. Leave the glue to dry.

4 Curve the card to fit around your head and glue the two ends of the strip together. Leave the glue to dry before trying the headdress on.

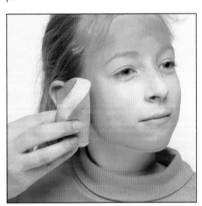

5 For the face, use a make-up sponge to apply an orange base all over.

Super Hero

Be a hero for a day and make your very own costume.

YOU WILL NEED
cardboard
scissors
tin foil
coloured foil papers
glue
silver cardboard
ribbon
sticky tape

FOR THE CAPE
leotard or catsuit
2 m (2 yd) fabric
needle and matching thread

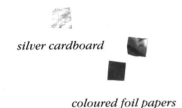

silver cardboard

coloured foil papers

scissors

glue

1 To make a wristband, first cut out a cardboard triangle and cover it in tin foil. Cut a smaller triangle in coloured foil paper and glue it onto the silver triangle. Cut out the letter 'S' in silver cardboard and glue it onto the coloured traingle. Cut a strip of silver cardboard 5 cm/2 in wide and long enough to fit around your wrist. Glue the two ends together to make a band and glue on the triangle. Make another wristband the same way.

2 To make the waistband, cut a piece of cardboard to fit around your waist. Cut a circle from cardboard and cover it in tin foil. Cut a star from coloured foil paper and glue it onto the silver circle. Cut out the letter 'S' in cardboard and glue it onto the star. Glue the circle onto the waistband.

3 At each end of the waistband, attach a piece of ribbon with sticky tape. To make the headband, cut a strip of silver cardboard to fit around your head. Glue it and leave to dry. You can decorate this in a similar way to the wristbands or cape.

4 Cut a circle in coloured foil paper. Cut a smaller circle in a different colour and glue it to the centre of the large circle. Cut out a silver letter 'S' and glue it on the circles. Cut a smaller 'S' in coloured foil paper and glue it onto the silver 'S'. Make a cape as opposite.

Super Heroine

Impress your friends and family with your heroic powers and dress up in this futuristic costume.

YOU WILL NEED
cardboard
scissors
tin foil
coloured foil papers
glue
silver cardboard
ribbon
sticky tape
coloured cardboard (optional)

FOR THE CAPE
leotard or catsuit
2 m (2 yd) fabric
needle and matching thread

scissors

coloured foil papers

glue

1 Make the wristbands, waistband and headband as for the Super Hero's outfit, varying the decorations, if you like.

2 To make the pendant, cut out a star in silver cardboard and glue the letter 'S' onto it. On the back of the star, attach a piece of ribbon in a loop with strong sticky tape.

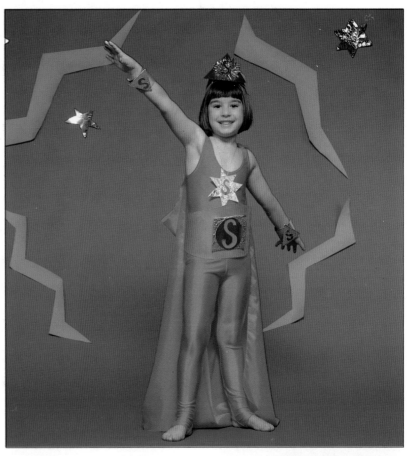

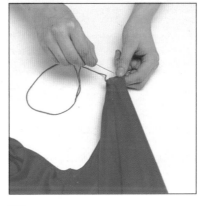

3 To make the cloak you will need a leotard or catsuit. Sew one end of the fabric onto the shoulder straps.

4 Where the fabric joins the straps, glue on silver cardboard triangles.

Regal Crown

Crown yourself King or Queen of the castle!

YOU WILL NEED
tape measure
card (cardboard)
pencil
ruler
scissors
shiny coloured paper
ribbon
glue
paintbrush
silver and gold paper
glitter

ruler

pencil

glitter

glue

silver paper

card (cardboard)

paintbrush

ribbon

scissors

shiny paper

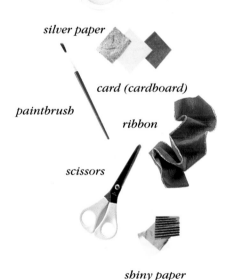

1 Measure around your head with a tape measure so that you know how long to cut the card (cardboard) band. Remember to allow a few centimetres (inches) for gluing the band together. Cut a strip of card 8 cm/3 in deep with a pair of scissors. Cover the card in shiny paper and stick on a piece of ribbon with glue.

2 Cut out two strips of card (cardboard) measuring 4 × 30 cm (1½ × 12 in). Cover them in silver paper.

3 Make six jewel circles from shiny paper and glitter and glue them onto the ribbon.

4 Attach the silver strips to the inside of the crown band using glue and leave to dry.

5 Trace out five more jewel shapes from card (cardboard) and cut them out. Cover each one in gold paper and decorate with circles of shiny paper and glitter.

6 When the jewels are dry, glue them onto the silver bands.

Fun with Food

The best thing about cooking is that you can eat
the finished product! It is also a great way to entertain
and impress your friends. All your favourite dishes are
here in this chapter, plus some original and witty new
ways with food.

Equipment

There are probably lots of weird and wonderful things in the kitchen cupboards and drawers. Here's a guide to help you find out what they do.

colander

nutmeg grater

baking sheet

Blenders

Also called liquidizers, these are usually attached to an electric whisk motor or a food processor and are tall and deep, with blades at the base. Ideal for turning things into liquid such as fruit for sauces and milk shakes. Hand-held blenders can be used in a small bowl or mug.

Bowls

Mixing bowls come in all sorts of sizes and the most useful are made from heatproof glass. Use large ones for pastry and whisking egg whites; smaller ones are better for smaller quantities, such as mixing dips.

Chopping boards

Lots of people use the same board for all their preparation, but it's much more hygienic to use a different one for each type of job. It is possible to buy boards with coloured handles, so the same one is always used for the same job. A wooden board is best for cutting bread. Scrub boards well after use.

Electric whisk

A whisk's main function is to beat in air and make the mixture bigger and thicker, as in, for example, cream and cake mixtures. But a whisk can also blend things together and make them smooth, such as sauces.

Food processor

This is actually a giant blender, with a large bowl and, usually, lots of attachments. The metal chopping blade is the one we use most, it's best with dry ingredients like vegetables and pastry. The plastic blade is for batters and cakes. Some processors also have grating blades and slicing plates.

Graters

A pyramid-shaped or box-shaped grater is the most useful type. Each side has a different grating surface, made up of small, curved, raised blades. Use the coarsest one for vegetables and cheese and the finer sides for grating orange and lemon rind. Stand the grater on a flat surface while you use it and grated food collects inside the pyramid. Scrub well with a brush after use. There are also very small graters, for whole nutmegs.

Measuring equipment

Most homes have some sort of measuring equipment, whether this is scales, spoons or cups.

Recipes seem to have lots of weights listed; this is because different countries use different ways to measure things. As long as you stick to the same ones for each recipe, you shouldn't have any problems.

The metric quantity is mentioned first, such as 115 g, followed by the imperial measurement – 4 oz – and these are ways to measure dry ingredients, such as flour, vegetables and chocolate.

When you measure liquids, there are three measurements to choose from. The metric measurement, such as 300 ml, followed by ½ pint – the imperial one; and, finally, 1¼ cups, which is the American measure. Most measuring jugs have all these measurements written on the side for easy measuring.

Small amounts of both dry and wet ingredients are often measured in millilitres (ml) and tablespoons (tbsp). 15 ml is the same as 1 tbsp and 5 ml is the same as 1 teaspoon (1 tsp). The spoon should be level.

Pans

Saucepans and frying pans can be made from different metals; some are even glass! The most popular are aluminium pans and stainless steel ones. Pans need to have a thick base to stop food from sticking.

Safety first for whisks, blenders and processors

Never put your hand in the processor to move something while it is plugged in. And keep your fingers away from whisks while they are whizzing round. Treat all electrical equipment very carefully and unplug everything before you fiddle around with blades.

bun tin (pan)

saucepans

saucepan

springform
cake tins
(pans)

frying pan

wire cooling
rack

grater

muffin
tin (pan)

measuring cups

weighing scales

whisks

food processor

mixing bowls

electric blender

measuring
spoons

chopping boards

measuring jug

Preparing Onions

Keeping the onions a similar size means they all cook at the same time, but we don't want any sliced fingertips, so take care. Keep a tissue nearby in case the onions make you cry!

Preparing Carrots

Although they are often just sliced in circles, carrots can look much more attractive cut in a different way. The fresher the carrot, the easier it is to cut and the nicer it looks!

1 Cut the onion in half with the skin still on. Lie the cut side flat on a board. Trim off both ends. Peel off the skin.

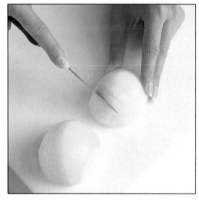

2 Make several parallel cuts lengthways (from trimmed end to end), but not cutting right to one end.

1 Peel the carrot, using this quick method with a swivel peeler, and trim the ends.

3 Make cuts at right angles to the first ones, at the same distance apart. The onion will be finely chopped. Finally, chop the end.

Cook's Tip
To slice an onion, cut down through each half to make lots of vertical slices.

2 Cut the carrot into short lengths and then into thin slices, lengthways. You will need a sharp knife for this job, so be very careful.

3 Cut each thin slice into fine strips, about the size of matchsticks.

Cook's Tip
Use tiny cutters to stamp out shapes from the thin carrot slices, to garnish soups or salads.

Separating Eggs

Meringues and some sauces call for just egg whites, so they must be separated from the yolk.

Grating

The most popular grater is the pyramid or box type, which offers different-sized blades.

I The very fine side is for grating whole nutmeg. Hold the nutmeg in one hand and rub it up and down the grater. Sometimes, it is easier to do this directly over the food.

2 The finer blades are best for citrus fruits. The blades only work downwards and you might need to brush out some of the rind from the inside with a dry pastry brush.

I Break the egg onto a saucer.

2 Stand an egg cup over the yolk and hold it firmly in place, taking care not to puncture the yolk.

3 Hold the saucer over the mixing bowl and let the egg white slide in, holding onto the egg cup. The yolk will be left on the saucer.

COOK'S TIP

The yolk may be needed for glazing, so check the recipe before you throw it away.

3 The coarsest side is best for cheese, fruit and vegetables. The blades work when you press downwards and the food will collect inside the grater.

COOK'S TIP

The jagged punched holes down one side of the grater are ideal for making breadcrumbs.

Most dishes need something to go with them, to turn them into a complete meal.
Here are some quick and easy ideas for accompaniments.

Making Mashed Potatoes

Check the labelling on the packets to see which potatoes are good for mashing: or ask your greengrocer.

Serves 4

INGREDIENTS
450 g/1 lb potatoes, peeled and
   quartered
25 g/1 oz/2 tbsp butter
30 ml/2 tbsp milk or cream
salt and pepper

COOK'S TIP
Add two crushed cloves of garlic or a handful of chopped fresh herbs, to make a real change.

1 Cook the potatoes in a pan with enough room to mash them. Cover with water, add a little salt and bring the water to the boil. Turn down the heat and simmer for 20–25 minutes. The potatoes should feel tender and fall off a sharp knife when cooked.

2 Drain them in a colander and return them to the pan. Add the butter, milk or cream and black pepper and use a potato masher to squash the potatoes and flatten all the lumps. Add more milk if you like them really soft.

Cooking Rice

Measure rice in a jug, by volume rather than by weight, for best results.

Serves 2

INGREDIENTS
10 ml/2 tsp oil
150 ml/¼ pint/⅔ cup long grain
   white rice
300 ml/½ pint/1¼ cups boiling water
   or stock
salt

COOK'S TIP
Some types of easy-cook rice may not take as long; check cooking times on the packet.

1 Heat the oil in a saucepan and add the rice. Stir to coat all the grains with the oil.

2 Pour on the boiling water or stock, add a little salt and stir once, before putting on the lid. Turn down the heat so the liquid is just simmering gently and walk away. Leave it alone for 15 minutes.

3 Lift the lid carefully (away from you) and check whether the rice is tender and that the liquid has almost gone. Fluff up the grains of rice with a fork and serve immediately.

Cooking Pasta

Pasta comes in lots of different shapes, sizes and colours. Green pasta has spinach in it, red pasta has tomato, and brown pasta is made from wholewheat flour. Egg pasta has extra eggs in the dough. Allow about 115 g/4 oz dried pasta per person if it is the main ingredient, and a little less if it is to accompany a meal, although this may vary according to how hungry you are!

Serves 4

INGREDIENTS
350–450 g/12 oz–1 lb dried pasta
salt

COOK'S TIP
Fresh pasta is also available, but its cooking times are shorter – check pack instructions.

1 Bring a large saucepan of water to boil. Add a little salt. Add the pasta to the pan, a little at a time so that the water stays at a rolling boil.

2 Cook for 8–12 minutes, depending on what type of pasta you are using – spaghetti will not take as long as the thicker penne pasta. It should be "al dente" when cooked, which means it still has some firmness to it and isn't completely soft and soggy.

3 Drain the pasta well in a colander and tip it back into the pan. Pour a sauce over or toss in a little melted butter.

Making Salad Dressing

Green or mixed salads add crunch and freshness to heavy meaty meals like lasagne or barbecued ribs, but they are bland and boring without a dressing like this one.

Serves 4

INGREDIENTS
15 ml/1 tbsp white wine vinegar
10 ml/2 tsp coarse-grain mustard
salt
freshly ground black pepper
30 ml/2 tbsp oil

COOK'S TIP
Mix 30 ml/2 tbsp oil with 15 ml/1 tbsp lemon juice, for a tangier dressing. Add chopped fresh herbs for extra flavour.

1 Put the vinegar and mustard in a bowl or jug. Whisk well, then add a little salt and pepper.

2 Add the oil slowly, about 5 ml/1 tsp at a time, whisking constantly. Pour the dressing over the salad just before serving so that the lettuce stays crisp. Use two spoons to toss the salad and coat it with the dressing.

Skinny Dips

Potato skins in disguise, with a delicious spicy dip.

Serves 4

INGREDIENTS
8 large potatoes, scrubbed
30–45 ml/2–3 tbsp oil
90 ml/6 tbsp mayonnaise
30 ml/2 tbsp natural (plain) yogurt
5 ml/1 tsp curry paste
15 ml/1 tbsp roughly chopped fresh
    coriander (cilantro)
salt

curry paste

potatoes

mayonnaise

fresh coriander
(cilantro)

natural (plain) yogurt

COOK'S TIP

If there is just one of you, prick one large potato all over with a fork and microwave on HIGH for 6–8 minutes, until tender. Scoop out the centre, brush with oil and grill (broil) till brown.

1 Preheat the oven to 190°C/375°F/ Gas Mark 5. Arrange the potatoes in a roasting tin (pan), prick them all over with a fork and cook for 45 minutes, or until tender. Leave to cool slightly.

2 Carefully cut each potato into quarters lengthways, holding it with a clean dish towel if it's still a bit hot.

3 Scoop out some of the centre with a knife or spoon and put the skins back in the roasting tin. Save the cooked potato for making fish cakes.

4 Brush the skins with oil and sprinkle with salt before putting them back in the oven. Cook for 30–40 minutes more, until they are crisp and brown, brushing them occasionally with more oil.

5 Meanwhile, put the mayonnaise, yogurt, curry paste and coriander (cilantro) in a small bowl and mix together well. Leave for 30–40 minutes for the flavour to develop.

6 Put the dip in a clean bowl and arrange the skins around the edge. Serve hot, sprinkled with the remaining coriander (cilantro).

See-in-the-Dark Soup

Stop stumbling around when the lights are off – eat more carrots! Serve with crunchy toast.

Serves 4

INGREDIENTS
15 ml/1 tbsp oil
1 onion, sliced
450 g/1 lb carrots, sliced
75 g/3 oz/½ cup split red lentils
1.2 litres/2 pints/5 cups vegetable
  stock
5 ml/1 tsp ground coriander
75 ml/3 tbsp chopped fresh parsley
salt and pepper

vegetable
stock

onion

parsley

red lentils

carrots

coriander

1 Heat the oil and fry the onion until it is starting to brown. Add the sliced carrots and fry gently for 4–5 minutes, stirring them often, until they soften.

3 Add the lentils, stock and coriander to the saucepan with salt and pepper. Bring the soup to the boil.

2 Meanwhile, put the lentils in a small bowl and cover with cold water. Pour off any bits that float. Tip the lentils into a sieve and rinse under cold running water.

4 Turn down the heat, put the lid on and leave to simmer gently for 30 minutes, or until the lentils are cooked.

5 Add the chopped parsley and cook for 5 minutes more. Remove from the heat and allow to cool slightly.

6 Carefully put the soup into a food processor or blender and whizz until it is smooth. (You may have to do this a half at a time.) Rinse the saucepan before pouring the soup back in and add a little water if it looks too thick. Heat up again before serving.

COOK'S TIP
Push the soup through a sieve with a wooden spoon or leave it chunky, if you don't have a food processor or blender.

Nutty Chicken Kebabs

A tasty Thai starter that's quick to make and uses everyone's favourite spread in the dip.

Serves 4

INGREDIENTS
30 ml/2 tbsp oil
15 ml/1 tbsp lemon juice
450 g/1 lb boneless, skinless chicken
    breasts, cut in small cubes

FOR THE DIP
5 ml/1 tsp chilli powder
75 ml/5 tbsp water
15 ml/1 tbsp oil
1 small onion, grated
1 garlic clove, peeled and crushed
30 ml/2 tbsp lemon juice
60 ml/4 tbsp crunchy peanut butter
5 ml/1 tsp salt
5 ml/1 tsp ground coriander
sliced cucumber and lemon wedges,
    to serve

lemon juice

crunchy peanut butter

onion

oil

chilli powder

chicken breast

ground coriander

garlic

1 Soak 12 wooden skewers in water, to prevent them from burning during grilling. Mix the oil and lemon juice together in a bowl and stir in the cubed chicken. Cover and leave to marinate for at least 30 minutes.

2 Thread four or five cubes on each wooden skewer. Cook under a hot grill (broiler), turning often, until cooked and browned, about 10 minutes. Cut one piece open to check it is cooked right through; this is very important, especially for chicken.

3 Meanwhile make the dip. Mix the chilli powder with 15 ml/1 tbsp water. Heat the oil in a small frying pan and fry the onion and garlic until tender.

4 Turn down the heat and add the chilli paste and the remaining ingredients and stir well. Stir in more water if the sauce is too thick and put it into a small bowl. Serve warm, with the chicken kebabs, cucumber slices and lemon wedges.

Eggs in a Blanket

A hearty brunch or lunch to tuck into on a chilly day, with chunks of wholewheat bread.

Serves 4

INGREDIENTS

1 aubergine (eggplant), sliced
5 ml/1 tsp salt
15 ml/1 tbsp oil
1 onion, sliced
1 garlic clove, peeled and crushed
1 yellow bell pepper, seeded and
   sliced
1 courgette (zucchini), sliced
400 g/14 oz can chopped tomatoes
120 ml/4 fl oz/½ cup water
10 ml/2 tsp dried mixed herbs
4 eggs

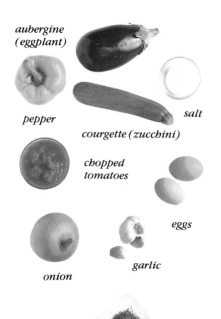

aubergine (eggplant)

pepper

courgette (zucchini)

salt

chopped tomatoes

eggs

onion

garlic

mixed herbs

1 Arrange the aubergine (eggplant) slices on a plate, sprinkle with salt and leave for 30 minutes. Rinse and squeeze out as much juice as you can.

2 Heat the oil in a large frying pan. Fry the onion until it starts to soften. Add the garlic, pepper, courgette (zucchini) and aubergine and fry for 3–4 minutes.

3 Add the chopped tomatoes, water and herbs. Stir in salt and pepper to taste. Simmer gently for 5 minutes.

4 Make four shallow dips in the mixture and break an egg into each one. Cover the pan with a lid or foil and simmer for 8–12 minutes, until the eggs are set and the vegetables are tender.

Bacon Twists

Making bread is always fun, so try this tasty version and add that extra twist to your breakfast. Serve with soft cheese with herbs.

Makes 12

INGREDIENTS
450 g/1 lb/4 cups strong white flour
6 g/¼ oz sachet easy-blend yeast
2.5 ml/½ tsp salt
400 ml/14 fl oz/1¾ cups hand-hot
   water
12 bacon rashers (strips)
1 egg, beaten

water
flour
egg
yeast
salt
bacon

1 Mix the flour, yeast and salt in a bowl and stir them together. Add a little of the water and mix with a knife. Add the remaining water and use your hands to pull the mixture together, to make a sticky dough.

2 Turn the dough on to a lightly floured surface and knead it for 5 minutes, or until the dough is smooth and stretchy.

3 Divide into 12 pieces and roll each one into a sausage shape.

4 Lay each bacon rasher (strip) on a chopping board and run the back of the knife down its length, to stretch it slightly. Wind a rasher of bacon round each dough "sausage".

5 Brush the "sausages" with beaten egg and arrange them on a lightly oiled baking sheet. Leave somewhere warm for 30 minutes, or until they have doubled in size. Preheat the oven to 200°C/400°F/ Gas 6 and cook the "sausages" for 20–25 minutes, until cooked and browned.

COOK'S TIP

This same basic dough mix can be used to make rolls or a loaf of bread. Tap the base of the breadstick – if it sounds hollow, it's cooked.

Give 'em a Roasting

Don't stick to roast potatoes! A good roasting brings out the colours and flavours of other vegetables too.

Serves 4

INGREDIENTS
1 aubergine (eggplant), cut in large
    chunks
15 ml/1 tbsp salt
1 red bell pepper, seeded and cut in
    thick strips
1 green bell pepper, seeded and cut in
    thick strips
1 yellow bell pepper, seeded and cut
    in thick strips
1 courgette (zucchini), cut in large
    chunks
1 onion, cut in thick slices
115 g/4 oz small mushrooms
225 g/8 oz plum tomatoes, quartered
75 ml/5 tbsp olive oil
4–5 thyme sprigs
2 oregano sprigs
3–4 rosemary sprigs
sea salt and freshly ground black
    pepper

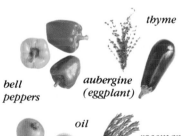
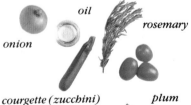

*bell
peppers*

thyme

*aubergine
(eggplant)*

oil

onion

rosemary

courgette (zucchini)

*plum
tomatoes*

mushrooms

oregano

1 Arrange the aubergine (eggplant) chunks on a plate and sprinkle them with the salt. Leave for 30 minutes.

2 Squeeze the aubergine to remove as much liquid as possible. Rinse off the salt. This process stops the aubergine tasting so bitter.

3 Preheat the oven to 200°C/400°F/ Gas 6. Arrange all the vegetables, including the aubergine, in a roasting tin (pan) and drizzle the oil over.

4 Scatter most of the herb sprigs in among the vegetables and season well. Put the tin into the hot oven and cook for 20–25 minutes.

5 Turn the vegetables over and cook them for 15 minutes more, or until they are tender and browned.

6 Scatter the remaining fresh herb sprigs over the cooked vegetables just before serving.

Wicked Tortilla Wedges

A tortilla is a thick omelette with lots of cooked potatoes in it. It is very popular in Spain, where it is cut in thick slices like a cake and served with bread. Try it with sliced tomato salad.

Serves 4

INGREDIENTS
30 ml/2 tbsp oil
675 g/1½ lb potatoes, cut in small
    chunks
1 onion, sliced
115 g/4 oz mushrooms, sliced
115 g/4 oz/1 cup frozen peas, thawed
50 g/2 oz/⅓ cup frozen corn kernels,
    thawed
4 eggs
150 ml/¼ pint/⅔ cup milk
10 ml/2 tsp Cajun seasoning
30 ml/2 tbsp chopped fresh parsley
salt and pepper

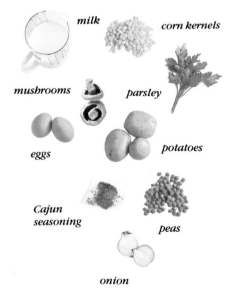

milk

corn kernels

mushrooms

parsley

eggs

potatoes

Cajun
seasoning

peas

onion

1 Heat the oil in a large frying pan and fry the potatoes and onion for 3–4 minutes, stirring often. Turn down the heat, cover the pan and fry gently for another 8–10 minutes, until the potatoes are almost tender.

2 Add the mushrooms to the pan and cook for 2–3 minutes more, stirring often, until they have softened.

3 Add the peas and corn and stir them into the potato mixture.

4 Put the eggs, milk and Cajun seasoning in a bowl. Add salt and pepper to taste and beat well.

5 Level the top of the vegetables and scatter the parsley on top. Pour the egg mixture over and cook over a low heat for 10–15 minutes.

6 Put the pan under a hot grill (broiler) to set the top of the tortilla. Serve hot or cold, cut into wedges.

COOK'S TIP

Use less Cajun seasoning if you don't like spicy food. Make sure the frying pan can be used under the grill (broiler).

Homeburgers

These look the same as ordinary burgers, but watch out for the soft cheese centre. Serve with chips (fries) and sliced tomatoes.

Serves 4

INGREDIENTS
450 g/1 lb lean minced (ground) beef
2 slices of bread, crusts removed
1 egg
4 spring onions (scallions), roughly
  chopped
1 garlic clove, peeled and chopped
15 ml/1 tbsp mango chutney
10 ml/2 tsp dried mixed herbs
50 g/2 oz/⅓ cup mozzarella cheese
salt and pepper
4 burger buns, to serve

1 Put the mince, bread, egg, spring onions (scallions) and garlic in a food processor. Add a little salt and pepper and whizz until evenly blended. Add the chutney and herbs and whizz again.

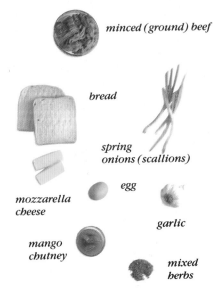

minced (ground) beef

bread

spring
onions (scallions)

mozzarella
cheese

egg

garlic

mango
chutney

mixed
herbs

2 Divide the mixture into four equal portions and pat flat, with damp hands, to stop the meat from sticking.

3 Cut the cheese into four equal pieces and put one in the centre of each piece of beef. Wrap the meat round the cheese to make a fat burger. Chill for 30 minutes. Preheat the grill (broiler).

4 Put the burgers on a rack under the hot grill, but not too close or they will burn on the outside before the middle has cooked properly. Cook them for 5–8 minutes on each side then put each burger in a roll, with your favourite trimmings.

Popeye's Pie

Tuck into this layered pie and you, too, can have bulging muscles!

Serves 4

INGREDIENTS

75 g/3 oz/⅓ cup butter
5 ml/1 tsp grated nutmeg
900 g/2 lb fresh spinach, washed and large stalks removed
115 g/4 oz/⅔ cup feta cheese, crumbled
50 g/2 oz Cheddar cheese, grated
275 g/10 oz filo pastry sheets
10 ml/2 tsp mixed ground cinnamon, nutmeg and black pepper

1 Melt 25 g/1 oz/2 tbsp of the butter in a large frying pan, add the nutmeg and the spinach and season well. Cover and cook for 5 minutes, or until the spinach is tender. Drain well, pressing out as much liquid as possible.

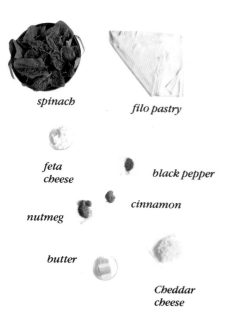

spinach

filo pastry

feta cheese

black pepper

nutmeg

cinnamon

butter

Cheddar cheese

2 Preheat the oven to 160°C/325°F/Gas 3. Melt the remaining butter in a small saucepan. Mix the cheeses together in a bowl and season them with salt and pepper. Unfold the pastry so the sheets are flat. Use one to line part of the base of a small, deep-sided, greased roasting tin (pan). Brush with melted butter. Keep the remaining filo sheets covered with a damp dish towel: they dry out very quickly.

3 Continue to lay pastry sheets across the base and up the sides of the tin, brushing each time with butter, until two-thirds of the pastry has been used. Don't worry if they flop over the top edges – they will be tidied up later.

4 Mix together the grated cheeses and spinach and spread them into the tin. Fold the pastry edges over. Crumple up the remaining sheets of pastry and arrange them over the top of the filling. Brush with melted butter and sprinkle the mixed spices over the top. Cook the pie for 45 minutes. Raise the oven temperature to 200°C/400°F/Gas 6, for 10–15 minutes more, to brown the top. Serve hot or cold.

Sticky Fingers

You have to like messy food to eat this popular dish, so plenty of napkins please! Juicy tomatoes make a refreshing accompaniment.

Serves 4

INGREDIENTS
30 ml/2 tbsp oil
1 onion, chopped
1 garlic clove, crushed
30 ml/2 tbsp tomato purée
15 ml/1 tbsp white wine vinegar
45 ml/3 tbsp clear honey
5 ml/1 tsp dried mixed herbs
2.5 ml/½ tsp chilli powder
150 ml/¼ pint/⅔ cup chicken stock
8 chicken thighs
375 g/12 oz spare ribs

FOR THE POTATOES
675 g/1½ lb potatoes, cubed
30 ml/2 tbsp oil
1 large onion, sliced
1 garlic clove, crushed
salt and pepper

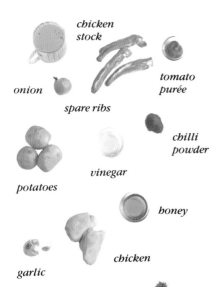

chicken stock
onion
tomato purée
spare ribs
chilli powder
vinegar
potatoes
honey
garlic
chicken
mixed herbs

1 Heat the oil in a saucepan and fry the onion and garlic until the onion starts to soften.

2 Add the tomato purée, vinegar, honey, herbs, chilli powder and stock and bring to the boil. Lower the heat and simmer for 15–20 minutes, when the sauce should have thickened.

3 Preheat the oven to 190°C/375°F/ Gas 5. Arrange the chicken and ribs in a roasting tin (pan).

4 Spoon the sauce evenly over the meat and cook for 30 minutes. Turn the meat over to ensure that it is coated evenly in the sauce.

5 Cook for 45 minutes more, turning the meat several times and spooning the sauce over. The meat should be really browned and sticky.

6 Meanwhile, put the potatoes in lightly salted water, bring to the boil, then drain well. Heat the oil in a large frying pan. Fry the onion until it starts to turn brown. Add the potatoes and garlic and fry for 25–30 minutes, until everything is cooked through, browned and crisp.

Something Very Fishy

If you like getting your hands messy, this is the recipe for you! Serve with green vegetables and new potatoes.

Serves 4

INGREDIENTS
450 g/1 lb old potatoes, cut in small chunks
25 g/1 oz/2 tbsp butter or margarine
15 ml/1 tbsp milk
412 g/14½ oz can pink salmon, drained with skin and bones removed
1 egg, beaten
60 ml/4 tbsp plain flour
2 spring onions (scallions), finely chopped
4 sun-dried tomatoes in oil, chopped
grated rind of 1 lemon
25 g/1 oz sesame seeds

1 Cook the potatoes in boiling lightly salted water until tender. Drain and return to the saucepan. Add the butter or margarine and milk and mash until smooth. Season well.

2 Put the mashed potato in a bowl and beat in the salmon. Add the egg, flour, spring onions (scallions), tomatoes and lemon rind. Mix well.

3 Divide the mixture into 8 equal pieces and pat them into fish cake shapes, using floured hands.

salmon

butter

potatoes

milk

egg

flour

spring onions (scallions)

lemon

sesame seeds

sun-dried tomatoes

4 Put the sesame seeds on a large plate and very gently press both sides of the fish cakes into them, until the cakes are lightly coated.

5 Pour oil into a frying pan to a depth of about 1 cm/½ in. Heat it gently. Put a small cube of bread in the pan and, if it sizzles, the oil is ready to cook the fish cakes. You will need to cook the fish cakes in several batches.

6 When one side is crisp and brown turn the cakes over carefully with a spatula and a fork, to cook the second side. The fish cakes are quite soft and need gentle treatment or they will break up. Lift them out and put them to drain on kitchen paper. Keep hot until they are all cooked.

COOK'S TIP
Use canned tuna instead of the salmon, if you prefer.

Pepperoni Pasta

Add extra zip to bland and boring pasta dishes with spicy pepperoni sausage.

Serves 4

INGREDIENTS

275 g/10 oz/2½ cups dried pasta
175 g/6 oz pepperoni sausage, sliced
1 small or ½ large red onion, sliced
45 ml/3 tbsp green pesto
150 ml/¼ pint/⅔ cup double (heavy) cream
225 g/8 oz cherry tomatoes, halved
15 g/½ oz fresh chives

cherry tomatoes

green pesto

pasta

double (heavy) cream

red onion

fresh chives

pepperoni sausage

1 Cook the pasta in a large pan of lightly salted, boiling water, following the instructions on the packet.

2 Meanwhile, gently fry the pepperoni sausage slices and the onion together in a frying pan until the onion is soft. The oil from the sausage will mean you won't need extra oil.

3 Mix the pesto sauce and cream together in a small bowl.

4 Add this mixture to the frying pan and stir until the sauce is smooth.

5 Add the cherry tomatoes and snip the chives over the top with scissors. Stir again.

6 Drain the pasta and tip it back into the pan. Pour the sauce over and mix well, making sure all the pasta is coated. Serve immediately.

COOK'S TIP

Use a mixture of red and yellow cherry tomatoes for a really colourful meal. Serve with sesame bread sticks.

Pizza Faces

These funny faces are very easy to make. The base is a crispy crumpet (English muffin) topped with tomato sauce and melted cheese. The toppings are just suggestions – you can use whatever you like to create the shapes for the smiley faces.

Makes 9

INGREDIENTS
30 ml/2 tbsp vegetable oil
1 onion, finely shredded
200 g/7 oz can chopped tomatoes
25 g/2 tbsp tomato purée (paste)
9 crumpets (English muffins)
220 g/7.5 oz packet of processed
  cheese slices
1 green bell pepper, seeded and
  chopped
4–5 sliced cherry tomatoes
salt and pepper

*crumpet
(English muffin)*

onion

cheese slices

*tomato purée
(paste)*

chopped tomatoes

! IMPORTANT
SAFETY NOTE
Make sure an adult helps make the sauce. Stand away from the frying pan so the hot oil doesn't splash out.

1 With the help of an adult, preheat the oven to 220°C/425°F/Gas 7. Heat the oil in a large pan, add the onion and cook for about 2–3 minutes.

2 Add the can of tomatoes, tomato purée (paste) and salt and pepper. Bring to a boil and cook for 5–6 minutes until the mixture becomes thick and pulpy. Leave to cool.

3 Lightly toast the crumpets (English muffins) under the grill (broiler). Lay them on a baking sheet. Put a heaped teaspoonful of the tomato mixture on the top and spread it out evenly. Bake in the preheated oven for 25 minutes.

4 Cut the cheese slices into strips and arrange them with the green pepper and the cherry tomatoes on top of the pizzas to make smiley faces. Return to the oven for about 5 minutes until the cheese melts. Serve the pizzas while still warm.

Roly Poly Porcupines

A meal in itself! Everyone loves frankfurter sausages (hot dogs) and they're especially good if skewered into hot baked potatoes. Always serve with a big bowl of tomato ketchup nearby.

Serves 4

INGREDIENTS
4 large baking potatoes
6–8 frankfurter sausages (hot dogs)
50 g/2 oz cherry tomatoes
50 g/2 oz mild Cheddar cheese
2 sticks (stalks) celery

TO SERVE
iceberg lettuce, shredded
small pieces of red bell pepper and
   black olive
1 carrot

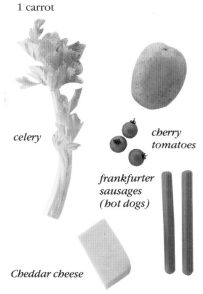

celery

cherry tomatoes

frankfurter sausages (hot dogs)

Cheddar cheese

IMPORTANT SAFETY NOTE

You may need an adult to help chop the vegetables. Make sure an adult takes the potatoes from the oven, and leave them to cool for a while before touching.

1 With the help of an adult, preheat the oven to 200°C/400°F/Gas 6. Scrub the potatoes and prick them all over. Bake in the oven for 1–1¼ hours until soft.

2 Meanwhile, prepare the frankfurters (hot dogs). Heat the frankfurter sausages in a large pan of boiling water for 8–10 minutes until they are warmed through. Drain and leave to cool slightly.

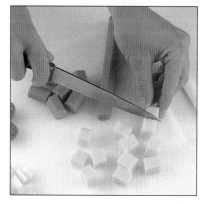

3 Cut the cherry tomatoes in half and when cool enough to handle, chop the sausages into 2.5 cm (1 in) pieces. Cut the cheese into cubes and slice the celery. Arrange them onto toothpicks.

4 When the potatoes are cooked, remove them from the oven. Pierce the skin all over with the toothpicks topped with the frankfurters, cheese cubes, cherry tomatoes and celery slices. Serve on shredded lettuce and decorate the porcupine's head with pieces of red pepper and olive, and a carrot snout.

Tasty Toasts

Next time friends come over to watch a video, surprise them with these delicious treats.

Serves 4

INGREDIENTS

2 red bell peppers, halved lengthways and seeded
30 ml/2 tbsp oil
1 garlic clove, peeled and
  crushed
1 French baton (short French
  stick)
45 ml/3 tbsp pesto
50 g/2 oz/⅓ cup soft goat's cheese

garlic

*French baton
(stick)*

*soft goat's
cheese*

*red bell
peppers*

pesto

oil

1 Put the pepper halves, cut-side down, under a hot grill (broiler) and let the skins blacken. Carefully put the halves in a plastic bag, tie the top and leave them until they are cool enough to handle. Peel off the skins and cut the peppers into strips.

2 Put the oil in a small bowl and stir in the garlic. Cut the bread into slanting slices and brush one side with the garlic-flavoured oil. Arrange the slices on a grill (broiler) pan and brown under a hot grill (broiler).

3 Turn the slices over and brush the untoasted sides with the garlic-flavoured oil and then with the pesto.

4 Arrange pepper strips over each slice and put small wedges of goat's cheese on top. Put back under the grill (broiler) and toast until the cheese has browned and melted slightly.

Chilli Cheese Nachos

Viva Mexico! Silence that hungry tummy with a truly spicy snack. Make it as cool or as hot as you like, by adjusting the amount of sliced jalapeno peppers. Olé!

Serves 4

INGREDIENTS
115 g/4 oz bag chilli tortilla
  chips
50 g/2 oz Cheddar cheese,
  grated
50 g/2 oz Red Leicester cheese,
  grated
50 g/2 oz pickled green
  jalapeno chillies, sliced

FOR THE DIP
30 ml/2 tbsp lemon juice
1 avocado, roughly chopped
1 beefsteak tomato, roughly
  chopped
salt and pepper

1 Arrange the tortilla chips in an even layer on a flameproof plate which can be used under the grill (broiler). Sprinkle all the grated cheese over and then scatter as many jalapeno chillies as you like over the top.

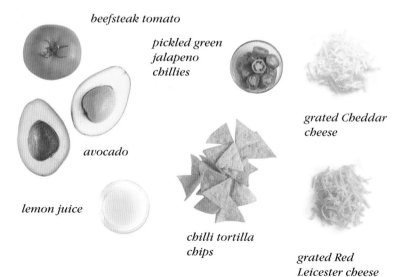

beefsteak tomato

pickled green jalapeno chillies

grated Cheddar cheese

avocado

lemon juice

chilli tortilla chips

grated Red Leicester cheese

2 Put the plate under a hot grill (broiler) and toast until the cheese has melted and browned – keep an eye on the chips to make sure they don't burn.

3 Mix the lemon juice, avocado and tomato together in a bowl. Add salt and pepper to taste and serve with the chips.

Pancake Parcels

Be adventurous with your pancakes! Don't just stick to lemon and sugar – try this savoury version for a real change.

Serves 4

INGREDIENTS

FOR THE PANCAKES

115 g/4 oz/1 cup plain (all-purpose)
  flour
1 egg
300 ml/½ pint/1¼ cups milk
2.5 ml/½ tsp salt
25 g/1 oz/2 tbsp butter,
  for frying
spring onions (scallions)

FOR THE FILLING

200 g/7 oz/scant 1 cup cream
  cheese with chives
90 ml/6 tbsp double (heavy) cream
115 g/4 oz ham, cut in strips
115 g/4 oz cheese, grated
salt and pepper
15 g/½ oz/¼ cup fresh
  breadcrumbs

breadcrumbs

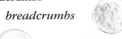

butter

double (heavy) cream

plain (all-purpose) flour

cheese

milk

ham

cream cheese with chives

egg

1 To make the pancakes, put the flour, egg, a little milk and the salt in a bowl and beat together with a wooden spoon. Gradually beat in the rest of the milk until the batter looks like double (heavy) cream. (The milk must be added slowly or the batter will be lumpy.)

2 Melt a little butter in a medium-size frying pan and pour in just enough batter to cover the base in a thin layer. Tilt and turn the pan to spread the batter out. Cook gently until set, then turn over with a palette knife and cook the second side. If you feel brave enough, try tossing the pancakes!

3 Slide the pancake out of the pan. Stack the pancakes in a pile, with a piece of greaseproof (wax) paper between each one to stop them sticking to each other. There should be enough batter to make four large pancakes. Preheat the oven to 190°C/375°F/Gas 5.

4 Make the filling. Beat the cream cheese and cream in a bowl. Add the ham and half the cheese; season well with salt and pepper. Put a spoonful of the mixture in the centre of a pancake.

5 Fold one side over the mixture and then the other. Fold both ends up as well to make a small parcel. Arrange the parcels on a baking sheet, with the joins underneath. Make three more parcels in the same way.

6 Sprinkle the remaining cheese and the breadcrumbs over the parcels and cover with foil. Cook for 20 minutes. Remove the foil. Cook for 10 minutes more, until browned. Tie green spring onion (scallion) leaves neatly around the parcels.

Chunky Cheesy Salad

Something to really sink your teeth into – this salad is chok-a-bloc with vitamins and energy. Serve on large slices of crusty bread.

Serves 4

INGREDIENTS
¼ small white cabbage, finely chopped
¼ small red cabbage, finely chopped
8 baby carrots, thinly sliced
50 g/2 oz small mushrooms, quartered
115 g/4 oz cauliflower, cut in small florets
1 small courgette (zucchini), grated
10 cm/4 in piece of cucumber, cubed
2 tomatoes, roughly chopped
50 g/2 oz sprouted seeds
50 g/2 oz/½ cup salted peanuts
30 ml/2 tbsp sunflower oil
15 ml/1 tbsp lemon juice
salt and pepper
50 g/2 oz cheese, grated
crusty bread, to serve

1 Put all the prepared vegetables and the sprouted seeds in a bowl and mix together well.

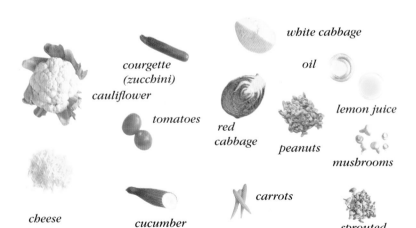

courgette (zucchini)
cauliflower
tomatoes
red cabbage
peanuts
white cabbage
oil
lemon juice
mushrooms
cheese
cucumber
carrots
sprouted seeds

2 Stir in the peanuts. Drizzle the oil and lemon juice over. Season well with salt and pepper and leave to stand for about 30 minutes to allow the flavour to develop.

3 Sprinkle grated cheese over just before serving on large slices of crusty bread. Have extra dressing ready, in case anybody wants more.

Yellow Chicken

An all-time Chinese favourite that you can stir-fry in a few minutes. Serve with boiled rice.

Serves 4

INGREDIENTS
30 ml/2 tbsp oil
75 g/3 oz/¾ cup salted cashew
  nuts
4 spring onions (scallions), roughly
  chopped
450 g/1 lb boneless, skinless
  chicken breasts, cut in strips
165 g/5½ oz jar Chinese yellow bean
  sauce

Chinese
yellow bean
sauce

spring
onions
(scallions)

chicken

cashew nuts

oil

1 Heat 15 ml/1 tbsp of the oil in a frying pan and fry the cashew nuts until browned. This does not take long, so keep an eye on them. Lift them out with a slotted spoon and put them to one side.

2 Heat the remaining oil and fry the spring onions (scallions) and chicken for 5–8 minutes, until the meat is browned all over and cooked.

3 Return the nuts to the pan and pour the jar of sauce over. Stir well and cook gently until hot. Serve at once.

COOK'S TIP

Cashew nuts are quite expensive, but you can buy broken cashews, which are cheaper and perfectly good for this dish. You could also use almonds, if you prefer.

Tiny Toads

Serve these mini-sized portions of toad-in-the-hole with peas.

Serves 4

INGREDIENTS
115 g/4 oz/1 cup plain (all-purpose)
  flour
1 egg
300 ml/½ pint/1¼ cups milk
45 ml/3 tbsp fresh mixed herbs,
  e.g. parsley, thyme and chives,
  roughly chopped
24 cocktail sausages
salt and pepper

FOR THE ONION GRAVY
15 ml/1 tbsp oil
2 onions, sliced
600 ml/1 pint/2½ cups stock
15 ml/1 tbsp soy sauce
15 ml/1 tbsp whole-grain mustard
25 g/1 oz/2 tbsp cornflour
  (cornstarch)
30 ml/2 tbsp water

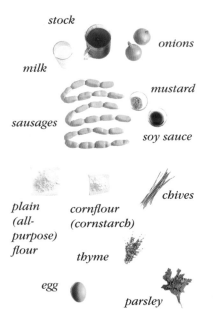

stock

onions

milk

mustard

sausages

soy sauce

chives

plain
(all-purpose)
flour

cornflour
(cornstarch)

thyme

egg

parsley

1 Preheat the oven to 200°C/400°F/ Gas 6. Put the flour, egg and a little milk in a bowl and mix well with a wooden spoon. Gradually mix in the rest of the milk to make a batter. Season well with salt and pepper and stir in the herbs.

2 Lightly oil eight 10 cm/4 in non-stick Yorkshire pudding tins and arrange three sausages in each. Cook in the hot oven for 10 minutes.

COOK'S TIP
Use vegetarian sausages for friends who don't eat meat.

3 Carefully take the tins out of the oven and use a ladle to pour batter into each tin. Put them back in the oven and cook for 30–40 minutes more, until the batter is risen and browned.

4 Meanwhile, heat the oil in a pan. Fry the onions for 15 minutes until browned. Add the stock, mustard and soy. Bring to the boil. Mix the cornflour (cornstarch) and water together in a cup and pour into the gravy. Bring to the boil, stirring. Serve with the toads.

Honey Chops

These tasty, sticky chops are very quick and easy to prepare and grill (broil), but they would be just as good barbecued. Serve with herby mashed potatoes or chips (fries).

Serves 4

INGREDIENTS
450 g/1 lb carrots
15 ml/1 tbsp butter
15 ml/1 tbsp soft brown sugar
15 ml/1 tbsp sesame seeds

FOR THE CHOPS
4 pork loin chops
50 g/2 oz/¼ cup butter
30 ml/2 tbsp clear honey
15 ml/1 tbsp tomato purée (paste)

carrots   honey

butter

tomato
purée
(paste)

pork loin
chops

sesame
seeds

soft brown
sugar

COOK'S TIP
If the chops are very thick, put under a medium-hot grill (broiler) for longer to make sure they are cooked in the middle.

1 Cut the carrots into matchstick shapes, put them in a saucepan and just cover them with cold water. Add the butter and brown sugar and bring to the boil. Turn down the heat and leave to simmer for 15–20 minutes, until most of the liquid has boiled away.

2 Line the grill (broiler) pan with foil and arrange the pork chops on the rack. Beat the butter and honey together and gradually beat in the tomato purée (paste), to make a smooth paste. Preheat the grill (broiler) to high.

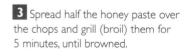

3 Spread half the honey paste over the chops and grill (broil) them for 5 minutes, until browned.

4 Turn the chops over, spread them with the remaining honey paste and return to the grill (broiler). Grill the second side for a further 5 minutes, or until the meat is cooked through. Sprinkle the sesame seeds over the top of the carrots and serve with the chops.

Raving Ravioli

Have a raving good time making your own pasta – get your friends to help.

Serves 4

INGREDIENTS

75 g/3 oz fresh spinach, torn
 up, with tough stalks removed
275 g/10 oz/2½ cups strong
 white (bread) flour
3 eggs, beaten
15 ml/1 tbsp oil
salt and pepper
300 ml/½ pint/1¼ cups
 double (heavy) cream
15 ml/1 tbsp chopped fresh
 coriander (cilantro)
30 ml/2 tbsp grated Parmesan
 cheese, plus extra to serve

FOR THE FILLING

115 g/4 oz trout fillet, poached
 and drained, skin and bones
 removed
50 g/2 oz/⅓ cup ricotta cheese
grated rind of 1 lemon
15 ml/1 tbsp chopped fresh
 coriander (cilantro)

eggs

*double
(heavy) cream*   *spinach*

oil

*trout
fillet*

*strong white
(bread) flour*

lemon

*Parmesan
cheese*

*ricotta
cheese*

*fresh
coriander
(cilantro)*

1 Steam the spinach over a pan of boiling water until it wilts. Allow to cool, and squeeze out as much water as you can. Put it into a food processor together with the flour, eggs, oil and salt and pepper and whizz until the mixture forms a dough.

2 Place the dough on a lightly floured surface and knead it for 5 minutes, until smooth. Wrap it in clear film and chill in the fridge for 30 minutes.

3 Sprinkle the work surface with flour. Roll out the dough to make a 50 x 46 cm (20 x 18 in) shape, so the dough is the thickness of card. Leave to dry for 15 minutes. Use a sharp knife or pastry wheel to trim the edges and cut the dough in half.

4 Put the trout in a small bowl. Add the ricotta cheese, lemon rind, the coriander (cilantro) and salt and pepper and beat together. Put four spoonfuls of the filling across the top of the dough, leaving a small border round the edge. Carry on putting the filling mixture in lines, to make eight rows. Lift up the second sheet of pasta on a rolling pin and lay it gently over the first sheet.

5 Run your finger between the bumps to remove any air and to press the dough together. Using a knife or pastry wheel, cut the ravioli into small parcels and trim round the edge as well, to seal each one. Cook in lightly salted boiling water for 8–10 minutes. Drain and return to the pan.

6 Put the cream, remaining coriander (cilantro) and the Parmesan in a small saucepan and heat gently, without boiling. Pour over the ravioli and stir until evenly coated. Serve immediately, garnished with a sprig of coriander and Parmesan. Hand extra Parmesan round, if you like.

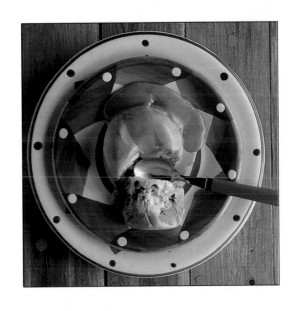

Sweet Treats

Who can resist monster meringues, ice cream bombes
and chunky choc bars? Make these delicious recipes
for a party, or gift wrap a box of cookies as a special
present for a friend. The only problem is not eating
them all yourself!

Chocolate Cups

Perfect for the chocoholics in the family. Serve with crisp dessert cookies.

Serves 4

INGREDIENTS

200 g/7 oz bar plain (semi-sweet) chocolate
120 ml/4 fl oz/½ cup double (heavy) cream
75 g/3 oz white chocolate

double (heavy) cream

white chocolate   *plain (semi-sweet) chocolate*

1 Break half the plain (semi-sweet) chocolate into pieces and put them in a bowl. Stand the bowl over a pan of hot, but not boiling, water and leave to melt, stirring occasionally. Make sure the water doesn't touch the bowl.

2 Line four ramekins, or similarly sized cups, with a piece of foil. Don't worry about it creasing or scrunching up.

3 Use a clean paintbrush to brush the melted chocolate over the foil in a thick layer. Chill in the fridge until set. Paint a second layer and leave to chill again.

4 Put the cream in a bowl and whisk until stiff. Melt the remaining plain chocolate as before and use a metal spoon to fold it into the cream.

5 Roughly chop the white chocolate and stir it gently into the chocolate and cream mixture.

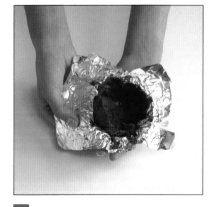

6 Carefully peel the foil off the chocolate cups and fill each one with the chocolate and cream mixture. Chill until set.

COOK'S TIP

Try using white chocolate drops, chocolate-covered raisins or a chopped chocolate bar, instead of the white chocolate.

Ice Cream Bombes

This chilly dessert with warm sauce will have you ready to explode – it's dynamite!

Serves 6

INGREDIENTS
1 litre/1¾ pints/4 cups soft-scoop
   chocolate ice cream
475 ml/16 fl oz/2 cups soft-scoop
   vanilla ice cream
50 g/2 oz/⅓ cup plain (semi-sweet)
   chocolate drops
115 g/4 oz toffees
75 ml/5 tbsp double (heavy) cream

double (heavy) cream

vanilla ice cream

chocolate drops

chocolate ice cream

toffees

1 Share the chocolate ice cream between six small cups. Push it roughly to the base and up the sides, leaving a small cup-shaped dip in the middle. Don't worry if it's not very neat; it will be frozen again before the ice cream melts too much. Return to the freezer and leave for 45 minutes. Take it out again and smooth the ice cream into shape. Return to the freezer.

2 Put the vanilla ice cream in a small bowl and break it up slightly with a spoon. Stir in the chocolate drops and then use this mixture to fill the dip in the chocolate ice cream. Return the cups to the freezer and leave overnight.

3 Put the toffees in a small saucepan and heat gently, stirring all the time. As they melt, add the double cream and keep mixing until all the toffees have melted and the sauce is warm.

4 Dip the cups in hot water and run a knife round the edge of the ice cream. Turn out on to individual plates and pour the toffee sauce over the top. Serve immediately.

Puffy Pears

An eye-catching dessert that is simple to make and delicious to eat, especially when served with whipped cream or natural (plain) yogurt.

Serves 4

INGREDIENTS
225 g/8 oz puff pastry
2 pears, peeled
2 squares plain (semi-sweet)
   chocolate, roughly chopped
15 ml/1 tbsp lemon juice
1 egg, beaten
15 ml/1 tbsp caster (superfine) sugar

puff pastry

pears

egg

caster
(superfine)
sugar

lemon
juice

plain
(semi-sweet)
chocolate

COOK'S TIP
Try the same thing using eating apples, especially when you have picked the fruit yourself.

1 Roll the pastry into a 25 cm/10 in square on a lightly floured surface. Trim the edges, then cut it into four equal smaller squares.

2 Remove the core from each pear half and pack the gap with the chopped chocolate. Place a pear half, cut-side down, on each piece of pastry and brush them with the lemon juice, to prevent them from going brown.

3 Preheat the oven to 190°C/375°F/ Gas 5. Cut the pastry into a pear shape, by following the lines of the fruit, leaving a 2.5 cm/1 in border. Use the trimmings to make leaves and brush the pastry border with the beaten egg.

4 Arrange the pastry and pears on a baking sheet. Make deep cuts in the pears, taking care not to cut right through the fruit, and sprinkle them with the caster sugar. Cook for 20–25 minutes, until lightly browned. Serve hot or cold.

Summer Fruit Cheesecake

Making this is much easier than it looks and it tastes so good, it's well worth the effort.

Serves 8–10

INGREDIENTS
175 g/6 oz/¾ cup butter
225 g/8 oz digestive biscuits (graham crackers)
rind and juice of 2 lemons
11 g/scant ½ oz sachet gelatine
225 g/8 oz/1 cup natural (plain) cottage cheese
200 g/7 oz/scant 1 cup cream cheese
400 g/14 oz can condensed milk
450 g/1 lb/4 cups strawberries
115 g/4 oz/1 cup raspberries

milk
butter
lemons
cottage cheese
raspberries
cream cheese
digestive biscuits (graham crackers)
strawberries
gelatine

COOK'S TIP

Always add gelatine to the liquid, never the other way round.

1 Cut a piece of greaseproof (wax) paper to fit the base of a 20 cm/8 in loose-bottomed springform cake tin (pan). Melt the butter in a saucepan over a low heat. Break the biscuits (graham crackers) in pieces, put them in a food processor and whizz until they are crumbs. Stir them into the melted butter until well mixed.

2 Tip the crumbs into the cake tin and use a spoon to spread the mixture in a thin, even layer over the base, pressing down well. Put the tin in the fridge while you make the filling.

3 Put the lemon rind and juice in a small bowl and sprinkle the gelatine over. Stand the bowl in a saucepan of water and heat gently, until the gelatine crystals have all melted. Stir the mixture and leave to cool slightly.

4 Put the cottage cheese in a food processor and whizz for 20 seconds. Add the cream cheese and condensed milk, fix the lid in place again and whizz the mixture. Pour in the dissolved gelatine mixture and whizz once more.

5 Roughly chop half the strawberries and scatter them over the base. Add half the raspberries, saving the rest for decorating the top. Pour the cheese mixture carefully over the fruit and level the top. Return to the fridge and leave overnight to set.

6 Carefully loosen the edges of the cheesecake with a palette knife. Then stand the cake tin on a large mug or can and gently open the clip at the side of the tin. Allow the tin to slide down. Put the cheesecake on a serving plate and decorate it with the reserved fruit.

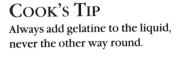

Carrot Cake

This is full of healthy fibre – yet moist and soft at the same time.

Serves 10–12

INGREDIENTS

225 g/8 oz/2 cups self-raising (rising) flour
10 ml/2 tsp baking powder
150 g/5 oz/1 scant cup soft brown sugar
115 g/4 oz ready-to-eat dried figs, roughly chopped
225 g/8 oz carrots, grated
2 small ripe bananas, mashed
2 eggs
150 ml/¼ pint/⅔ cup sunflower oil
175 g/6 oz/¾ cup cream cheese
175 g/6 oz/1½ cups icing (confectioner's) sugar, sifted
small coloured candies, nuts or grated chocolate, to decorate

sunflower oil
dried figs
cream cheese
self-raising (rising) flour
baking powder
icing (confectioner's) sugar
eggs
carrots
bananas
soft brown sugar

1 Lightly grease an 18 cm/7 in round, loose-based springform cake tin (pan). Cut a piece of baking parchment or greaseproof (wax) paper to fit the base of the tin.

2 Preheat the oven to 180°C/350°F/Gas 4. Put the flour, baking powder and sugar into a large bowl and mix well. Stir in the figs.

3 Using your hands, squeeze as much liquid out of the grated carrots as you can and add them to the bowl. Mix in the mashed bananas.

4 Beat the eggs and oil together and pour them into the mixture. Beat together with a wooden spoon.

5 Spoon into the prepared tin and level the top. Cook for 1–1¼ hours, until a skewer pushed into the centre of the cake comes out clean. Remove the cake from the tin and leave to cool.

6 Beat the cream cheese and icing (confectioner's) sugar together, to make a thick frosting. Spread it over the top of the cake. Decorate with small coloured candies, nuts or grated chocolate. Cut in small wedges, to serve.

COOK'S TIP

Because this cake contains moist vegetables and fruit, it will not keep longer than a week, but you probably won't find this a problem!

Gingerbread Jungle

Snappy cookies in animal shapes, which can be decorated in your own style.

Makes 14

INGREDIENTS

175 g/6 oz/1½ cups self-raising (rising) flour
2.5 ml/½ tsp bicarbonate of soda
2.5 ml/½ tsp ground cinnamon
10 ml/2 tsp caster (superfine) sugar
50 g/2 oz/¼ cup butter or margarine
45 ml/3 oz/3 tbsp golden (corn) syrup
50 g/2 oz/½ cup icing (confectioner's) sugar
5–10 ml/1–2 tsp water

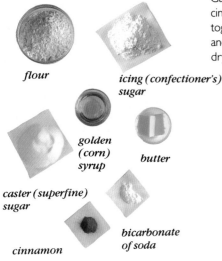

flour

icing (confectioner's) sugar

golden (corn) syrup

butter

caster (superfine) sugar

cinnamon

bicarbonate of soda

1 Preheat the oven to 190°C/375°F/Gas 5. Put the flour, bicarbonate of soda, cinnamon and sugar in a bowl and mix together. Melt the butter or margarine and syrup in a saucepan. Pour over the dry ingredients.

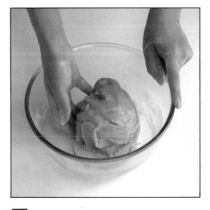

2 Mix together well and then use your hands to pull the mixture together to make a dough.

3 Turn onto a lightly floured surface and roll out to a 5 mm/¼ in thickness.

4 Use animal cutters to cut shapes from the dough and arrange them on two lightly oiled baking sheets, leaving enough room between them to rise. Press the trimmings back into a ball, roll it out and cut more shapes. Continue to do this until the dough is used up. Cook for 8–12 minutes, until lightly browned.

5 Leave the shapes to cool slightly, before lifting them on to a wire rack, with a palette knife. Sift the icing (confectioner's) sugar into a small bowl and add enough water to make a fairly soft frosting. Put the icing in a piping bag fitted with a small, plain nozzle and pipe decorations on the cookies.

COOK'S TIP

Any cutters can be used with the same mixture. Obviously the smaller the cutters, the more cookies you will make.

Hot Chocolate & Choc-tipped Cookies

Get those cold hands wrapped round a steaming hot drink, and tuck into choc-tipped cookies.

Serves 2

INGREDIENTS

FOR THE HOT CHOCOLATE
90 ml/6 tbsp drinking chocolate powder, plus a little extra for sprinkling
30 ml/2 tbsp sugar, according to taste
600 ml/1 pint/2½ cups milk
2 large squirts canned whipped cream

FOR THE CHOC-TIPPED COOKIES
115 g/4 oz/½ cup soft margarine
45 ml/3 tbsp icing (confectioner's) sugar, sifted
150 g/5 oz/1¼ cups plain (all-purpose) flour
few drops of vanilla essence
75 g/3 oz plain (semi-sweet) chocolate

milk

sugar

vanilla essence

drinking chocolate powder

soft margarine

canned whipped cream

flour

icing (confectioner's) sugar

plain (semi-sweet) chocolate

1 To make the hot chocolate, put the drinking chocolate powder and the sugar in a saucepan. Add the milk and bring it to the boil, whisking all the time. Divide between two mugs. Add more sugar if needed. Top with a squirt of cream.

2 To make the choc-tipped cookies, put the margarine and icing (confectioner's) sugar in a bowl and beat them together until very soft. Mix in the flour and vanilla essence. Preheat the oven to 180°C/350°F/Gas Mark 4 and lightly grease two baking sheets.

3 Put the mixture in a large piping bag fitted with a large star nozzle and pipe 10–13 cm/4–5 in lines on the baking sheets. Cook for 15–20 minutes, until pale golden brown. Allow to cool slightly before lifting on to a wire rack. Leave the cookies to cool completely.

4 Put the chocolate in a small bowl. Stand in a pan of hot, but not boiling, water and leave to melt. Dip both ends of each cookie in the chocolate, put back on the rack and leave to set.

COOK'S TIP
Make round cookies if you prefer, and dip half of each cookie in melted chocolate.

Strawberry Smoothie & Stars-in-your-Eyes Cookies

A real smoothie that's lip-smackingly special, when served with crunchy stars-in-your-eyes cookies.

Serves 4–6

INGREDIENTS
FOR STARS-IN-YOUR-EYES COOKIES
115 g/4 oz/½ cup butter
175 g/6 oz/1½ cups plain (all-purpose) flour
50 g/2 oz/¼ cup caster (superfine) sugar
30 ml/2 tbsp golden (corn) syrup
30 ml/2 tbsp preserving sugar

FOR THE STRAWBERRY SMOOTHIE
225 g/8 oz/2 cups strawberries
150 ml/¼ pint/⅔ cup natural (plain) yogurt
475 ml/16 fl oz/2 cups ice-cold milk
30 ml/2 tbsp icing (confectioner's) sugar

milk
flour
natural (plain) yogurt
icing (confectioner's) sugar
golden (corn) syrup
strawberries
caster (superfine) sugar
preserving sugar
butter

1 First make the stars-in-your-eyes cookies: put the butter, flour and sugar in a bowl and rub in the fat with your fingertips, until the mixture looks like breadcrumbs. Stir in the caster (superfine) sugar and then knead together to make a ball. Chill in the fridge for 30 minutes.

2 Preheat the oven to 180°C/350°F/Gas 4 and lightly grease 2 baking sheets. Roll out the dough on a floured surface to a 5 mm/¼ in thickness and use a 7.5 cm/3 in star-shaped cutter to stamp out the cookies.

3 Arrange the cookies on a baking sheet, leaving enough room for them to rise. Press the trimmings together and keep rolling out and cutting more cookies until all the mixture has been used. Bake for 10–15 minutes, until they are golden brown.

4 Put the syrup in a small, microwave-safe bowl and heat it on HIGH for 12 seconds. Or heat for a minute or two over simmering water. Brush over the cookies while they are still warm. Sprinkle a little preserving sugar on top of each one and leave to cool.

5 To make the strawberry smoothies, reserve a few of the strawberries for decoration and put the rest in a blender with the yogurt. Whizz until fairly smooth.

6 Add the milk and icing (confectioner's) sugar, process again and pour into glasses. Serve each glass decorated with one or two of the reserved strawberries.

Peanut Cookies

Packing up a picnic? Got a birthday party to go to? Make sure some of these nutty biscuits are on the menu.

Makes 25

INGREDIENTS

225 g/8 oz/1 cup butter
30 ml/2 tbsp smooth peanut
   butter
115 g/4 oz/1 cup icing
   (confectioners') sugar
50 g/2 oz/scant ½ cup cornflour
   (cornstarch)
225 g/8 oz/2 cups plain (all-purpose)
   flour
115 g/4 oz/1 cup unsalted peanuts

plain (all-purpose) flour

cornflour (cornstarch)

peanut butter

butter

unsalted peanuts

icing (confectioners') sugar

1 Put the butter and peanut butter in a bowl and beat together. Add the icing (confectioners') sugar, cornflour (cornstarch) and flour and mix together with your hands, to make a soft dough.

2 Preheat the oven to 180°C/350°F/ Gas 4 and lightly oil two baking sheets. Roll the mixture into 25 small balls, using floured hands, and place the balls on the two sheets. Leave plenty of room for the cookies to spread.

3 Press the tops of the balls of dough flat, using either the back of a fork or your fingertips.

4 Press some of the peanuts into each of the cookies. Cook for about 15–20 minutes, until lightly browned. Leave to cool for a few minutes before lifting them carefully onto a wire rack with a palette knife (metal spatula). When they are cool, pack them in a tin.

COOK'S TIP

Make really monster cookies by making bigger balls of dough. Leave plenty of room on the baking sheets for them to spread, though.

Five-Spice Fingers

Light, crumbly biscuits (cookies) with an unusual Chinese five-spice flavouring.

Makes 28

INGREDIENTS

115 g/4 oz/½ cup margarine
50 g/2 oz/½ cup icing
  (confectioners') sugar
115 g/4 oz/1 cup plain (all-purpose)
  flour
10 ml/2 tsp five-spice powder
oil, for greasing
grated rind and juice of
  ½ orange

orange

icing (confectioners') sugar

five-spice powder

margarine

plain (all-purpose) flour

1 Put the margarine and half the icing (confectioners') sugar in a bowl and beat with a wooden spoon, until the mixture is smooth, creamy and soft.

2 Add the flour and five-spice powder and beat again. Put the mixture in a large piping bag fitted with a large star nozzle.

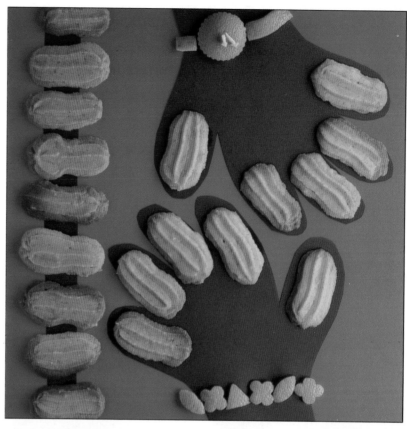

3 Preheat the oven to 180°C/350°F/ Gas 4. Lightly grease two baking sheets and pipe short lines of mixture, about 7.5 cm/3 in long, on them. Leave enough room for them to spread. Cook for about 15 minutes, until lightly browned. Leave to cool slightly, before lifting them onto a wire rack with a palette knife (metal spatula).

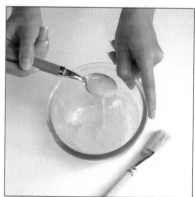

4 Sift the remaining amount of icing (confectioners') sugar into a small bowl and stir in the orange rind. Add enough juice to make a thin icing and brush it over the fingers while they are still warm. Leave to cool a little and serve.

COOK'S TIP
Delicious served with ice cream or creamy desserts.

Monster Meringues

A mouth-watering dessert made from meringue, whipped cream and tangy summer fruits.

Serves 4

INGREDIENTS

3 egg whites
175 g/6 oz/¾ cup caster (superfine)
  sugar
15 ml/1 tbsp cornflour (cornstarch)
5 ml/1 tsp white wine vinegar
few drops vanilla essence (extract)
225 g/8 oz assorted red summer
  fruits
300 ml/½ pint/1¼ cups
  double (heavy) cream
1 passion fruit

double (heavy) cream

caster (super-fine) sugar

strawberries

cornflour (cornstarch)

passion fruit

redcurrants

vanilla essence (extract)

eggs

white wine vinegar

raspberries

COOK'S TIP
Draw six 7.5 cm (3 in) circles and pipe smaller meringues, if you aren't hungry enough for a monster dessert.

1 Preheat the oven to 140°C/275°F/ Gas 1. In pencil, draw eight 10 cm/4 in circles on two separate sheets of baking parchment (parchment paper) that will fit on two flat baking sheets.

2 Put the egg whites into a very clean, dry bowl and whisk until stiff. This will take about 2 minutes with an electric whisk; peaks made in the meringue should keep their shape when it's ready. Add the sugar gradually and whisk well each time. The mixture should now be very stiff.

3 Use a metal spoon to gently stir in the cornflour (cornstarch), white wine vinegar and vanilla essence (extract). Put the meringue into a large piping bag, fitted with a large star nozzle.

4 Pipe a solid layer of meringue in four of the drawn circles and then pipe a lattice pattern in the other four. Put the meringues in the oven and cook for 1¼–1½ hours, swapping shelf positions after 30 minutes, until lightly browned. The paper will peel off the back easily when the meringues are cooked.

5 Roughly chop most of the summer fruits, reserving a few for decoration. Whip the cream and spread it over the solid meringue shapes. Scatter the fruit over. Halve the passion fruit, scoop out the seeds with a teaspoon and scatter them over the fruit. Put a lattice lid on top of each and serve with the reserved fruits.

Chocolate Puffs

These are always a firm favourite and so easy and cheap to make.

Serves 4–6

INGREDIENTS
150 ml/¼ pint/⅔ cup water
50 g/2 oz/¼ cup butter
65 g/2½ oz/generous ½ cup
  plain (all-purpose) flour, sifted
2 eggs, beaten

FOR THE FILLING AND ICING
150 ml/¼ pint/⅔ cup double (heavy)
  cream
225 g/8 oz/1½ cups icing
  (confectioners') sugar
15 ml/1 tbsp cocoa powder
30–60 ml/2–4 tbsp water

water

plain (all-purpose) flour

double (heavy) cream

icing (confectioners') sugar

cocoa powder

butter

eggs

COOK'S TIP
If the unfilled puffs go soggy, put them back into a hot oven for a few minutes and they will crisp up again.

1 Put the water in a saucepan, add the butter and heat gently until it melts. Bring to the boil and remove from the heat. Tip in all the flour at once and beat quickly until the mixture sticks together, leaving the side of the pan clean. Leave to cool slightly.

2 Add the eggs, a little at a time, to the mixture and beat well each time, by hand with a wooden spoon or with an electric whisk, until the mixture is thick and glossy and drops reluctantly from a spoon (you may not need to use all of the egg). Preheat the oven to 220°C/425°F/Gas 7.

3 Dampen two baking sheets with cold water and put walnut-sized spoonfuls of the mixture on them. Leave some space for them to rise. Cook for 25–30 minutes, until golden brown and well risen. Use a palette knife (metal spatula) to lift them onto a wire rack and make a small hole in each one with the handle of a wooden spoon to allow the steam to escape. Leave to cool.

4 To make the filling and icing, whip the cream until thick. Put it into a piping bag fitted with a plain or star nozzle. Push the nozzle into the hole in each puff and squirt a little cream inside. Put the icing (confectioners') sugar and cocoa in a small bowl and stir together. Add enough water to make a thick glossy icing. Spread a spoonful of icing on each puff and serve.

Let's Get Tropical

Supermarkets are full of weird and wonderful fruits that make a really tangy salad when mixed together. Serve with cream or yogurt.

Serves 4

INGREDIENTS
1 small pineapple
2 kiwi fruit
1 ripe mango
1 watermelon slice
2 peaches
2 bananas
60 ml/4 tbsp tropical fruit juice

tropical fruit juice

watermelon

mango

pineapple

peaches

kiwi fruit

bananas

1 Cut the pineapple into 1 cm/½ in slices. Work round the edge of each slice, cutting off the skin and any spiky bits. Cut each slice into wedges and put them in a bowl.

2 Use a potato peeler to remove the skin from the kiwi fruit. Cut them in half lengthways and then into wedges. Add to the fruit bowl.

3 Cut the mango lengthways into quarters and cut round the large flat stone. Peel the flesh and cut it into chunks or slices.

4 Cut the watermelon into slices, cut off the skin and cut the flesh into chunks. Remove the seeds. Cut the peaches in half, remove the stones and cut the flesh into wedges. Slice the bananas. Add all the fruit to the bowl and gently stir in the fruit juice.

Chocolate Brownies

Scout out these delicious, moist and chewy cakes, and guide yourself to a chocolate treat!

Makes 9

INGREDIENTS
65 g/2½ oz/⅓ cup butter
50 g/2 oz plain (semi-sweet)
  chocolate
150 g/5 oz/scant 1 cup soft
  brown sugar
2 eggs, beaten
65 g/2½ oz/generous ½ cup
  plain (all-purpose) flour
50 g/2 oz/½ cup roughly
  chopped pecans or walnuts
25 g/1 oz/¼ cup icing
  (confectioners') sugar

icing (confectioners') sugar

soft brown sugar

butter

plain (all-purpose) flour

eggs

plain (semi-sweet) chocolate

pecans

1 Put the butter and chocolate in a bowl and stand it over a saucepan of hot, but not boiling water. Make sure the water doesn't touch the bowl. Leave until they have both melted and then stir them together.

2 Stir the sugar into the butter and chocolate mixture and leave for a while to cool slightly.

3 Cut a piece of baking parchment or greaseproof (wax) paper to fit the base of an 18 cm/7 in square cake tin (pan).

4 Preheat the oven to 180°C/350°F/ Gas 4. Beat the eggs into the chocolate mixture, then stir in the flour and nuts.

5 Pour the mixture into the lined cake tin (pan) and level the top. Cook for 25–35 minutes, until firm around the edges but still slightly soft in the middle.

6 Cut into nine squares and leave to cool in the tin (pan). Dredge with a little icing (confectioners') sugar and serve hot or cold, whichever you prefer.

Blueberry Muffins

These monster muffins contain whole fresh blueberries that burst in the mouth when bitten.

Makes 9

INGREDIENTS

375 g/13 oz/3¼ cups plain (all-
 purpose) flour
200 g/7 oz/scant 1 cup caster
 (superfine) sugar
25 ml/1½ tbsp baking powder
175 g/6 oz/¾ cup butter,
 roughly chopped
1 egg, beaten
1 egg yolk
150 ml/¼ pint/⅔ cup milk
grated rind of 1 lemon
175 g/6 oz/1½ cups fresh
 blueberries

milk

*caster
(superfine)
sugar*

*plain (all-
purpose) flour*

*baking
powder*

egg

egg yolk

lemon

blueberries

butter

1 Preheat the oven to 200°/400°F/
Gas 6. Line a muffin tin (pan) with nine
large paper muffin cases (cups).

3 In a separate bowl, beat the egg, egg
yolk, milk and lemon rind together.

2 Put the flour, sugar, baking powder and butter in a bowl. Use your fingertips to
rub the butter into the flour, until the mixture looks like breadcrumbs.

4 Pour the egg and milk mixture into
the flour mixture, add the blueberries
and mix gently together.

5 Share the mixture among the paper
cases and cook for 30–40 minutes, until
they are risen and brown.

6 Push a skewer into the middle of
one of the muffins. The muffins are
cooked if it comes out clean. Lift them
onto a wire rack to cool.

COOK'S TIP

As the muffins have fresh fruit in
them, they will not keep for longer
than four days, so best eat them
immediately!

Chunky Choc Bars

This no-cook cake is a smash hit with everyone.

Makes 12

INGREDIENTS
350 g/12 oz plain (semi-sweet)
  chocolate
115 g/4 oz/½ cup butter
400 g/14 oz can condensed milk
225 g/8 oz digestive biscuits,
  (graham crackers) broken
50 g/2 oz/⅓ cup raisins
115 g/4 oz ready-to-eat dried
  peaches, roughly chopped
50 g/2 oz hazelnuts or pecans,
  roughly chopped

condensed milk

digestive biscuits (graham crackers)

hazelnuts

butter

plain (semi-sweet) chocolate

dried peaches

raisins

1 Line an 18 × 28 cm/7 × 11 in cake tin (pan) with clear film (plastic wrap).

2 Put the chocolate and butter in a large bowl over a pan of hot but not boiling water (the bowl must not touch the water) and leave to melt. Stir until well mixed.

3 Beat the condensed milk into the chocolate and butter mixture.

4 Add the biscuits (crackers), raisins, peaches and nuts and mix well, until all the ingredients are coated in chocolate.

5 Tip the mixture into the prepared tin, making sure it is pressed well into the corners. Leave the top craggy. Put in the fridge and leave to set.

6 Lift the cake out of the tin using the clear film (plastic wrap) and then peel it off. Cut into 12 bars and keep chilled – until you are ready to eat them.

Lemon Meringue Cakes

This is a variation on cupcakes – soft lemon sponge topped with crisp meringue.

Makes 18

INGREDIENTS
115 g/4 oz/½ cup margarine
200 g/7 oz/scant 1 cup caster
   (superfine) sugar
2 eggs
115 g/4 oz/1 cup self-raising
   (rising) flour
5 ml/1 tsp baking powder
grated rind of 2 lemons
30 ml/2 tbsp lemon juice
2 egg whites

self-raising (rising) flour   *caster (superfine) sugar*   *lemon juice*

baking powder   *eggs*   *lemons*

margarine

1 Preheat the oven to 190°C/375°F/ Gas 5. Put the margarine in a bowl and beat until soft. Add 115 g/4 oz/½ cup of the sugar and continue to beat until the mixture is smooth and creamy.

2 Beat in the eggs, flour, baking powder, half the lemon rind and all the lemon juice.

4 Whisk the egg whites in a clean bowl, until they stand in soft peaks.

3 Stand 18 small paper cases (cups) in two bun tins (muffin pans), and share the mixture between them all.

5 Stir in the remaining sugar and lemon rind.

COOK'S TIP

Make sure that you whisk the egg whites enough before adding the sugar – when you lift out the whisk they should stand in peaks that just flop over slightly at the top. Use a mixture of oranges and lemons, for a sweeter taste.

6 Put a spoonful of the meringue mixture on each cake. Cook for about 20–25 minutes, until the meringue is crisp and brown. Serve hot or cold.

Kooky Cookies

Easy to make and yummy to eat! Let your imagination run wild with the decorating. If it's easier, you can use coloured icing pens.

Makes about 15

INGREDIENTS
115 g/4 oz/1 cup self-raising (rising) flour
5 ml/1 tsp ground ginger
5 ml/1 tsp bicarbonate of soda (baking soda)
50 g/2 oz/4 tbsp granulated sugar
50 g/2 oz/4 tbsp softened butter
25 g/2 tbsp golden syrup (corn syrup)

ICING
115 g/4 oz/½ cup softened butter
250 g/8 oz/2 cups sifted icing (confectioners') sugar
5 ml/1 tsp lemon juice
few drops of food colouring (optional)
coloured icing pens
brightly coloured sweets (candies)

sugar

self-raising (rising) flour

butter

golden syrup (corn syrup)

ginger

icing (confectioners') sugar

1 Sift the flour, ginger and bicarbonate of soda (baking soda) into a bowl. Add the sugar, then rub in the butter with your fingertips until the mixture resembles fine breadcrumbs.

2 Add the golden syrup (light corn syrup) and mix to a dough. Preheat the oven to 190°C/375°F/Gas 5.

3 Roll out to 3 mm (⅛ in) thick on a lightly floured surface. Stamp out the shapes with biscuit (cookie) cutters and transfer to a lightly greased baking sheet. Bake for 5–10 minutes before transferring to a wire rack to cool.

4 To make the icing, beat the butter in a bowl until light and fluffy. Add the icing (confectioners') sugar a little at a time and continue beating. Add lemon juice and food colouring (if using).

5 Spread the icing over the cooled cookies and leave to set.

6 When the icing has set, make patterns on the icing with coloured icing pens and decorate with coloured sweets (candies).

Jolly Orange Boats

These are so easy to make and fun to eat. The only difficult thing is waiting for the jelly (gelatine) to set! These boats make a yummy dessert or party treat. You could serve with ice cream for something extra special.

Serves 4

INGREDIENTS
2 oranges
1 packet orange-flavoured jelly
　(gelatine)
4 sheets rice paper or coloured paper

orange

jelly (gelatine)

rice paper

1 Cut the oranges in half lengthways. Scrape out the flesh, taking care not to pierce the skins. Chop up the flesh.

2 Make the jelly (gelatine) according to the packet instructions. Add the orange flesh while the jelly cools.

3 Place the orange shells onto a baking sheet and pour in the jelly mixture. Leave for 1 hour to set. Once set, cut the skins in half again using a sharp knife to create little boats.

4 Cut the rice paper or coloured paper sheets into eight squares. Pierce each corner with a toothpick and attach the sail to the middle of the orange boat.

IMPORTANT SAFETY NOTE

You may need an adult's help cutting the oranges. Be very careful whenever you handle knives.

Chocolate Witchy Apples

These chocolate witches are great fun. Be careful with the melted chocolate, though, as it has a nasty habit of getting everywhere!

Serves 6

INGREDIENTS
6 small eating apples
6 wooden lollipop sticks
250 g/8 oz/8 squares milk chocolate
6 ice cream cones
sweets (candies) for decorating

apple

milk chocolate

sweets (candies)

lollipop stick

ice cream cone

1 Peel and thoroughly dry the apples. Press a wooden lollipop stick into the core of each one.

2 In the microwave or over a pan of boiling water, gently melt the chocolate.

IMPORTANT SAFETY NOTE

Melted chocolate is very hot! Make sure an adult helps you melt it.

3 When melted, tilt the pan and dip the apple into it, coating it thoroughly. Place it on a baking sheet lined with baking paper. Press the sweets (candies) into the chocolate to decorate before the chocolate sets.

4 Holding the stick, use a little melted chocolate to attach the cone for a hat. The cone can also be decorated by sticking sweets on with spare melted chocolate. Repeat with the other five apples.

TEMPLATES

*These templates are used in some of the projects in the book.
You can either trace them directly from the page,
or enlarge them to the size required following the instructions
at the beginning of the book.*

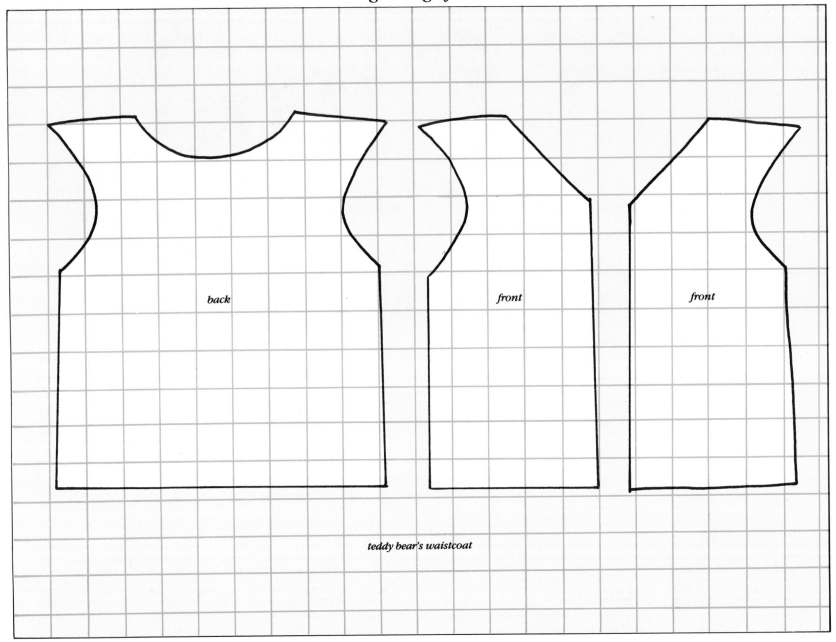

back

front

front

teddy bear's waistcoat

Christmas wreath

dressing-up doll

Christmas wreath

eye mask

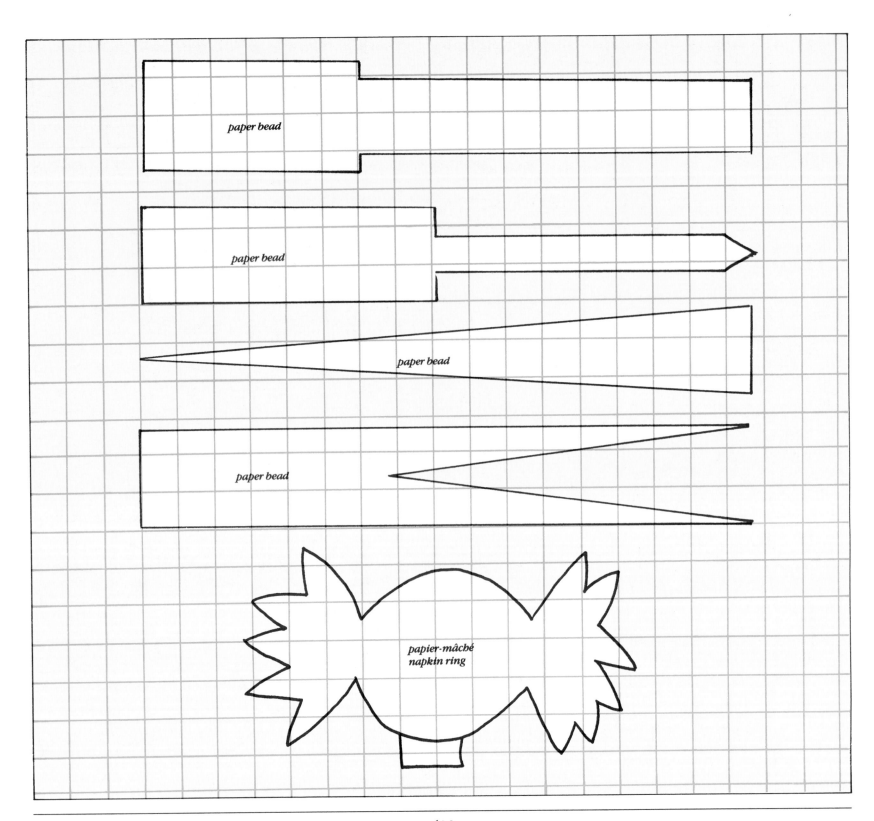

paper bead

paper bead

paper bead

paper bead

papier-mâché napkin ring

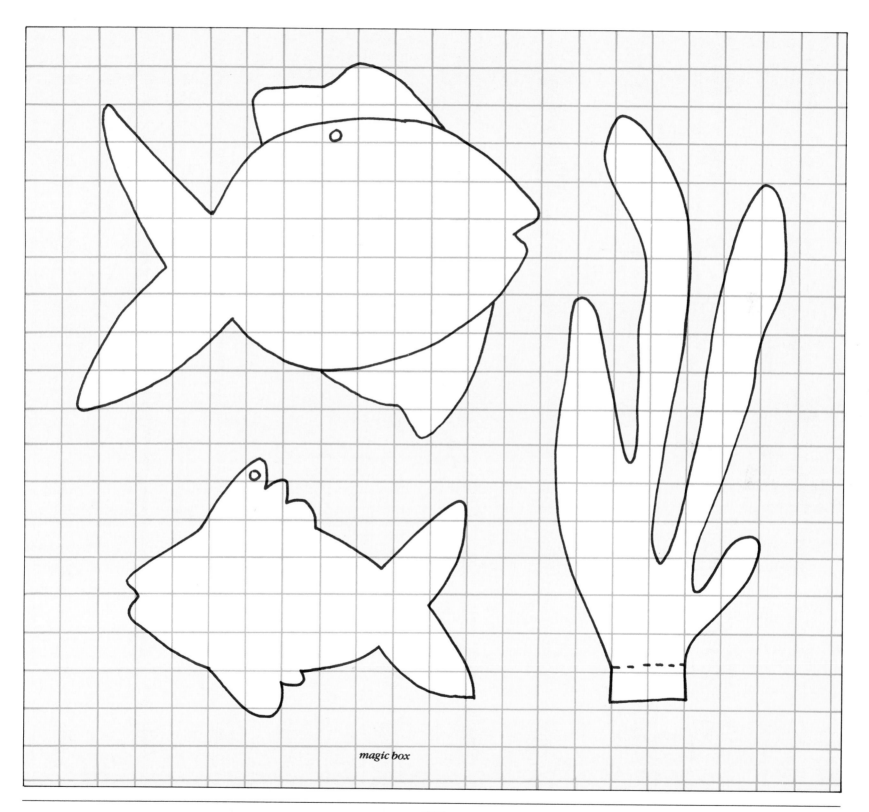

magic box

jewel handle for
papier-mâché
treasure box

paper doll

origami water bomb

magic box

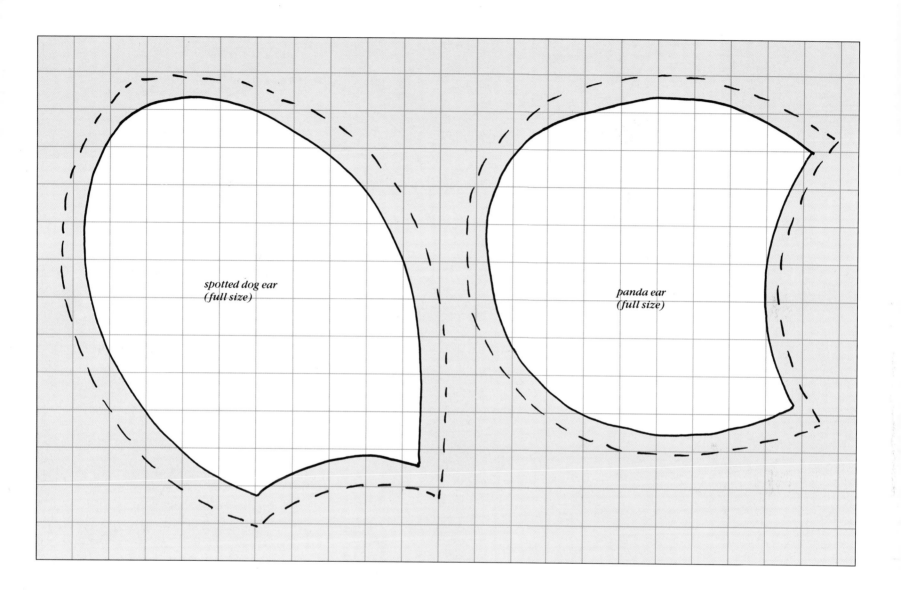

spotted dog ear
(full size)

panda ear
(full size)

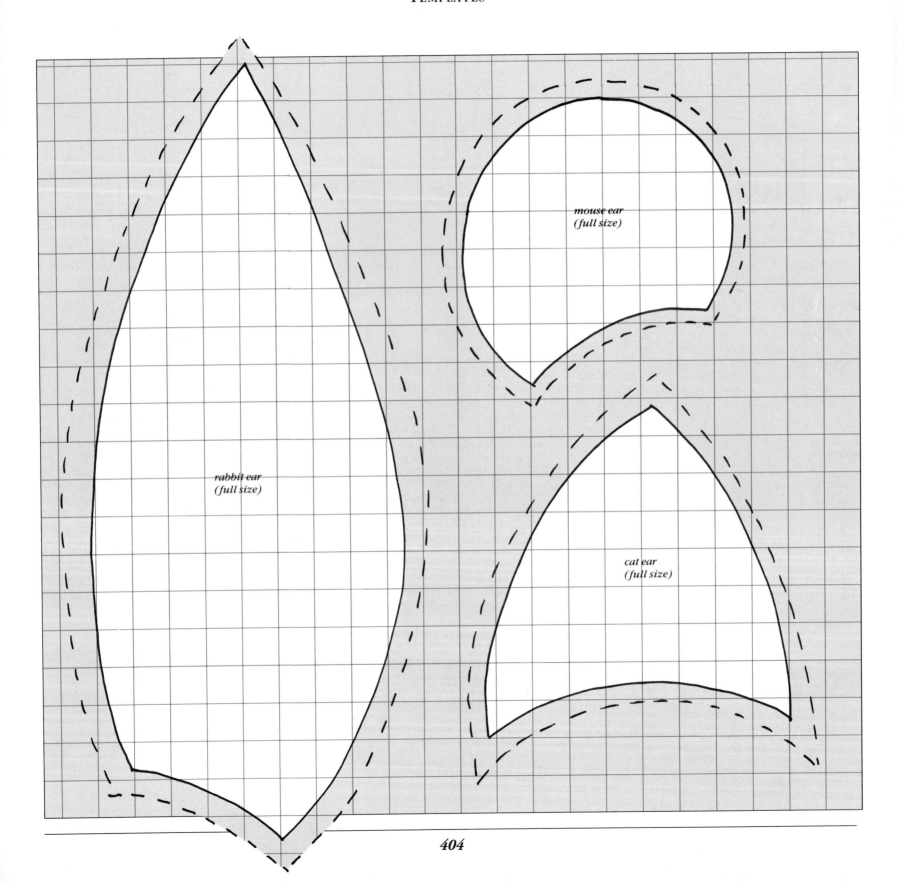

*rabbit ear
(full size)*

*mouse ear
(full size)*

*cat ear
(full size)*

Templates

hippy flower
(half size)

cowboy pocket
(half size)

cowboy pocket detail
(half size)

clown button
(half size)

wizard pendant
(half size)

cowboy badge
(half size)

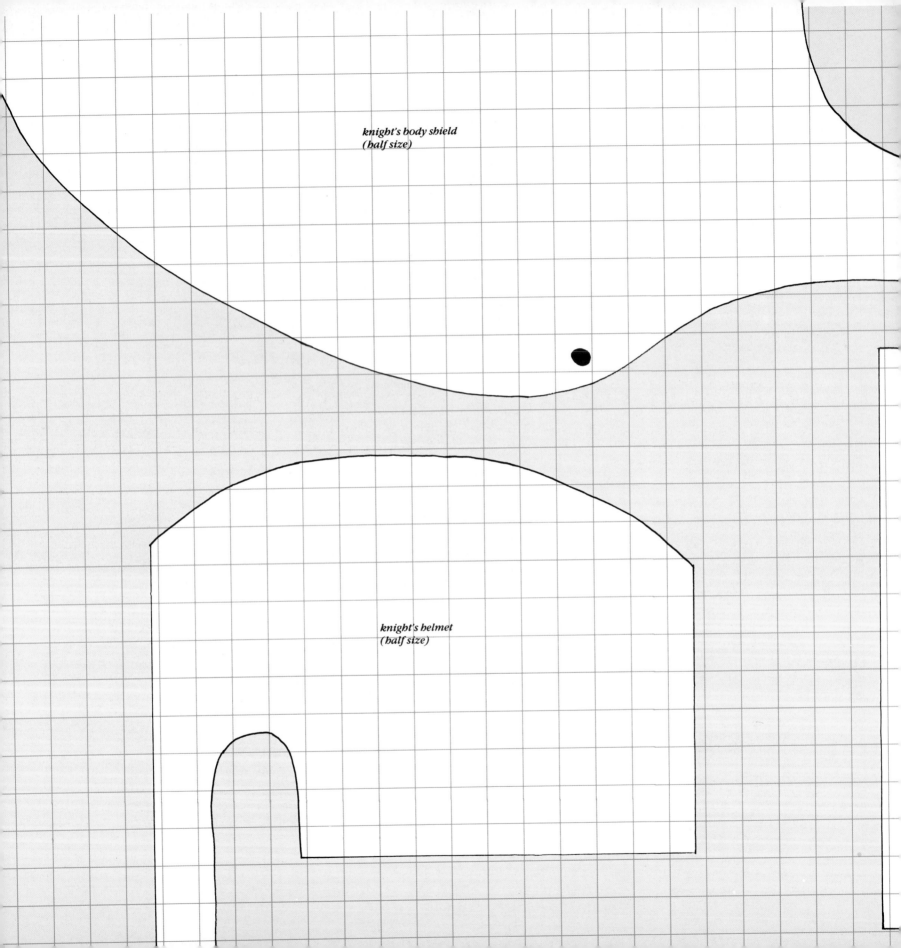

knight's body shield
(half size)

knight's helmet
(half size)

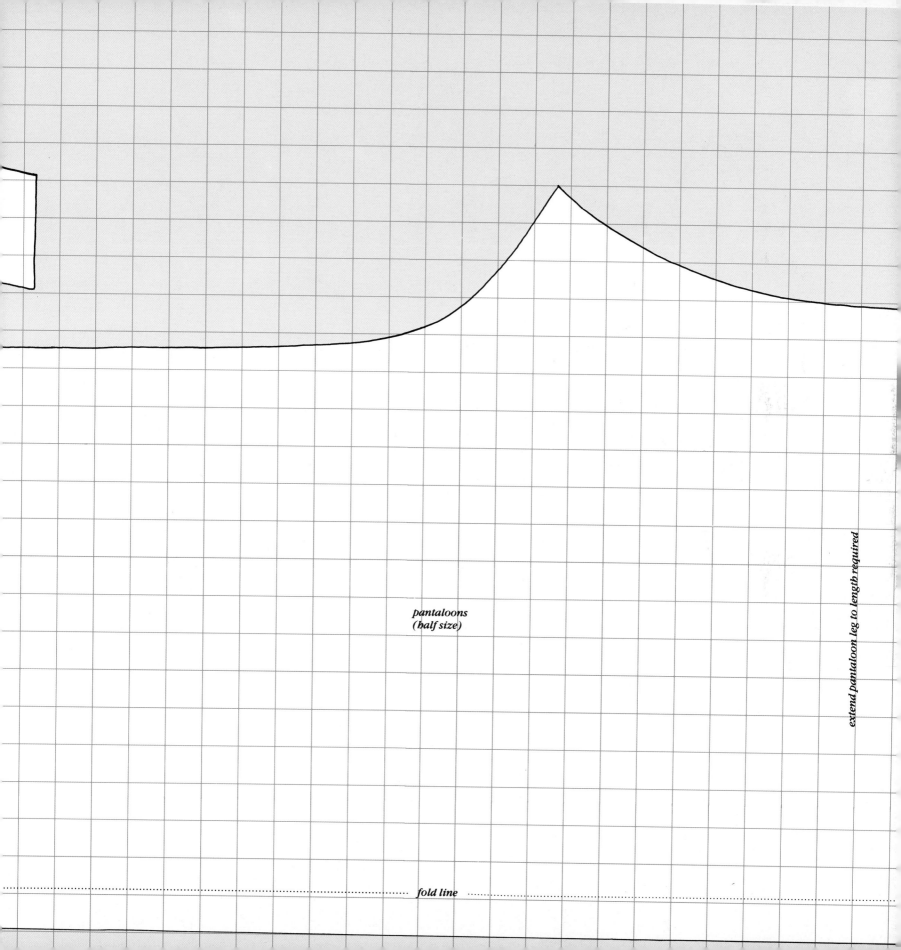

pantaloons
(half size)

extend pantaloon leg to length required

fold line

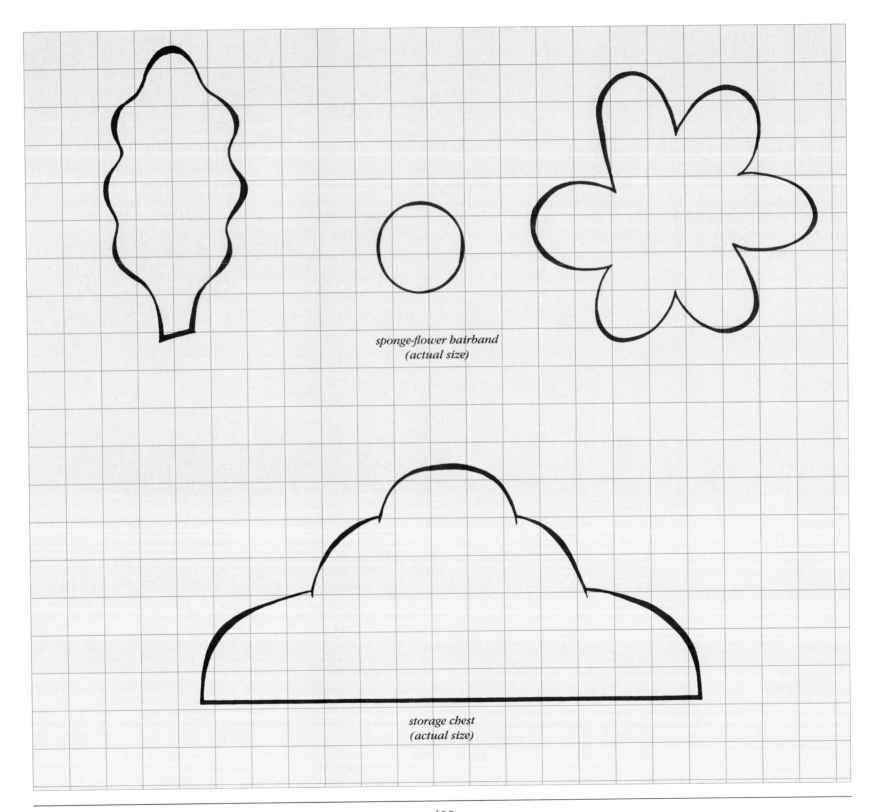

sponge-flower hairband
(actual size)

storage chest
(actual size)

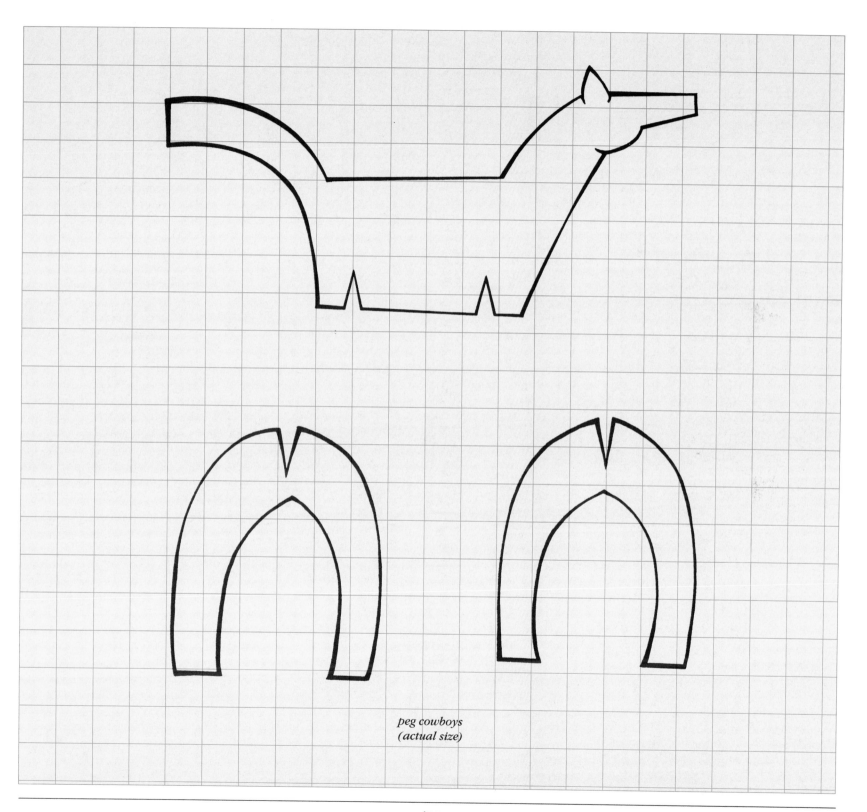

peg cowboys
(actual size)

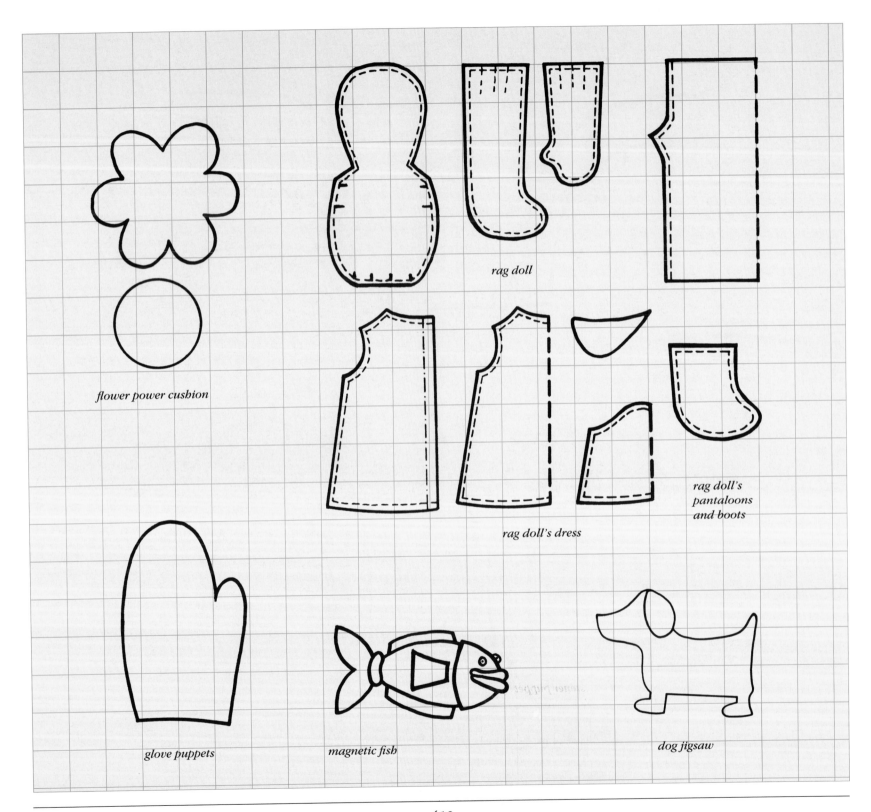

flower power cushion

rag doll

rag doll's dress

rag doll's pantaloons and boots

glove puppets

magnetic fish

dog jigsaw

dog and bone mobile

felt picture book

paper fastener puppet

felt game

toy bag

INDEX

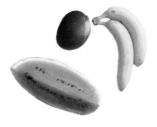

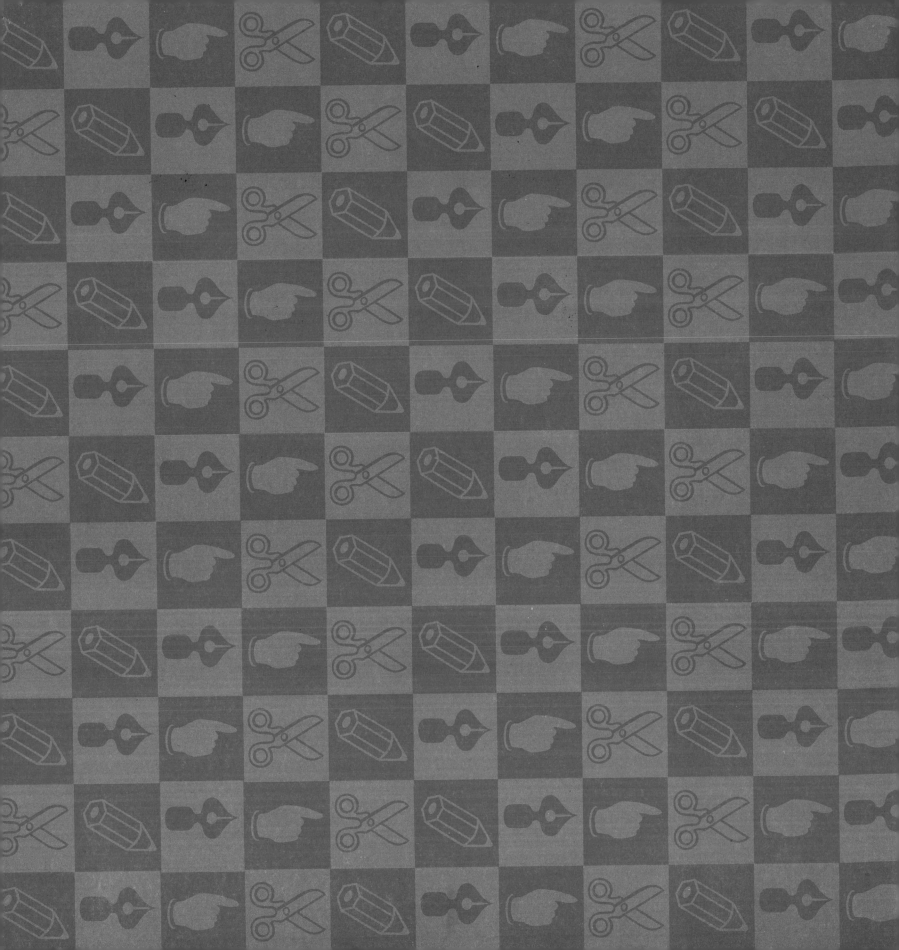